ALSO BY DIANE RAVITCH

Reign of Error

The Death and Life of the Great American School System

The Language Police

Left Back

National Standards in American Education

The Schools We Deserve

The Troubled Crusade

The Revisionists Revised

The Great School Wars

Slaying Goliath

Slaying Goliath

The Passionate Resistance to
Privatization and the Fight to Save
America's Public Schools

DIANE RAVITCH

ALFRED A. KNOPF New York
2020

THIS IS A BORZOI BOOK
PUBLISHED BY ALFRED A. KNOPF

Copyright © 2020 by Diane Ravitch

All rights reserved. Published in the United States by Alfred A. Knopf,
a division of Penguin Random House LLC, New York, and distributed
in Canada by Penguin Random House Canada Limited, Toronto.

www.aaknopf.com

Knopf, Borzoi Books, and the colophon are registered trademarks
of Penguin Random House LLC.

Library of Congress Cataloging-in-Publication Data
Names: Ravitch, Diane, author.
Title: Slaying Goliath : the passionate resistance to privatization and the fight
to save America's public schools / Diane Ravitch.
Description: First edition. | New York : Alfred A. Knopf, [2020] |
Includes bibliographical references and index
Identifiers: LCCN 2019022776 (print) | LCCN 2019022777 (ebook) |
ISBN 9780525655374 (hardcover) | ISBN 9780525655381 (ebook)
Subjects: LCSH: Privatization in education—United States. | Public schools—
United States. | Education and state—United States.
Classification: LCC LB2806.36 .R385 2020 (print) | LCC LB2806.36 (ebook)
DDC 371.010973—dc23 LC record available at https://lccn.loc.gov/2019022776
LC ebook record available at https://lccn.loc.gov/2019022777

Jacket photograph by Gregor Schuster /
Photographer's Choice / Getty Images

Jacket design by Adalis Martinez

Manufactured in the United States of America
First Edition

For Mary

Money never sleeps. Follow the money.

—PROFESSOR MAURICE CUNNINGHAM,
University of Massachusetts

I believe in standardizing automobiles. I do not believe in standardizing human beings. Standardization is a great peril which threatens American culture.

—ALBERT EINSTEIN

Everybody can be great, because everybody can serve. You don't have to have a college degree to serve. You don't have to make your subject and your verb agree to serve. You don't have to know about Plato and Aristotle to serve. You don't have to know Einstein's theory of relativity to serve. You don't have to know the second theory of thermodynamics in physics to serve. You only need a heart full of grace, a soul generated by love.

—DR. MARTIN LUTHER KING JR., "The Drum Major Instinct,"
delivered at the Ebenezer Baptist Church, Atlanta, Georgia,
February 4, 1968

A parody of the Reagan administration's famous 1983 report *A Nation at Risk:* "If a foreign country had inflicted upon our public education system what Ed Reform plutocrats and their toadying political sycophants have imposed upon it, we would have considered it an act of war."

—ANONYMOUS

Contents

Slaying Goliath

Disruption Is Not Reform!

I started to write this book in the spring of 2018 at an unusual moment in our nation's history. In state after state, tens of thousands of teachers walked out of their schools and marched to their state capitols to protest low pay, poor working conditions, and the persistent underfunding of public education. The walkouts and strikes continued into 2019, spreading from district to district and state to state. Teachers were marching not just for themselves but for the students they taught, who were in overcrowded classes, using obsolete textbooks, in long-neglected buildings. In the Republican-dominated states where the walkouts began, education spending had been sharply reduced in the previous decade. Faced with thousands of irate teachers and closed schools, legislators made concessions to placate the striking teachers, even in states where unions were weak and strikes were forbidden.

Most commentators were shocked by teacher militancy. They never imagined that teachers would rise up spontaneously, but they did. Across the nation, teachers were demoralized by stagnant wages, budget cuts, soaring health care costs, crowded classrooms, punitive evaluation systems, attacks on teachers' job security and pensions, and public funding of privately managed schools, which reduced the funding of public schools. Many teachers decided they could no longer remain in their chosen profession because a draconian standards-and-testing regime mandated by federal law stole weeks, sometimes months, from classroom instruction, distorted the goals of education, and made it impossible for them to teach with autonomy, passion, and creativity.

Persistent insults and legislative attacks on the teaching profession and public schools caused many experienced teachers to abandon their classrooms long before they were due to retire, creating teacher shortages and causing a sharp drop in the number of applicants to teacher preparation institutions. At a time when fake "Reformers" were casting teachers as villains, the number of people entering the profession went into free fall. How can a nation educate its young without well-qualified, experienced teachers?

The teacher walkouts were a nail in the coffin of what has falsely been called "education reform" for at least two decades. By the bold act of walking out in mass numbers and marching to their state capitols, even where doing so was forbidden by law, teachers were educating the public about the mean-spiritedness, ignorance, and shortsightedness behind the facade of "education reform." Teachers were working second and third jobs to make ends meet. Some teachers were paid so little that they were eligible for government food stamps. Even with their low wages, teachers laid out or raised hundreds of dollars each year to buy essential school supplies for their students. These conditions, graphically illustrated in newspapers, magazines, and on websites, educated the public about the causes of widespread teacher shortages and the dramatic underfunding of public schools.

This was the wreckage that the so-called "reform" movement had created by demonizing teachers as if they were adversaries of their students and treating them as malingerers who required constant evaluation lest they fail to do their duty. This was the damage inflicted on public schools, their students and teachers, by heedless billionaires who had decided to disrupt, reinvent, and redesign the nation's public schools. This was the work of some of the richest people in the nation: the Walton family, Bill Gates, Betsy DeVos, the Koch brothers, Michael Bloomberg, Laurene Powell Jobs, Reed Hastings, Eli Broad, and a bevy of other billionaires, most of whom had made their fortunes on Wall Street, in Silicon Valley, or in the tech industry.

For nearly two decades, the "reformers" had promised a dramatic transformation in American education, based on their strategy of high-stakes testing, teacher evaluation by test scores, charter schools, and closing low-scoring public schools. They confidently claimed that they knew the answers to all the vexing problems in education. They asserted that they were leading the civil rights movement of our time, funded by billionaires, Wall Street titans, and the federal government, as if the elites would be leading a civil rights movement against the powerful (themselves!). They insisted that when their remedies were imposed, America's test scores would soar to the top of international rankings. No longer would poor children be "trapped in failing schools." No more would children's success be determined by their ZIP code or social status. They all sang from a common hymnal about the failures of public education and proclaimed their certainty that they knew how to turn failure into high test scores for all.

But despite the investment of billions of federal, state, local, and philanthropic dollars, these malign efforts came up empty. The leaders of this charade had confidently predicted that success was just beyond the horizon. But as so often happens with mirages, the horizon kept receding farther away. None of their promises and claims came true. Judged by their own chosen metrics—standardized test scores—the fake "reformers" failed.

In this book, I will not call these activities and their leaders by the honorable word *reform,* which they have brazenly appropriated. The individuals and groups who promote test-based accountability, school closings, and school choice as remedies for low test scores are not reformers. What to call them? Others call them "deformers" or the "financial privatization cabal" or the "Destroy Public Education Movement" or "privateers." Such groups and individuals often say their goal is to "disrupt" public education, and I think in this instance they have accurately named themselves. They are Disrupters. They are masters of chaos, which they inflict on other people's children, without a twinge of remorse. They are most certainly not reformers, the title they have deceptively claimed. The old and true sense of the word "reform" has positive connotations; most people hear the word and think of "improvement," "progress," and "uplift." This does not describe the current disruption movement, which is in fact a calculated, insidious, and munificently funded campaign to privatize America's public schools, to break teachers' unions, to tear apart communities, and to attack teacher professionalism. The rhetoric used by this campaign is so similar from place to place that I assume it was concocted by marketing and branding professionals to deceive the public. I will not allow the term "reform" to be hijacked by those who have a hidden agenda.

Disrupters are proponents of privatization. They distrust the public sector. They don't like local control. They like to close public schools. They belittle teachers. They use their vast resources to transfer public assets to the private sector and to demean those who teach our children despite their low wages and poor working conditions.

Disrupters say that schools should be run like businesses. They think that students, teachers, principals, and schools need to be externally motivated by carrots and sticks, by bonuses and penalties, tied to standardized test scores. They believe that because businesses succeed by having private ownership, profit and loss statements, and data-driven decision making, so should schools. They believe that standardized testing is an essential tool for making objective decisions about which teachers are effective or ineffective and which schools should be rewarded or closed.

The Disrupters view education as an entrepreneurial activity that should be "scalable" and should produce "return on investment." They encourage new businesses to enter the education marketplace. The schools, once seen solely as institutions of teaching and learning, have been reimagined by corporations and entrepreneurs as places of commerce and profit. There is money to be made in selling tests, hardware, software, professional development, new curricula, new ways to analyze and utilize data, and consulting services for all of the above. There is money to be made by opening charter chains, buying real estate under one name and leasing it back to the new charter under another name, establishing related corporations to supply goods and services to one's own charter schools, using the charter school's credit card to fly first-class, eat in pricey restaurants, and buy luxury cars and clothing. Frequent conferences are convened to explore how equity investors can make a profit in the education industry. Many people have figured out how to make money from public education dollars, but these people are not teachers. Teachers meet their classes several times a day, do their jobs for an average wage of $60,000, far below the salaries of their peers with the same credentials in other professions in the same states. They are definitely not in education for the money.

In the new era of Disruption, it seems quaint, antique actually, to speak of "love of learning" as a goal of education, to speak of education as personal development and preparation for citizenship in a democratic society. Where is the profit in such fuzzy goals? How could those be measured?

The disruption and privatization movement was codified into law by George W. Bush's No Child Left Behind Act (passed by Congress in 2001 and signed by the president in 2002) and extended its control of state and local policy by Barack Obama's Race to the Top program (2009). The marketing of Disruption reached a large national audience in 2010 with the release of the documentary *Waiting for "Superman,"* which falsely asserted that America's public schools had failed, extolled the virtues of privately managed charter schools, and ridiculed public schools and their teachers.

I wrote two books about the emergence of this new movement. The first appeared in 2010 and was called *The Death and Life of the Great American School System: How Testing and Choice Are Undermining Education.* Having worked as assistant secretary of education for the Office of Educational Research and Improvement in the administration of President George H. W. Bush and for many years in some of the nation's leading conservative think tanks, I had hoped that privatization and testing would produce sweeping improvement, especially for the neediest students. It didn't. I couldn't pretend otherwise. I came to realize that the privatization movement was a continuation of a decades-long campaign by right-wingers who hated public schools, which they derisively called "government schools." I renounced my own past views and determined to expose the well-funded smear campaign against American public schools and their teachers.

In 2013, watching the privatization movement grow to become the status quo, embedded in federal and state policy and supported by billionaires and major foundations, I published *Reign of Error: The Hoax of the Privatization Movement and the Danger to America's Public Schools,* which contained not only an indictment of privatization and teacher-bashing, but also a detailed list of research-based actions that would improve schools and help poor and needy students, their families, and their communities.

What I had come to understand was that the root cause of poor performance in school is not "bad schools" or "bad teachers" but poverty. Closing schools and firing their teachers and principals does not help students. If anything, it introduces damaging instability into their lives. The privatizers hail disruption and call it "creative," but it is neither creative nor beneficial.

The Corporate Disrupters are indifferent to poverty and racial segregation. They refuse to acknowledge the impact of poverty on students' lives. They insist that poverty can be cured by "great teachers" or "great schools." It is true that teachers can change children's lives; time and again, remarkable and dedicated teachers have enabled students to emerge from difficult circumstances because of their influence. But uplifting individual stories are not proof of a large-scale remedy. There is neither research nor evidence to support the Disrupters' belief that intergenerational, systemic poverty can be eliminated by teachers and schools. Lasting social change requires a new direction in public policy, one that directly reduces economic inequality and poverty.

Disrupters wreak havoc on urban school districts, where test scores are lowest and where poverty and racial segregation are concentrated. In some cities, such as New Orleans, Indianapolis, Philadelphia, and Washington, D.C., the very existence of public education has been put at risk by the growth of charter schools. Others, like Oakland, teeter on the brink of insolvency due to the diversion of state funds to charter schools. The privatizers gloss over two fundamental facts: first, every dollar that goes to a charter school is taken away from public schools; second, public schools have fixed costs that cannot be reduced, requiring them to lay off teachers, increase class sizes, and cut programs. Thus, the great majority of students suffer from budget cuts so that a small minority of students can attend charter schools, which may abruptly close due to mismanagement or low enrollment.

Because the Disruption movement was promoted by the Obama administration, supporters of public education were caught off guard. If Democrats, the traditional defenders of public education, gave their approval to the strategies of the Disruption movement, how bad could it be? President Obama's secretary of education Arne Duncan frequently pointed to successful charter schools, but never acknowledged such factors as attrition rates, exclusion of students with disabilities or English learners, or the large number of charter schools that failed or that closed after a year or two.

The remedies imposed by the Obama administration were no different from those of the George W. Bush administration. Actually, they were worse. None had any evidence to support them. None achieved the promised outcomes. When the Obama administration was followed by the Trump administration, the failed Bush-Obama policies remained in place. The Disruption agenda remained the same whether the secretary of education was Rod Paige, Margaret Spellings, Arne Duncan, John King, or Betsy DeVos.

After two decades of the same failed federal policies, it became clear that the Disruption movement was running out of steam. Even the Disrupters felt the slow but steady shift of the pendulum away from the stale and unpopular policies of the Bush and Obama administrations. Since test scores were stagnant, some moved the goalposts and said that test scores didn't really matter after all; instead, graduation rates mattered, or parental satisfaction mattered, or choice was an end in itself and nothing else mattered. Secretary of Education Betsy DeVos claimed that as long as parents were choosing their children's schools, the outcomes were unimportant. The sense of an era coming to an end was palpable.

The Disruption movement is dying. It is not yet dead, but it is nonetheless on its last legs, stumbling and defensive. Its strategies of high-stakes testing, standardization, and privatization have not succeeded. Yet its adherents press on because the money keeps flowing in from billionaires and the federal government. The Disruption combine is like a giant creature whose heart and brain have died, but whose tentacles keep reaching out and strangling whatever it can get hold of.

As I was writing this book, I read about a man who decapitated a rattlesnake in his backyard; he waited ten minutes, then picked up the detached head, and it bit him, nearly killing him. The snake was dead, but it still had poisonous venom and still was capable of grievous harm. That is like the Disrupters today. Not one of their efforts has succeeded, as I will show in this book. Based on glorious promises, Disruption has managed to undercut and damage public education in many urban districts by replacing public schools with ones that are privately managed. But taking control is not the same as being successful. Disruption has failed to achieve any of its goals. It is kept alive by its vast resources and by its lock on federal policy: every child must be tested every year, and test results are used to hold teachers, administrators, and schools accountable. States must intervene in the lowest-performing schools, either closing or privatizing them. Closing schools does not make them better nor does it help the students who are sent to distant schools.

Disruption in education gives off the same aura as did the Soviet Union in the late 1980s. The faithful had fallen away. No one believed in the promises anymore. People walked in lockstep, doing the same things they did last year, not because they had faith, but because doing so was habitual or because they were paid to do their job, to go through the motions.

The creature continues to live, not only because it has become the status quo, but also because its backers are very, very rich. It has the support of billionaires who don't mind wasting a few million dollars here or there, buying a local or state election for like-minded Disrupters and funding new organizations to give the illusion of mass action when there is none. As masters of the universe, they never admit failure.

In this book, I will document the failures of Corporate Disruption.

And I will tell stories of the heroic teachers, students, parents, and activists who stood up to unaccountable power and bravely fought for the common good.

There is a long way to go before the last of the dread tentacles of the Disruption beast stops grabbing public schools, but the end is in sight. The Disrupters—from George W. Bush to Donald J. Trump—have had two decades to prove their ideas, and they have failed. They can keep on going for a while, but their time is running out. Meanwhile, communities and their schools are under assault, and millions of students have been cheated of the joy of learning, and millions of teachers have been stripped of their autonomy and creativity, forced to kneel before the false gods of standardized testing.

A democratic society needs a strong public sector and a strong private sector. The public sector exists to serve the needs of the commonweal. It belongs to all of us. The public sector includes not only public schools, but police, firefighters, hospitals, libraries, highways, beaches, parks, transit, and oversight of the air and water. Depending on the state and community, the public sector may address more or fewer of those needs. When people are not satisfied with the police, we do not use public funds to hire private security guards for them. When people do not like their community pool, we do not give them public funds to build their own private pool. When people do not like the local public school, they may transfer to another public school, or they may decide to send their child to a private or religious school, which is their right, but not the responsibility of the public. I admire Catholic schools, which have a long history of providing good education to poor and middle-income students, but I do not believe it is in their interest or the public interest for such schools to be funded by the government. They should be funded by their alumni and by wealthy philanthropists who appreciate their mission.

The public schools belong to the public, and they should be properly supported by the public because they are our investment in the future of our democracy. They must provide an appropriate, well-resourced education for all children who enroll. All children have the right to be educated at public expense in public schools.

Corporate Disruption has failed. It has diminished the status of the teaching profession. It has created national teacher shortages. It has discouraged creative and thoughtful teaching. It has undermined the transmission of knowledge and skill in history, science, literature, foreign languages, and the arts. It has reduced time for physical education, recess, and play and given it to testing and test preparation. It has demoralized students and teachers alike. It has crushed the spirit of learning. It has failed to produce the miracles and benefits that it promised.

But perhaps worst among the Disrupters' sins is that they have changed the subject, drawing attention away from root causes and substituting fake solutions. The festering sores in our society are firmly rooted in poverty and inequality, coupled with racial segregation. About 19 percent of our nation's children live in poverty and another 22 percent are "near poor," according to the National Center for Children in Poverty. This is a proportion higher than in any other modern industrialized society. Disrupters avoid talking about poverty, inequality, and racial segregation. To do so would certainly mean raising the taxes of the wealthiest to pay the cost of healing our social order. The Disrupters have persuaded the American political establishment that high-stakes testing and school choice would lead to the just and good society we all theoretically hope to see. The Disrupters distracted our attention, trying to convince us that charters and vouchers are the path to equality and justice. They are not. Even if they produce higher test scores (and they usually don't), charters and vouchers are fake substitutes for policies that increase equality and provide a decent standard of living for all Americans.

Can schools alone change the social order? It is naive to expect them to solve structural problems that require sustained and large-scale government action. The privatization movement distracts the public from problems that require a concerted effort by all of us to solve. It is an effort to change us from citizens to consumers, interested only in our own well-being, not in the common good.

The purpose of public schools is to encourage students to think and act as citizens of a democratic society, prepared to do their part in making it better for everyone. Public schools belong to the public, not to entrepreneurs or corporate chains. They belong to all of us. We dare not lose them.

Ordinary heroes among us have stood up to the Corporate Disrupters. Time and again, the Resistance has won. They spoke out, they stood up, they organized, they voted. I will celebrate their accomplishments in this book.

CHAPTER 2

The Odious Status Quo

Today, no one is satisfied with the status quo. The Corporate Disrupters want to blow up the public schools and start from scratch. Bill Gates says that they are obsolete; Laurene Powell Jobs, Mark Zuckerberg, and Charles Koch want to reinvent them, as do other billionaires, despite their lack of experience in the field of education. Back in the mid-nineteenth century, Ralph Waldo Emerson said that every reformer had a plan in his vest pocket to reinvent society. Fortunately, none of the reformers of Emerson's day were so rich and powerful that they could impose their untested ideas on unwilling people; they had to go through the democratic process to persuade people to adopt their reforms. Today, it seems that every billionaire has a plan in his or her vest pocket to reinvent or reimagine the public schools.

In his book *Winners Take All: The Elite Charade of Changing the World*, Anand Giridharadas warned that billionaires use their philanthropy to control other people under the guise of helping. Their "gifts" appear well-meaning but are Trojan horses, meant to protect the status quo. So it is with the Disrupters. Their efforts to capture public schools, which belong to the public, undermine democracy. The billionaires don't like public schools; they don't like unions; they don't like elected school boards. They don't like grassroots democracy, so they spend millions of dollars to win control of state and local school boards.

The people who try to protect the public schools from the Disrupters don't like the status quo. They are tired of the time and money spent on standardized testing; tired of the annual rankings of students, teachers, and schools based on standardized test scores; and tired of the endless bashing of teachers and public schools. They are tired of seeing their public schools lose good students and precious resources to charter schools that compete with the local public schools. They are tired of seeing their public schools replaced by corporate chains. They are tired of the sales pitches for the latest technological fads; they are tired of seeing their children, too young to read, put in front of computer screens; and they are tired of their children's data being mined by mega-corporations for sale to other mega-corporations.

No one likes the status quo. Disrupters claim to oppose the status quo, but they *are* the status quo. After all, they control the levers of power in federal and state governments. They write the laws and mandates. They control policy. They define the status quo. They own it.

The purpose of public education, from its inception, was threefold: first, to teach the basics of learning—reading, writing, and mathematics; second, to teach the elements of citizenship in a democracy, to prepare the younger generation to vote, serve on juries, and participate in the lives of their communities; and third, to enable them to make wise choices after they finish their schooling so that they can take care of themselves and their families and improve our society. What matters most in pursuing these goals is the cultivation of character, that is, the development of such attributes as integrity, honesty, civility, industriousness, responsibility, and ethics. Character matters more than test scores.

For many generations, Americans were proud of their public schools. They knew they were not perfect, but they took pride in the fact that every child had the right to go to a free public school. They believed in this ideal long before it was realized. Controversies were never far removed from the schoolhouse door. The schools were in many ways a reflection of American society. Society was racist, and the schools were racially segregated. It required a historic decision by the United States Supreme Court in 1954 to declare that states could not use the force of law to segregate students by race. To be sure, ending de jure (legally recognized and enforced) segregation did not end de facto segregation: the problems of racism, racial isolation, and segregation persist in the

schools and the larger society to this day. Schools have been tasked by law
with the education of children whose native language is not English, and
they have been similarly required to educate students with disabilities.
When Disrupters speak nostalgically of the "good old days," they harken
back to schools that were not racially integrated and did not enroll non-
English-speaking students or students with disabilities.

There was never a time in the past when the public schools were
all excellent. That is a fantasy. There were always great teachers, good
teachers, and bad teachers. There were always excellent students, average
students, and problem students who came to school reluctantly. Useful
correctives to fantasy thinking are the film *The Blackboard Jungle* (1955)
and Bel Kaufman's *Up the Down Staircase* (1964), both of which depict
dysfunctional urban public schools in that era. It was far from idyllic.
There were well-resourced schools in affluent communities, and poorly
resourced schools in poor communities. We can't say whether students in
those days knew more or less than students do today. We have no common yardstick by which to compare. From my knowledge as a historian
of education, from my experience as a high school student in the 1950s,
as well as my experience as a member of the governing board of the
federal testing agency, the National Assessment of Educational Progress,
I believe that students today certainly know far more mathematics and
science than students in the 1940s and 1950s did. Students today are less
likely to have read great literature than their grandparents were, because
English teachers in the 1930s, 1940s, and 1950s were expected to teach
classic literature and were not forced to rely on homogenized textbooks
that contain snippets of literature to prepare students for standardized
tests.

So much for the fantasy of the days when education was allegedly at
its apex.

Fast-forward to the early 1980s.

Ronald Reagan was elected president in 1980. He appointed Terrel
Bell, a career educator from Utah, as his secretary of education. Bell had
served previously as U.S. commissioner of education under Presidents
Richard Nixon and Gerald Ford. Reagan had three goals in education:
he wanted to abolish the U.S. Department of Education (created by his
predecessor President Jimmy Carter), he wanted to restore school prayer

(once common in the public schools but prohibited by the Supreme Court in 1962), and he wanted to introduce school vouchers to allow students to attend religious and private schools at public expense. Reagan was advised by his friend Milton Friedman, a libertarian economist who did not believe in public schools and advocated vouchers. Commissioner Bell did not share President Reagan's passion for vouchers and school prayer or his disdain for public schools.

In 1981, hoping to save the new U.S. Department of Education, Secretary Bell established a National Commission on Excellence in Education. In 1983, the commission released its report, called *A Nation at Risk: The Imperative for Educational Reform.* As Bell had hoped, the report did not recommend school prayer or vouchers. However, its central theme—blaming the public schools for the nation's economic woes—was no less destructive to public education. The report's bombastic rhetoric asserted that the public schools were failing and were mired in "a rising tide of mediocrity."

It warned:

If an unfriendly foreign power had attempted to impose on America the mediocre educational performance that exists today, we might well have viewed it as an act of war. As it stands, we have allowed this to happen to ourselves. . . . We have, in effect, been committing an act of unthinking, unilateral educational disarmament.

The report sparked a sense of national alarm. It blamed the public schools for the nation's economic woes, including the loss of American industries to Japan, Germany, and South Korea. It mentioned standards only as a general principle, ignored vouchers and school choice, and only briefly mentioned standardized testing (it recommended that such tests should be administered "at major transition points from one level of schooling to another and particularly from high school to college or work"). It did not recommend testing every student every year, which is now the federally mandated policy.

In 2018, on the thirty-fifth anniversary of *A Nation at Risk,* NPR reporter Anya Kamenetz interviewed surviving members of the commission. They candidly admitted that the conclusions of the report were predetermined and that the data cited were "cherry-picked" to make American public schools look as bad as possible. That is what the Reagan administration wanted. The public schools did not cause the recession of the early 1980s. While Detroit continued to manufacture gas-guzzling automobiles, the Japanese built fuel-efficient cars that the public wanted at a time of rising fuel prices. The economy was in the doldrums, and it was easy to blame the schools for the outsourcing of industries to other nations even though doing so was nonsensical. When the economy improved, no one thanked the schools or apologized for slandering them.

The report turned education into a national political football, with governors and even presidents feeling obliged to take charge and find solutions to problems they did not understand. Southern governors called for common tests by which to gauge where their states stood when compared with one another. President George H. W. Bush convened a summit of the nation's governors in 1989, which set six ambitious "national goals" for the year 2000 (Arkansas governor Bill Clinton was personally involved in drafting the national goals).

Contrary voices were ignored. The U.S. Department of Energy commissioned a study of the current status of American education by the Sandia National Laboratories in 1990, which criticized the alarmism of *A Nation at Risk.* The engineers at Sandia studied test scores, graduation rates, and other indicators. They concluded that achievement was holding steady or improving, and that the biggest challenge the nation faced was to upgrade the education of poor and minority youth in urban districts.

At the time, I was assistant secretary of education for education research and improvement, and in 1992, I attended the Energy Department's briefing about the Sandia report. I accompanied David Kearns, former CEO of Xerox, who was deputy secretary of education, to the meeting. He was outraged by the Sandia report, which contradicted the view of the U.S. Department of Education that American public schools were failing and needed radical change. The Energy Department never published the report, but it was immediately leaked to hundreds of influential researchers, who wrote about its findings. In retrospect, the Sandia report got it right. The late Gerald Bracey, a prolific and outspoken education researcher, was also highly critical of the conventional wisdom, which I was then defending. I hereby personally apologize to him. He was right. The "crisis in education" was a politically inspired hoax, or as the eminent researchers David Berliner and Bruce Biddle later called it, a *"Manufactured Crisis."*

Nonetheless, it was a hoax that appealed to politicians, because it gave them a defenseless scapegoat and enabled them to replace educators in the driver's seat. Both political parties endorsed the crisis narrative and claimed to have solutions, all of which involved standards, testing, and accountability. Both Republicans and Democrats agreed that it was time to get tough on the kids. It was time to get tough on the teachers. It was time to hold them accountable to meet high standards or face stern consequences.

Since the federal government, by law and tradition, exercised very little control over education, it was not clear how any of this might happen. But step by step, those at the top pushed for leverage.

In 1991, the George H. W. Bush administration launched a program called America 2000, which urged voluntary compliance with the ambitious national goals agreed upon at President Bush's Charlottesville summit in 1989. Some of the goals were wildly unlikely (e.g., "American students will be first in the world in science and math by the year 2000"). But others made sense ("All children will start school ready to learn by the year 2000"), which encouraged programs for maternal health, child nutrition and health, and early childhood education, though such necessary programs were out of reach due to lack of funding.

The Clinton administration, elected in 1992, agreed with President George H. W. Bush's standards-testing-and-accountability regime and presented its own program, called Goals 2000. It was enacted into law and—mindful that federal law prohibits any federal agency from attempting to direct or control the curriculum or instruction of any school—it offered money to every state to write its own standards and choose its own tests. Predictably, the quality and rigor of state standards and tests varied.

The template for Disruption was created by Florida's Governor Jeb Bush. After his election in 1998, he put forward his A+ Plan, which combined choice, competition, high-stakes testing, grading schools (A–F), and accountability as its formula for "excellence" in education. Governor

Bush substituted choice and testing for equitable and adequate funding. Two decades after the A+ Plan was launched, his amply funded publicity machine crowed about a "Florida miracle," but the only miracle was that anyone believed it. Florida's schools continued to have ill-maintained and overcrowded buildings, high teacher attrition, low teachers' salaries, and numerous unfilled positions. The state's public schools lose billions of dollars each year to privately managed charter schools and vouchers for religious schools. The state holds back third grade students who have low test scores, which predictably inflates the state's fourth grade performance on national tests; but the state's eighth grade students rank no better than average on the National Assessment of Educational Progress. No miracle, just hype and propaganda, but other states with Republican leaders eagerly adopted the tenets of the "Florida Model."

When George W. Bush was narrowly elected in 2000 as a self-described "compassionate conservative," his first priority was to revise the federal education law. He offered a twenty-seven-page document called "No Child Left Behind," the centerpiece of which was the idea that every student in grades 3–8 should take annual tests in reading and mathematics. Their scores, he asserted, would show whether they were making progress and whether their schools were doing a good job. This simple formula, Bush insisted, had wrought a miracle in Texas. He claimed during the campaign that annual testing had led to higher test scores, higher graduation rates, and the closing of gaps between white and nonwhite students. During the campaign, several scholars said there had been no Texas miracle, but no one listened to them. In the fall of 2001, Congress enacted Bush's No Child Left Behind (NCLB) proposal, which had turned into a one-thousand-page law; it was passed by large majorities of both houses of Congress and cosponsored by leading Democrats, including Senator Ted Kennedy of Massachusetts and Congressman George Miller of California. President Bush signed it into law on January 8, 2002. The law was due to be reauthorized in 2007, but Congress could not agree on what to change. It remained on the books until December 2015, long past its expiration date, even though none of its promises and goals was met.

No Child Left Behind allowed states to choose their own standards. It required every state to set achievement levels on its tests of basic, pro-

George W. Bush, forty-third president of the United States. His No Child
Left Behind program vastly expanded the federal role in education and
created a regime of testing and accountability that led to the closure of
many public schools, whose chief fault was that they enrolled high numbers
of impoverished students.

ficient, and advanced. It mandated that 100 percent of students must
become proficient by the year 2014, a dozen years after enactment of the
law. This was a patently absurd goal, but its sponsors didn't care. At the
time, I attended an event in Washington, D.C., at the Willard Hotel,
sponsored by the conservative Hoover Institution, where my former boss
in the George H. W. Bush administration, Senator Lamar Alexander
of Tennessee, was on a panel discussing the new law. I stood up in the
audience and asked whether he truly expected that "every student" would
be proficient by 2014. He responded, "No, Diane, we don't expect that,
but it's good to have goals." Little did he know that many schools would
be closed and many teachers and principals would be fired because they
could not accomplish what was patently impossible.

The law required states to make "adequate yearly progress" toward
meeting that impossible goal of 100 percent proficiency. States were
required to disaggregate test scores by race, ethnicity, gender, disability
status, poverty status, and so on and to report them to the public. Disag-
gregation, it was assumed, would increase the pressure on educators to
produce good results for low-performing groups.

The theory of action behind NCLB was that schools and districts that didn't get the expected results should be punished. Fear of punishment, fear of failure, and fear of losing one's job and career were supposed to cause the staff to try harder and the schools to get better.

The law included what were called "cascading remedies." In the first year that a school did not meet its goals, its students would be offered the option to transfer to another public school. If a school continued to miss its goal of steadily increasing test scores, students would be entitled to tutoring. If the school still fell short, it was subject to "corrective action," which included new curricula, a longer school day or school year, replacing staff or management, or other steps meant to shake up the school. After the fifth year of failing to meet its goals, the federal axe would fall on the school. It might be closed and reopened as a charter school. Its staff might be fired and replaced. The state might hire an "educational management organization" to take charge of the school. The state itself might take over the school.

None of these "remedies" had any prior evidence of success.

If lawmakers and policymakers had stuck to the NCLB timetable of 100 percent proficiency by 2014, nearly every public school in the nation would have been declared a failure and subject to privatization or closure. No national legislature in the world had ever passed such an insanely punitive law directed at their nation's schools.

No Child Left Behind was a massive federal intrusion into state and local control of education. For the first time in the history of the nation, the federal government shifted from supporting states and localities to telling them what to do and how to do it. The law did this in the complete absence of any evidence that its policies and mandates were likely to be successful.

NCLB locked the nation's public schools into an ironclad regime of annual testing of every student in two basic subjects from grades 3–8. It also locked policymakers at the federal and state levels into a mindset that they could not escape. When they thought about schools, they could only think about accountability, test scores, and the incentives and punishments that they hoped would produce results.

As NCLB became the status quo, student test scores were all that mattered. They became both the measure and the goal of education.

Schools cut back on civics, history, the arts, and physical education, even recess, to make more time for testing and test preparation. Districts purchased interim assessments to prepare for the consequential annual tests. Testing and test preparation extended down to kindergarten and first grade, even to preschool, since every year was preparation for the rigors of the following year.

The only national measure of student achievement was the National Assessment of Educational Progress (NAEP), a testing program launched in the late 1960s and administered by the federal government. NCLB authorized NAEP to test reading and mathematics every two years, as an audit of state reports on their progress. NAEP showed that the greatest improvements in student test scores occurred before the enactment of NCLB. There were additional gains from 2003 to 2007, as testing and test preparation took up more of the school year. But after 2007, the gains slowed to a halt, and achievement gaps remained stubbornly large. By the measure that Corporate Disrupters love best—standardized test scores—NCLB failed.

When Barack Obama came into office in 2009, his secretary of education, Arne Duncan, made clear that he considered American public education to be a disaster. He repeatedly claimed that teachers and administrators were "lying" to students about their progress in school. His program—Obama's program—was called Race to the Top. It was layered on top of NCLB, and its overriding goal was the same: raising test scores. Duncan asserted that more testing and more accountability would surely propel the nation to the "top" of international test score rankings. Like NCLB, Race to the Top failed.

In 2009, the nation was in the depths of a dire economic crisis. Congress expended many billions of dollars to promote an economic recovery. Congress gave the U.S. Department of Education $100 billion to help the schools survive the economic recession. Of that sum, $95 billion was sent to schools to pay staff and keep their doors open. The remaining $5 billion was given to Secretary Duncan to use as he wished to promote education reform. Never in history had the U.S. Department of Education had $5 billion in discretionary funds, unencumbered by congressional mandates. Duncan was not an educator, although he had served as superintendent of the low-performing Chicago Public Schools, where he initiated a program in 2004 called Renaissance 2010, in which he closed schools with low test scores and opened new schools, including charter schools. Duncan learned in Chicago to ignore parent and student protests when neighborhood schools were closed and to charge ahead, dispersing the students and enabling private charter organizations to open new schools.

Secretary Duncan and his colleagues at the U.S. Department of Education (many of them drawn from the Bill & Melinda Gates Foundation and the Eli and Edythe Broad Foundation) devised a competition for the states called Race to the Top, which offered a prize of billions of dollars in a time of fiscal austerity. To be eligible to compete, the states had to change their laws and agree to certain conditions. Almost every state agreed to do what Duncan wanted in hopes of winning part of the Race to the Top prize money, but only eighteen states actually got a share of the bonanza. It was a brilliant plan that accelerated widespread adoption of Duncan's ideas about standards, testing, accountability, and choice, but it ultimately failed because its remedies were no more effective than those in Bush's NCLB.

To be eligible, the states had to agree to increase the number of privately managed charter schools in their state. They had to accept "college-and-career-ready standards," which everyone understood were the Common Core State Standards, a set of national standards in reading and mathematics that were not yet finished in 2009 when the competition was announced. They had to agree to restructure or close or privatize the lowest-performing schools in their states. They had to agree to evaluate their teachers based on the test scores of their students. They also had to collect data on every student and build a longitudinal "data warehouse."

This was No Child Left Behind on steroids. The central purpose of Race to the Top was to raise test scores, and Duncan believed that these policies would do it. Federal law forbade the U.S. Department of Education from meddling in the curriculum or instruction in schools, yet here was the secretary of education bribing the states to adopt new standards that would invariably change their standards, their curriculum, their assessments, their textbooks, and their ways of evaluating teachers and principals. Without congressional approval, Duncan managed to escalate federal control of the nation's schools, imposing the same remedies that Republicans had long favored.

The result of Race to the Top: More charter schools. More high-stakes testing. Evaluation of teachers and principals by test scores, with their jobs on the line every year. Almost every state adopted the new and untested Common Core State Standards. Only two signatures were required: those of the governor and the state superintendent. Most agreed to adopt the Common Core without ever reading them, because they were not yet completed when the two top state officials signed on.

Like No Child Left Behind, Race to the Top assumed that the nation's public schools were in crisis and that only drastic disruption could save them. Constant testing was necessary to identify lagging students and bad teachers. Low-performing schools had to be closed or turned over to privately run charters. Everyone needed to adopt a common set of national standards, which would be tightly aligned with common national tests, teacher education, professional development, and curricular materials.

To manage the Race to the Top program and ultimately to be his chief of staff, Duncan hired Joanne Weiss, the former chief operating officer of the NewSchools Venture Fund, an organization that funds charter schools and educational technology. In an article for the *Harvard Business Review* blog, Weiss explained the Race to the Top competition as a spur to developing a new marketplace for educational materials, matching "smart capital" and innovation. She wrote:

> The development of common standards and shared assessments radically alters the market for innovation in curriculum development, professional development, and formative assessments. Previously, these markets operated on a state-by-state basis, and often on a district-by-district basis. But the adoption of common standards and shared assessments means that education entrepreneurs will enjoy national markets where the best products can be taken to scale.

Once all the pieces of the educational system were woven into a common framework, once everyone was using common standards and tests, once bad teachers were removed, once bad schools were closed, once there was a national marketplace for entrepreneurs, then the test scores of American students would soar to the top of international assessments, and America would be number one again! Or so Arne Duncan and his allies in the department, the corporate sector, the philanthropic world, the media, and Wall Street believed.

No Child Left Behind and Race to the Top were kissing cousins. There was not a dime's worth of difference between them, except that Race to the Top was even more punitive than NCLB. The ideas behind the two crystallized into federal policy that became known as the "education reform movement," but was in fact a movement to disrupt and privatize public education. This movement brought together centrist Democrats and conservative Republicans in common cause, wreaking havoc on American public education, its students, and its teachers.

By the end of 2015, Congress finally arrived at a compromise to replace the failed NCLB law. Republican senator Lamar Alexander of Tennessee and Democratic senator Patty Murray of Washington State and their staffs drafted the Every Student Succeeds Act. It curtailed the most punitive aspects of NCLB, such as requiring schools to make adequate yearly progress toward an unattainable goal of 100 percent proficiency (a goal that no state reached). But the law continued to require annual testing in grades 3–8 in reading and mathematics, a practice not found in any high-performing nation in the world. Other nations typically test students at the transition points between different levels of schooling, from elementary grades to middle school, from middle school to high school, and/or at the end of high school.

The new law provided modest relief, but not much. It left in place the heavy hand of the federal government. Did the federal law enacted in 2002 "leave no child behind"? No. The children who were left behind in 2002 were still left behind many years later. Did Race to the Top succeed in raising test scores to "the top"? No, test scores on the NAEP remained flat despite years of punishments and incentives, as did scores on international tests.

Will "every student succeed" because there is a federal law called the Every Student Succeeds Act? No. To add to the irony, the first secretary of education to judge the wisdom of state plans under the new ESSA act was Betsy DeVos, a noneducator who is actively opposed to the very concept of public schools and has spent many years promoting charter schools, vouchers, for-profit schools, religious schools, and online schools, while funding candidates for political office who share her views.

At the bottom of this avalanche of misguided policies was the purported Texas miracle of the 1990s that helped to elect George W. Bush to the presidency. There was no Texas miracle. On the NAEP for 2017, Texas students performed slightly below the national average.

And yet, many years later, long after it was obvious that this regime of standards, testing, and accountability had failed, the mythical Texas miracle continued to drive national policy. Every public school in the United States was compelled by federal law to continue following the dictates of a law built on a hoax. No national figure had the wisdom, intellect, or courage to stand up and say, "This must stop."

Plenty of parents and teachers did. Even students did.

How did they figure out what eluded our leaders?

CHAPTER 3

What Do the Disrupters Want?

The Disrupters believe that American public education is broken beyond repair, and they want the public to believe it. They rely on a tactic known in the public relations world as FUD (fear, uncertainty, and doubt). The goal of FUD is to sow doubt about a competitor in order to beat it. Disrupters have skillfully deployed FUD to undermine the public's long-standing belief that its public schools are valued community institutions. They want to persuade the public to agree with them on the necessity of closing public schools and turning them over to private management. Disrupters do not like neighborhood public schools and welcome the dispersion of students to schools across the district, even across district lines. They see no value in the bonds among schools, families, and communities.

Before the current era, true reformers wanted to make public schools better. They wanted public schools to have more resources. They wanted better prepared teachers or better curriculum or better teaching materials. They wanted teachers to have higher salaries and smaller classes. They wanted districts to have modern buildings and better playing fields and better physical equipment. They wanted schools to be racially integrated so that all children had the chance to learn alongside others who were different from themselves. They wanted schools to have nurses, health clinics, social workers, psychologists, librarians and libraries, up-to-date technology, and programs for students with disabilities and English language learners. They wanted all children to have equality of educational opportunity. They wanted all children to have good schools with good teachers.

Such were the reformers of old.

Today's Disrupters don't fight for these improvements. They want to reinvent education, reimagine it, replace it with another approach, either through technology or a market-driven choice system in which government supplies the funds and parents send their children wherever they want.

Not every Disrupter believes exactly the same thing about every point in the canon of Disruption. Some believe that test scores are the goal of education. Any school that produces high test scores, they think, is good enough to be funded by the public. Others, like Betsy DeVos, believe that choice is an end in itself. They don't care whether students attend religious schools or private schools or public schools or home schools, and they don't care whether students get higher scores, so long as families make the choice.

The corporate leaders of this campaign admire disruptive innovation, because high-tech businesses do it, so it must be good. They don't consider whether disruption is good for children. Disrupters admire the gig economy, like Uber and Airbnb, and think that reinvented schools should operate on demand and eliminate any job security for employees. They love charter schools because charters are start-ups without histories, just like many new businesses in the modern corporate world. The fact that so many charter schools close every year does not concern them, since frequent openings and closings of businesses are a feature of the modern economy. The concept of "creative destruction" is derived from the work of Austrian economist Joseph Schumpeter. Whether or not it is useful in the business world, it is not useful in the lives of children, who need stability, not disruption.

Corporate Disrupters approve of schools hiring inexperienced teachers with little or no training, such as Teach for America (TFA) recruits, who have only five weeks of preparation, because it cuts costs. Such teachers are paid less than experienced teachers, and few will stay long enough to expect a pension or expensive health benefits. Disrupters want to replace teachers with computers, which cost even less than inexperienced teachers do. Machine teaching is euphemistically called "blended learning" or "personalized learning." This is a peculiar use of the term "personalized," because only a human-to-human interaction can be described accurately as "personalized," while a student's interaction with a machine is by definition impersonal and should be properly called computer-based instruction or "depersonalized learning."

Disrupters like to move fast and break things, including school systems, historic schools, communities, and the lives of students, families, and education professionals. They take pride in disrupting established institutions and other people's lives, though they don't like people to disrupt their lives or private clubs or the exclusive schools that their children attend. Disrupters don't care if teachers and principals object to their strategies, because they are sure that professionals are protecting their self-interest while Disrupters claim that they are "putting students first." Disrupters are unmoved when students and parents plead for the life of a community school slated for closure.

Corporate Disrupters do not respect the teaching profession. They think that anyone can teach, anyone can run a school, and anyone can be a superintendent. Disrupters want to eliminate any job security for teachers, so teachers will live in fear of termination and thus be easier to control. They believe that schools with low test scores have many "incompetent" teachers—protected by their unions—who are acting against the best interests of their students.

Disrupters don't like democratic control of education by elected local school boards (unless they manage to buy control of them). They like mayoral control, where one person is in charge; the mayor can usually be counted on to listen to business leaders, ignore parents, and use his or her power to impose the changes that Disrupters want. They support state takeovers of entire school districts, as happened in New Orleans, Ohio, and Michigan, or state creation of special districts that hand low-performing schools over to charter corporations, as happened in Tennessee. Billionaire Reed Hastings, the founder of Netflix, spent many millions of dollars in California to elect Disrupters to state and local offices; he has said that he looks forward to the day when all schools are controlled by large nonprofit corporations, not by elected school boards.

The Disrupters oppose teacher tenure and seniority, which they con-

sider to be barriers to removing ineffective teachers. They prefer unten-
ured teachers who are willing to work long hours without extra pay and
who are likely to change careers after two or three years of teaching. They
don't like teachers' pensions, which cost a lot and encourage longevity
in the job. The Laura and John Arnold Foundation is determined to
eliminate defined benefit pensions for public sector employees, which
John Arnold considers a threat to the nation's solvency. (Teachers in
fifteen states receive pensions, but not Social Security, when they retire.)
Disrupters don't like teachers' unions, because they organize teachers
to fight for higher pay, smaller classes, and job rights, which Disrupters
oppose. Disrupters believe that standardized test scores can be reliably
used to identify the best and the worst teachers; once the worst teachers
are fired, then every teacher (they assume) will be great.

The teachers' strikes and walkouts that began in early 2018 called
attention to a decade of underinvestment in education. Not only did
teachers in many states have low salaries, well below those of other professionals with comparable education and experience, but public schools
in general had been placed on an austerity diet. In the states where the
strikes occurred, the governors and legislatures had systematically cut
corporate taxes and cut school spending. The corporations and billionaires who supported this agenda followed a similar playbook: Demonize
the public schools as failing. Cut spending on public schools because of
declining state revenues. As class sizes rise and programs are cut in the
public schools, offer school choice as an escape route for those who want
better schools. Tout charter schools and vouchers as superior to the cash-
strapped public schools. Divert public funding from the public schools
to the charter and voucher schools. Ignore evidence that school choice
does not produce superior results.

What do the billionaire funders of privatization want? In their public
statements, they speak of "excellence" and "closing achievement gaps,"
but their actions belie these goals. They are devoted to cutting taxes, cutting spending on public schools, and turning control of public schools
over to private corporations and individuals without prior experience in
education, individuals who are free to hire anyone regardless of credentials, and who can operate schools with minimal or no accountability.

Who are the Disrupters?

John Arnold made his fortune as a natural gas trader at Enron and a hedge fund manager. He has invested heavily in organizations that promote charter schools and privatization of public schools.

Let's start with government officials.

Donald Trump is a Disrupter, who promised during the 2016 campaign to shift $20 billion in federal funding to a school choice program and frequently lambasted public schools as a "disaster." His secretary of education, Betsy DeVos, is a lifelong Disrupter. She has spent decades advocating on behalf of alternatives to public schools. Her organization, the American Federation for Children, promotes her political agenda by lobbying and supporting candidates who favor school choice, not public schools. She is an active member and sponsor of the American Legislative Exchange Council (ALEC), the far-right bill-mill, which supports her views.

Rod Paige and Margaret Spellings, who served consecutively as secretary of education in the administration of George W. Bush, are Disrupters. They adamantly believed that standards, testing, and accountability would produce high performance. They were all-in for the test-and-punish regime of the No Child Left Behind Act, which they (with the assistance of Bush's education advisor, Sandy Kress) designed.

Arne Duncan, Barack Obama's secretary of education for seven years, is a Disrupter. During his time in office, he often lamented how terrible

Betsy DeVos's family fortune is derived from Amway. President Donald Trump appointed her to be secretary of education after his election in 2016. She is a passionate advocate of charter schools and vouchers for religious schools. She has long been active in Republican politics and gives generously to politicians who share her views about school choice.

American public schools are, how inadequate their teachers are, and how amazing are the miracles wrought by charter schools, free of union rules and most state regulations. He never endorsed vouchers but made no effort to stop their proliferation in state after state when he was in office. He was an enthusiastic booster of standardized testing, the Common Core standards, and the use of standardized tests to measure teacher quality. Duncan and Obama gave lip service to unions, but when Wisconsin's governor Scott Walker introduced legislation in 2011 to eliminate collective bargaining, and thousands of public sector employees encircled the state capitol in Madison to protest, neither Duncan nor Obama showed up to support the endangered unions. Wisconsin became a "right to work" state. "Right to work" is right-wing doubletalk, like using the term "personalized learning" as a euphemism to describe replacing teachers with computers. *Right to work* is a prohibition of agreements that require union membership or payment of union dues as a condition of employment. Its purpose is to cripple unions by reducing their membership and eliminating any worker voice in the workplace.

Every Republican governor is a Disrupter, because they actively support privatization by charters and vouchers. Republicans once supported local control as a matter of principle; now, whether in Indiana or Michigan or Ohio or Tennessee, they endorse state takeovers of local schools and districts. With the exception of elected officials from rural districts, the Republican Party seems to have written off public schools, even though at least 80 to 90 percent of the children of their constituents are enrolled in public schools. Rural Republicans tend to understand that the public schools are the anchors of their communities and don't betray them by supporting charters or vouchers. The list of Republican Disrupters is long. It includes such notables as Scott Walker of Wisconsin, Rick Scott and Ron DeSantis of Florida, Rick Snyder of Michigan, Bobby Jindal of Louisiana, Mitch Daniels and Mike Pence of Indiana, John Kasich of Ohio, Doug Ducey of Arizona, Bruce Rauner of Illinois, Nathan Deal of Georgia, Matt Bevin of Kentucky, and Bill Haslam and Bill Lee of Tennessee, as well as virtually every Republican member of the United States Senate, the House of Representatives, and the Trump administration. Support for privatization is not guaranteed among Republicans in Congress, however, because they refused to fund the radical budget proposals of the Trump administration, which would have shifted $20 billion from federal programs meant for needy children to school choice programs.

Among Democratic elected officials, there are Disrupters who support charter schools over public schools. Their number is not as great as those in the Republican Party. These include former Chicago mayor Rahm Emanuel, former governor Jerry Brown of California (who opened two charter schools when he was mayor of Oakland), Senator Michael Bennet and Governor Jared Polis of Colorado, Governor Andrew Cuomo of New York, former governor Dannel Malloy of Connecticut, and Senator Cory Booker of New Jersey.

Now let's consider the philanthropists.

Disrupters dominate the world of philanthropy. Many foundations have followed the lead of billionaires like Bill Gates, the DeVos family, the Walton family, Eli Broad, Michael Bloomberg, and the Koch brothers. Bill Gates has a fortune of more than $100 billion, based on his role in cofounding Microsoft. The Walton family collectively has a fortune of nearly $200 billion, derived from the Walmart and Sam's Club warehouse stores. Its family foundation has spent more than $1 billion to open and support charter schools; it claims to have opened at least one of every four charter schools in the nation. The right-wing, anti-union Walton Family Foundation has also been a major funder of the KIPP charter chain and Teach for America, which supplies low-wage temporary teachers for some public and many charter schools.

The Eli and Edythe Broad Foundation is a major donor to charter schools, even though Eli Broad is a graduate of the Detroit Public Schools. Eli Broad (net worth: more than $7 billion) made his fortune in home building and the insurance industry. He created the Broad Academy, an unaccredited program that trains would-be superintendents in his top-down management philosophy of closing public schools and

Three billionaires meet: Michael Bloomberg (*right*), former mayor of New York City, is CEO of technology and media giant Bloomberg Inc.; Bill Gates (*left*) is the principal founder of Microsoft and the Bill & Melinda Gates Foundation, which has made many forays into education policy; Richard Branson is a British magnate and entrepreneur who has launched numerous ventures.

Mark Zuckerberg, founder of Facebook, has used his vast fortune to promote "personalized learning," which is computer-based instruction and is thus "depersonalized learning." In many communities, students have rebelled against Zuckerberg's instructional ideas.

opening charter schools; its graduates are referred to as "Broadies," and they have a poor track record.

Dick and Betsy DeVos (net worth: $5 billion plus) support school choice, whether for profit or not; the DeVos billions were made primarily by ownership of the Amway Corporation. Charles and the late David Koch, whose net worth exceeds $100 billion, are libertarian supporters of privatization; their fortune derives from many sources, including the fossil fuel industry. The Bezos Family Foundation, representing the family of billionaire Jeff Bezos of Amazon (net worth: more than $100 billion), has contributed to Disrupter causes, including charter schools and Teach for America. Mark Zuckerberg of Facebook is a Disrupter whose net worth exceeds $50 billion; his Chan Zuckerberg Initiative (named for his wife, Priscilla Chan, and himself) promotes computer-based "personalized learning" in schools (CZI is actually a limited liability corporation, not a foundation). Michael Bloomberg, former mayor of New York City, became a multibillionaire in the technology industry; with a net worth of more than $50 billion, he gives generously to charter schools and like-minded candidates in state and local school board races across the nation. Laurene Powell Jobs, widow of Apple's legendary founder, Steve Jobs, has a net worth of nearly $20 billion; she established the Emerson Collective, which aims to reinvent public education.

Many other foundations support the privatization of public schools by charters or vouchers. Their numbers and their wealth are staggering. These organizations include the Lynde and Harry Bradley Foundation (which singlehandedly sponsored vouchers in Milwaukee and kept the voucher schools open when they were under challenge in court in the 1990s), Bloomberg Philanthropies, the Leona M. and Harry B. Helmsley Charitable Trust, the MacArthur Foundation, the Lilly Endowment (Indiana), the Adolph Coors Foundation (Colorado), the Laura and John Arnold Foundation, the Michael and Susan Dell Foundation (the computer manufacturer), the Ewing Marion Kauffman Foundation (Kansas City), the Doris and Donald Fisher Fund (The Gap, Banana Republic, and Old Navy stores), the Anschutz Foundation (Philip Anschutz is a billionaire evangelical who has funded anti-gay initiatives, produced the film *Waiting for "Superman,"* and is a major figure in the fossil fuel and fracking industry), the Thomas A. Roe Foundation (Roe, a successful businessman, was an ardent conservative), the William and Flora Hewlett Foundation (a usually liberal foundation), the W. K. Kellogg Foundation, the Scaife Foundations (created by billionaire Richard Scaife, an archconservative), and the Joyce Foundation. Others include the Charles and Helen Schwab Foundation (founder of a brokerage firm), the Bill and Susan Oberndorf Foundation (a Republican financier), the U.S. Chamber of Commerce Foundation, the Charles and Lynn Schusterman Family Foundation (wealth from the oil and gas industry), the Jacqulin Hume Foundation (devoted to right-wing and libertarian causes), the Daniels Fund, the David Herro Charitable Foundation, the Ballmer Group, the Louis Calder Foundation, the Robertson Foundation (Julian Robertson is a financier whose assets exceed $4 billion), the Wasserman Foundation, the Hunt Family Foundation (El Paso), the Marcus Foundation, the Lumina Foundation, the Overdeck Family Foundation, the William E. Simon Foundation, the Kovner Foundation (New York–based financier Bruce Kovner has a net worth exceeding $5 billion), the Donnell-Kay Foundation (Colorado), the Hyde Family Foundation

Philip Anschutz, a billionaire whose fortune derives from many industries, including oil, gas, and fracking; he produced the celebrated pro-charter, anti-union film *Waiting for "Superman."*

(Memphis), the Hastings/Quillin Fund, the J. A. and Kathryn Albertson Family Foundation (Idaho), the Karsh Family Foundation, the Kern Family Foundation, the KLE Foundation, Park Avenue Charitable Trust, Omidyar Network (Pierre Omidyar founded eBay and has a net worth of about $10 billion), the Raikes Foundation (Jeff Raikes was former head of the Gates Foundation), the Carnegie Corporation of New York, the Sackler Foundation (the family's net worth exceeds $14 billion, generated by Purdue Pharmaceuticals, which manufactures and markets opioids), the California Community Foundation, the Triad Foundation, City-Bridge Foundation, and Gen Next Foundation.

The conservative foundations have their own organization, called the Philanthropy Roundtable. It holds annual meetings, where funders learn where to target their donations to advance school choice and their anti-union views.

In addition, there are corporate donors who support Disruption, such as ExxonMobil, AT&T, Target, Pearson, JP Morgan Chase, Citigroup, ETS, the College Board, and News Corporation (Rupert Murdoch's corporation). Their gifts to charter schools are tax-exempt. The fossil fuel industry (oil, gas, coal, fracking) supports charter schools and vouchers because it prefers to keep its taxes low instead of funding public schools.

The power of the large foundations is enhanced by large contributions from individuals, both Republicans and Democrats, who are multimillionaires and billionaires. Such individuals include Charles and David Koch; venture capitalist Arthur Rock, a generous contributor to Teach for America; Reed Hastings, founder of Netflix; Richard Riordan, former mayor of Los Angeles; and Michael Steinhardt, who founded a chain of Hebrew-language charter schools.

The Disrupters include a large number of hedge fund managers, venture capitalists, and leaders of the technology sector. They believe in competition and the free market, they like start-ups, and they don't like government regulations.

In 2005, several hedge fund managers—Whitney Tilson, Ravenel Boykin Curry IV, John Petry, and Charles Ledley—launched Democrats for Education Reform at a posh party on Central Park South in Manhattan, where the inaugural speaker was a young senator from Illinois named Barack Obama. DFER, as it is deceptively called, was founded by Wall Street hedge fund managers to influence the Democratic Party to support school privatization by making strategic campaign contributions. Inspired by DFER, charter schools became the pet passion of Wall Street.

DFER is a political action committee or PAC. DFER endorses candidates who agree with its views about charter schools and high-stakes testing. Each election cycle, it issues a list of preferred candidates and encourages its members across the country to donate to them. A DFER appeal can raise a significant amount of campaign cash. The Democratic Party in both California and Colorado denounced DFER as a front for corporate America and called on it to remove the D from its title, but DFER ignored them.

DFER has a 501(c)3 twin called Education Reform Now. While DFER raises money for political candidates, ERN is on the ground in several key states, encouraging support for the privatization cause. The board of ERN is populated by hedge fund managers, whose campaign contributions are welcomed by political candidates. ERN is active in

Colorado, New York, Massachusetts, D.C., Louisiana, Connecticut, and New Jersey.

Supporting charter schools and serving on the board of KIPP or Eva Moskowitz's Success Academy or some other charter chain confers social cachet in the hedge fund world. It is a way to meet other hedge fund managers and to show that you too are part of the "in-crowd." The charter-loving equity investors and hedge fund managers include Julian Robertson (who made a gift of $25 million to the Success Academy charter chain), Daniel Loeb (who served as chair of the Success Academy charter chain and donated millions to it), John Paulson (a Trump supporter who gave $8.5 million to Success Academy), former Apple CEO John Sculley, David Einhorn, Christopher Gabrieli, Joel Greenblatt, Paul Tudor Jones, Nick Hanauer, Steve Ballmer, William Bloomfield, Stanley Druckenmiller, Ken Langone (founder of Home Depot), Seth Klarman, John Doerr, Carl Icahn, Rex Sinquefield (a Missouri billionaire), and dozens more very wealthy individuals. It is likely difficult to throw a beanbag in a corporate or Wall Street boardroom without hitting a member of the board of a charter chain. They seem to love the fun, sport, and excitement of being involved in redesigning the nation's education system, believing that what is needed most are incentives, competition, disruption, deregulation, and innovation.

Why do so many individuals and organizations support disruption of public schools? Some want lower taxes and less government spending. Some want to blow up the current system and replace it with privately run schools. Some hate government-run schools because they prefer free enterprise to anything run by the government. Some believe that disruption is what modern corporations do as often as possible. Some believe that the free market efficiently solves all problems, and they want to introduce a free market of schooling.

The radical right-wing American Legislative Exchange Council (ALEC) is the key organization in the world of Disruption advocacy. It is funded by dozens of major corporations. Some two thousand state legislators are members of ALEC. In his book *The One Percent Solution: How Corporations Are Remaking America One State at a Time,* Gordon Lafer lists over one hundred major corporations that are past or present members of ALEC (some dropped out of ALEC because of adverse publicity). The list includes such major corporations as AT&T, Altria, Amazon, Blue Cross Blue Shield, Boeing, Ford, General Electric, Home Depot, IBM, McDonald's, Merck, Microsoft, and many more. ALEC drafts legislation that is pro–charter school and pro-voucher, as well as anti–teacher certification, anti-union, and anti-regulation. Its members return to their home states and introduce ALEC bills as their own, simply inserting the name of their state on the ALEC bill. ALEC is passionately committed to deregulation and lower corporate taxes; it writes legislation opposing environmental regulations, gun control, and any government regulation of business. ALEC is a libertarian bill-mill for conservative state legislators yet has somehow been designated by the Internal Revenue Service as a charitable organization, meaning that donations to it are tax-exempt even though its work directly influences legislation. ALEC has long relied on the financial contributions of the DeVos family and the Koch brothers.

Betsy DeVos's American Federation for Children funds the Great Lakes Education Project, an advocacy group for school choice and the Mackinac Center for Public Policy in Michigan, which promotes lower taxes, right-to-work laws, and school choice. The Koch brothers created Americans for Prosperity, which opposes public spending and public schools across the nation, as well as the Charles Koch Institute. In 2019, Charles Koch and his powerful donor network unveiled plans to disrupt and privatize public schools and launched a new organization called Yes Every Kid. The Kochs have donated to create institutes in more than three hundred universities to spread their libertarian ideology.

The State Policy Network is a network that advocates for charter schools and vouchers. SourceWatch.org, a media watchdog of extremist groups, describes SPN as "a web of rightwing 'think tanks' and tax-exempt organizations in 49 states, Puerto Rico, Washington, D.C., Canada, and the United Kingdom." Founded in 1992, SPN describes itself as a "state-based free market think tank movement" devoted to finding free market solutions to policy issues. SourceWatch says that the SPN groups "operate as the policy, communications, and litigation arm of ALEC, giving the cookie-cutter ALEC agenda a sheen of academic legitimacy and state-based support." SPN member groups write bills

Charles Koch is among the most influential libertarian philanthropists in the nation. He and his late brother David are worth about $100 billion. Their fortune was initially established in the oil and chemical industries but has since expanded to multiple businesses. The Koch brothers invested strategically in think tanks and universities to build a cadre of libertarian intellectuals to provide support for their belief in minimal government.

for ALEC, and "peddle cookie-cutter 'studies' to back the cookie-cutter ALEC agenda, spinning that agenda as indigenous to the state." Source-Watch reports that SPN is funded by the Koch brothers, the DeVos family, the same corporations that fund ALEC, especially Big Tobacco and Big Oil, and the Walton Family Foundation, the Roe Foundation, the Coors family, the Bradley Foundation, and Searle Freedom Trust.

Conservative think tanks supply academic veneer to the offensive against public education. They provide research and policy documents to arm the school choice warriors. At the top of the list are the far-right Heritage Foundation, along with the libertarian Cato Institute. Then come the Thomas B. Fordham Institute of Ohio and D.C. and the Center for Education Reform, which likes every choice in schooling except public schools. Other prominent conservative think tanks include the American Enterprise Institute, the Heartland Institute, the Goldwater Institute, the Pioneer Institute, the Manhattan Institute for

Policy Research, the Center on Reinventing Public Education at the University of Washington, the Friedman Foundation for Educational Choice (now called EdChoice), the Reason Foundation, and the Mercatus Center at George Mason University. Almost every state has a free market conservative think tank specific to that state, such as the Texas Public Policy Foundation, the Oklahoma Council of Public Affairs, the Bluegrass Institute for Public Policy Solutions (Kentucky), the Cardinal Institute (Kentucky), the John Locke Foundation (North Carolina), and the Show-Me Institute in Missouri. The state-level think tanks are associated with the State Policy Network and amplify ALEC's free enterprise, anti-regulation, anti-tax messages. You can recognize the state-level think tanks by their mission statements, which usually laud liberty, free markets, and free enterprise. They promote state legislation for charters and vouchers, budget cuts for public schools, and legislation that reduces the working conditions and professional status of teachers. In North Carolina, when Tea Party extremists took control of the state legislature in 2010, one of their first actions was to kill the North Carolina Teaching Fellows program, a successful six-year program based in the state's public universities to prepare career teachers, and transferred its $6 million in state funding to Teach for America, whose teachers make no more than a two-year commitment and are often imported from out of state. The change had no rationale other than to cut off the pipeline of career teachers in the state.

The work of the right-wing and conservative think tanks is augmented by centrist think tanks that represent what is now called "neoliberal" thought. They straddle ideological divides and support privatization by charters but not by vouchers. The leaders in this camp are Education Trust, which advocates for high-stakes testing and charters, and the Center for American Progress, which served as an echo chamber for the Obama administration and now supports test-based accountability for teachers and applauds charters, no matter how much they damage existing public schools. Both are based in D.C. and are influential with Democratic legislators and their staffs. The Brookings Institution, also based in D.C., was long thought of as a liberal think tank, but its education program was led from 2010 to 2015 by Grover (Russ) Whitehurst, the former education research director for the George W. Bush administra-

The Sackler family became billionaires as a result of their ownership of Purdue Pharmaceuticals, the manufacturer of OxyContin. Multiple lawsuits have been filed against the corporation for its failure to warn about the addictive qualities of the painkiller, which has been responsible for more than 200,000 deaths. Jonathan Sackler (*standing, second from right*) is a major funder of charter schools in Connecticut and across the nation.

tion, during which time it promoted pro-choice education policies, even grading cities by their willingness to adopt alternatives to public schools.

Some activist organizations, like Stand for Children, are openly political, having both a charitable designation by the IRS (C3) and a political action committee (C4). Stand for Children was founded by Jonah Edelman, son of civil rights icon Marian Wright Edelman; it began its life as a progressive organization but turned into a well-funded front for Corporate Disrupters and a pass-through for campaign contributions to candidates who are pro-charter and critical of teacher tenure. Stand for Children engages in local election campaigns in support of charter-friendly school board candidates.

Foundations that want to give money to an all-purpose bundler of funds for charter school start-ups donate to the NewSchools Venture Fund, The Silicon Valley Foundation, or the Charter School Growth Fund, which are amply funded by billionaires like Gates, Walton, and

Broad. If they want to help a group working to promote charter schools across the nation, they can support 50CAN. 50CAN started in 2011, building on the foundation of ConnCAN, a Connecticut-based group created in 2005 to win political support for charter schools in that state. Given the pool of hedge fund managers in the affluent Fairfield County region (Greenwich, Darien, New Canaan), Connecticut was fertile territory. Billionaire Jonathan Sackler (the opioid manufacturer) was a key funder of both ConnCAN and 50CAN.

Organizations funded by billionaires to promote disruption and privatization pop up like mushrooms, with a similar cast of players migrating from one group to another. The money available to sustain them is seemingly endless. Education Cities, Inc., is a billionaire-funded organization promoting charters in thirty cities. It grew out of The Mind Trust, which began as a charter advocacy group in Indianapolis. The Mind Trust has been so effective in Indianapolis that the survival of public schools hangs in the balance as charter schools expand and public schools close. Education Cities has morphed into The City Fund, whose purpose is to spread the idea of "portfolio districts" to targeted cities; it injects money into local elections to help charter proponents gain control by outspending supporters of public schools. A portfolio district is one where the local board (or some entity operating in its stead) acts like a stockbrokerage, holding on to winners (schools with high test scores) and getting rid of losers (schools with low test scores), replacing them with charter schools. The City Fund began its life with nearly $200 million collected from the usual billionaires. Its stated goal of intervening in local school board elections by funding pro-charter candidates is deeply undemocratic.

Charter-friendly foundations have launched teacher organizations to support their agenda. Typically, these groups are led by Teach for America alumni who found a new career in advocacy for the Disruption agenda. Their representatives are sometimes called upon to testify in legislative hearings against tenure, seniority, unions, and other perks and rights that most teachers value. Groups like Teach Plus and Educators for Excellence, funded generously by Gates and Walton, fill this role.

If you are looking for a graduate school that exists solely to award advanced degrees to charter teachers, there is Relay Graduate School of Education. It is an odd "graduate school," which has offices in several cities but no campus, no library, no professors with doctorates, no research, and no critical studies of the history or sociology or economics of education. Its faculty consists primarily of former charter teachers and administrators, not scholars. Relay awards master's degrees to future charter teachers who major in the tricks of strict student discipline and the arcane subject of test score raising.

Teach for America is a favorite of the disruption-friendly foundations. It is handsomely funded by Walton, Gates, Broad, and many others. It currently has more than $350 million in assets, gathered not only from foundations and corporate donors, but also from payments it receives from districts that hire its inexperienced "corps members." TFA recruits recent college graduates, bright young people with an ample supply of energy and idealism, gives them five weeks of training in a summer institute, and then sends them to teach in challenging urban and rural classrooms. TFA used to boast that its newly minted teachers, during their two-year commitment to the classroom, were more successful than experienced teachers and would "make history" by their unique ability to change the "trajectory" of lives of poor children. However, the boasting has died down in recent years, as the examples of success have diminished in number and plausibility. Some TFA teachers remain in the classroom beyond the two years they signed on for, but most use their TFA connections as a stepping-stone to higher positions in education, the financial sector, or other fields. TFA's political organization, Leadership for Educational Equity, trains TFA alumni to run for state and local offices, where they can promote charter-friendly policies.

TFA alums have served as state commissioners (in Louisiana, North Carolina, Tennessee, and Rhode Island) and on local and state school boards, where they usually advocate for charter schools and sometimes for vouchers. With millions of dollars of funding from billionaire Arthur Rock of California, TFA places interns in key congressional staff offices to protect the interests of TFA and charter funding. TFA founded an international organization, Teach for All, with branches across the world, where its recruits undermine certified teachers and their unions. In 2019, ProPublica published an investigative article about the close ties between TFA and the charter school movement. Its high-powered national board of directors includes a member of the Walton family and the former Republican governor of Tennessee, Bill Haslam, a billionaire who supports vouchers. The small board of directors of Leadership for Educational Equity includes two billionaires: Emma Bloomberg (daughter of Michael Bloomberg) and Arthur Rock.

The National Council on Teacher Quality (NCTQ) was created in 2000 by the conservative Thomas B. Fordham Foundation, with the purpose of promoting alternative certification and discrediting teachers' colleges, which conservatives disliked and considered too "touchy-feely" and too progressive. At the time, I was on the board of the foundation (now renamed the Thomas B. Fordham Institute). NCTQ floundered at first, unsure of its strategy, but was rescued in 2001 by a $5 million grant from Rod Paige, George W. Bush's secretary of education. By 2012, NCTQ was funded by the Gates Foundation and a long list of other foundations; its advisory committee included Disruption stars like Michelle Rhee and Joel Klein, who served as chancellor of the New York City public schools from 2002 to 2010, during the mayoralty of Michael Bloomberg. NCTQ's biggest coup occurred when *U.S. News & World Report* invited it to rank the nation's teachers' colleges; that publication regularly publishes rankings of colleges, high schools, and graduate schools. Many of the well-established teachers' colleges refused to cooperate with NCTQ because they were already accredited by reputable associations that had no political agenda. NCTQ gives low grades to almost all teachers' colleges based on their course catalogues without bothering to visit them.

The Disrupters have a strong presence in the mainstream media, not only among conservative pundits on Fox News, *The Wall Street Journal*, and other outlets for conservative opinion (billionaire Rupert Murdoch has contributed to Success Academy and loves school privatization). They can count on glowing editorials in *The New York Times* and *The Washington Post* about the value of privately managed charter schools and standardized testing. Opinion writers such as Nicholas Kristof, David Leonhardt, David Brooks, Jonathan Chait, and Jonathan Alter are outspoken advocates for charter schools. *Time* and *Newsweek* devoted cover stories to disruption hero Michelle Rhee long before any evidence was available about her record.

Michelle Rhee, chancellor of the Washington, D.C., schools from

2007 to 2010, was the national face of the "reform" movement. During her time in office, she demeaned teachers and principals, reduced their professional autonomy, made standardized test scores the measure of all things, attacked the teachers' union, and promoted privatization.

After the 2010 defeat of Adrian Fenty, the mayor of D.C. who had hired her, Rhee resigned as chancellor and formed an organization called StudentsFirst. The very name "StudentsFirst" implied that students and teachers were on opposing sides and that experienced teachers were hostile to the interests of their students. Only Rhee and her allies, she implied, actually cared about students, and their teachers did not. Rhee declared that she would enroll one million members in her new organization and raise $1 billion to promote her brand of Disruption.

It is hard to overstate the extent of media adulation that Rhee attracted as chancellor of the school system in D.C. She was featured on the cover of national magazines and on national television programs, articulating the anti-public-school, anti-teacher, anti-union message of Corporate Disruption. PBS correspondent John Merrow devoted twelve programs to Rhee's aggressive efforts to reform the D.C. public schools. She appeared on *Oprah* as the savior of American education and had a starring role in *Waiting for "Superman."*

However, a cloud arose on the horizon in 2009, when the test publisher CTB/McGraw-Hill flagged more than forty D.C. schools that had an unusually high wrong-to-right erasure rate on their tests. District officials never investigated, and the media paid no attention. Then in 2011, *USA Today* identified 103 schools with suspicious erasure rates. One school stood out for its dramatic gains, the Crosby S. Noyes Education Campus, which Rhee considered the "shining star" of the district. She promoted its principal, Wayne Ryan, to be an instructional supervisor for other principals. Ryan was succeeded by Adell Cothorne, who was thrilled to become the leader of the district's top-performing school. But as the new principal visited classrooms, she was surprised to see "mediocre teaching and faltering student performance." In November 2010, only hours after students had taken a practice exam, Cothorne walked unannounced into a room where test booklets were scattered on a table, and "three staffers were poised above test answer sheets." She believed they were in the midst of changing answers. She reported

Michelle Rhee served as chancellor of the D.C. Public Schools from
2007 to 2010 and was featured on the cover of national newsmagazines
for her tough policies toward teachers and principals.

what she saw to two higher-ups. They disregarded her and later claimed
that she never said anything to them. In April 2011, at the next test
administration, Cothorne changed the locks on the room where the tests
and answer sheets were stored. As Jay Matthews of *The Washington Post*
reported: "Scores dropped dramatically. The portion of Noyes students
proficient in reading fell from 61 to 32 percent, and in math from 54 to 28
percent." For courageously challenging the cheating culture, Cothorne
became a pariah; she resigned from the district at the end of the spring
2011 semester. The district's inspector general conducted an investigation and found no evidence of cheating; curiously, he did not interview
Cothorne. In his final episode on PBS about Rhee, called "The Education of Michelle Rhee," John Merrow exposed the cheating scandal,
interviewed Cothorne, and cast doubt on the legitimacy of Rhee's legacy.

Rhee ignored the allegations of cheating. Nonetheless, her post-
D.C. career fizzled. During its brief heyday, her organization purchased
a television commercial that ran on network television during the 2012
Olympics and portrayed American students in the person of a flabby,
effeminate athlete who fell on his back when trying to perform in a

competition intended for female athletes. This was her ugly, homophobic, sexist portrayal of our nation's students. After funding right-wing candidates who supported her agenda, she retired from her organization, and it was absorbed by 50CAN.

After Michelle Rhee's star faded, Campbell Brown emerged as the public face of the Disruption movement. Brown, a former television news anchor, led the fight against teacher tenure and seniority. Although she lacked any experience in public schools as a student, teacher, or parent, Brown declared war on what she decided was the biggest problem in education: lazy, incompetent teachers who were protected by their unions and by tenure. Brown wrote editorials in Rupert Murdoch's publications (the *New York Post* and *The Wall Street Journal*) alleging that unions and tenure were shielding significant numbers of teachers who were sexual predators. She supported the Vergara lawsuit in California, which sought to eliminate teacher tenure in that state, and created her own organization called the Partnership for Educational Justice to continue the fight against tenure and seniority in state courts. The Vergara lawsuit was eventually dismissed by the state's highest court. Her lawsuits were tossed out by state courts in Minnesota and New Jersey, which didn't see any connection between teacher tenure and student test scores. Brown founded an online media outlet called "The 74," funded by charter-friendly billionaires. (The "74" refers to the millions of children under eighteen in the nation.) After Brown moved on to work for Facebook, in charge of its relationships with the media, The 74 remained active on the side of charters and Disruption.

With Rhee in retirement and Brown otherwise occupied, the new face of the "Education Reform" movement became Donald Trump's secretary of education Betsy DeVos, who never bothered to disguise her contempt for the nation's public schools.

The expansion of charters and the war on unions and experienced teachers appeared unstoppable because of the money and political power funding its activities. Supporters of public schools began to wonder whether they could survive these constant assaults.

I will argue in the pages to come that they not only will survive but will prevail. They will prevail because the Disruption movement is imploding. None of its ideas has been successful. Every promise it made has gone unfulfilled. Every initiative it has launched has failed. Its victories are ephemeral. Most are fanciful triumphs of public relations and marketing.

Aside from the true believers on the fringes of the right, the Disruption movement has reached the point of intellectual and moral exhaustion. Most of its followers are paid employees. Money is the fuel of the movement. I have often thought that if the Disruption movement held a convention in Madison Square Garden or some comparable large arena and excluded paid employees, there would be a few rows of billionaires and hedge fund managers socializing about their next big deal, a pack of friendly journalists, and the rest of the hall would be empty.

The Corporate Disruption movement is actually not a movement at all. It pretends to be one. It is an illusion created by elites and plutocrats, writing checks. No social movement in American history depended on the bounty and leadership of its richest citizens; genuine social movements are built by ordinary people, not powerful elites.

As Michael Edwards, a former Ford Foundation executive, wrote in his brilliant book *Small Change: Why Business Won't Save the World,* "the hype that surrounds philanthrocapitalism runs far ahead of its ability to deliver real results. . . . There have always been areas of life that we deliberately protect from the narrow calculations of competition, price, profit, and cost—such as our families and community associations—but in the rush to privatize and commercialize social action and activity, there is a danger that these firewalls will be forgotten. . . . Why should the rich and famous decide how schools are going to be reformed, or what kinds of drugs will be supplied at prices affordable to the poor, or which civil society groups get funded for their work? . . . Social transformation is not a job to be left to market forces or to the whims of billionaires."

Edwards added: "Would philanthrocapitalists have helped to finance the civil rights movement in the United States? One hopes so, but it didn't fit any of the criteria that are at the top of the philanthrocapitalists' agenda: It wasn't data driven, it didn't operate through competition, it couldn't generate much revenue, and it didn't measure its impact in terms of the number of people who were served each day—yet it changed the world forever. Real social change happens by deepening this kind of broad, democratic movement and when disadvantaged groups gain enough power to effect structural changes in politics and economics."

And yet, the world bows to those with the most money. They have an inordinate influence on public decision making because of their great wealth. This is corrosive to democracy, to the fundamental concept that we the people choose our rulers, with each person having one vote only.

So long as billionaires, hedge fund managers, and their allies are handing out money, there will be people lined up to take it. But their transactions cannot be confused with a social movement. Years from now, historians will look back and wonder why so many very wealthy people spent so much money in a vain attempt to disrupt and privatize public education and why they ignored the income inequality and wealth inequality that were eating away at the vitals of American society.

CHAPTER 4

Meet the Resistance

Who belongs to the Resistance?

Members of the Resistance have some genuine connection to education as teachers, administrators, students, parents or grandparents of students, graduates of public schools, scholars, religious leaders who believe in the separation of church and state, citizens who recognize that public schools are an essential foundation stone of a democratic society.

The Resistance agrees on several central ideas. First, it opposes the privatization of public schools. Second, it opposes the misuse and overuse of standardized testing. Third, it respects the teaching profession and believes that teachers and other school staff should have appropriate professional compensation. Fourth, it wants public schools to have the resources needed for the children they enroll. Fifth, it wants schools to cultivate the joy of learning and teaching. Sixth, it places the needs of children and the value of knowledge above the whims and theories of politicians and philanthropists. Last, it understands that students' lives are influenced by conditions outside the control of the school, including their access to good housing, medical care, nutrition, and safe neighborhoods.

The Resistance does not have access to vast reservoirs of cash. The Resistance relies primarily on the voluntarism and individual donations of those who believe in public education and oppose privatization.

Almost everyone who works for the Resistance does so without pay. (I do not include here the staff of teachers' unions, who are paid by the dues of teachers, not corporations, billionaires, foundations, or Wall Street.) The number of foundations that support the Resistance is in the single digits, led by the Schott Foundation for Public Education.

This is truly a David vs. Goliath matchup. If ever there was a mismatch, it is the contest between Disrupters and the Resistance.

And yet, the Resistance is winning the war. It is winning for two reasons. First, everything the Disrupters have imposed on the public schools has failed. Facts and evidence matter. The Disrupters' policies have not produced stunning improvements for any district or state, not even those they completely controlled, like Louisiana or New Mexico or Florida or the District of Columbia or Milwaukee or Detroit. Disrupters boast about the test scores of specific charter chains, but none of the high-flying charter chains has ever successfully managed an entire school district. In 1999, the for-profit Edison Project took over a three-school district in Inkster, Michigan, and failed, and in 2001, Edison took over nine of the ten schools in Chester-Upland in Pennsylvania, suspended nearly half the students, and failed. The charter model works best when the schools choose the students they want and exclude or push out those they don't want. Some charters have been known to discourage students by failing to offer transportation or by requiring an essay or by requiring parents to contribute money to the school. Even when they admit students by lottery, they can discourage unwanted students (those with disabilities or low test scores) from enrolling by telling them that the school is not "the right fit" for them; they can shed students by repeatedly suspending them for behavior issues, calling their mothers to conferences day after day, and using other tactics to push them out. The only all-charter district in the nation is New Orleans, which is a below-average district in one of the lowest-performing states in the nation. The story of the Disruption movement is a story of failed experiments on other people's children.

Second, the Resistance is persistent and highly motivated. The Resistance is powered not by money but by passion and conviction. The Resistance has what the Disrupters do not: millions of allies willing to work for no pay. Its values and ideals are shared by millions of teachers and principals who work every day in America's classrooms. It enjoys the support of millions of parents who oppose school closings and community disruption and who reject the narrow emphasis on standardized testing that is now written into federal law. The Resistance is dedicated to the principle of public education as a common good, one that should not be handed off to entrepreneurs, for-profit corporations, corporate chains, and amateurs. The Resistance believes that educators should be professionals, that children should be treated as individuals, not data points, and that real education cannot be measured by standardized tests.

The Resistance challenged the consensus among politicians of both parties and corporate leaders who claimed that American education was failing and that the only way to fix it was with standards, tests, competition, and accountability. Disrupters believed that schools should compete for students just as businesses compete for customers. They never understood the difference between a school and a shoe store. They never understood that competition produces a few winners and many losers. They believed that one could manage only what could be measured. For them, measurement was at the core of every successful business. Corporate executives need data, hard data, big data, to pinpoint success or failure, to give out rewards and sanctions. It never occurred to them that what presumably worked in the corporate world was not appropriate for measuring children, each of whom was unique, or for measuring learning, which was far more complex, nuanced, and idiosyncratic than what could be assessed by standardized tests. What, after all, is a standard unit when measuring learning? I have never forgotten being told by Peter Cunningham, who was then Secretary of Education Arne Duncan's chief spokesman, "We measure what we treasure." I was taken aback because I could not imagine how to measure what I treasure: my family, my friends, my pets, my colleagues, my work, the art and books I have collected. How do you measure what you really treasure?

Michael Edwards, whom I quoted earlier, contrasts what philanthrocapitalists value (data, outputs, test scores, measurable outcomes) with the relationships and qualities that civil society values: "There are no standard metrics for caring, solidarity, compassion, tolerance, and mutual support." Yet these are the bonds among citizens that produce lasting change.

Long before the passage of No Child Left Behind in 2001, the seeds of the Resistance were planted by outspoken authors and scholars.

In the 1960s, Jonathan Kozol wrote powerful books about the poverty, neglect, and segregation that harmed children in America's urban schools; his best-selling book *Death at an Early Age* is a classic. Susan Ohanian, a teacher in Vermont and a prolific author, warned about the misuse of standardized testing, its danger to the professional autonomy of teachers, and its threat to the well-being of children. In his books, Alfie Kohn attacked the misguided emphasis on standardized testing, grades, competition, and other extrinsic motivators of students.

Deborah Meier, an outspoken leader of the progressive education movement, was a teacher and principal who led by example, opposing standardized tests and the standardization of education. She opened schools of choice, but only within the public school systems of New York City and Boston.

Prominent scholars have refuted the claim that American public education was broken and that the way to fix it was with testing, competition, and punitive accountability. Scholars do not self-identify as members of the Resistance, but many have produced solid research demonstrating that a strong, equitable, and well-funded public school system is in the best interests of the nation and that standardized tests are ineffective, even harmful measures of both teachers and students.

In 1995, two eminent researchers, David C. Berliner and Bruce J. Biddle, challenged the conventional wisdom about "failing schools" in *The Manufactured Crisis: Myths, Frauds, and the Attack on America's Public Schools.* Berliner and Gene V. Glass, another respected scholar, published *50 Myths and Lies That Threaten America's Public Schools: The Real Crisis in Education,* which refuted the conventional wisdom about the alleged failure of public education. Richard Rothstein skewered the flawed mainstream narrative in *The Way We Were?: The Myths and Realities of America's Student Achievement,* which showed that the schools of the past were not superior to the schools of the present. Rothstein demonstrated how poverty negatively affects students in *Class and Schools: Using Social, Economic, and Educational Reform to Close the Black-White Achievement Gap.* Christopher A. Lubienski and Sarah Theule Lubienski documented the superiority of public schools over private schools in *The*

Public School Advantage: Why Public Schools Outperform Private Schools.
Economist Helen F. Ladd published major peer-reviewed studies demonstrating that test-based accountability, such as No Child Left Behind, is
"highly unrealistic," and insufficient to overcome the burdens of poverty.
Bruce Baker has demonstrated in his studies that equitable and adequate
funding matters. Soon after the launch of President Obama's Race to the
Top competition, a group of eminent education scholars issued a joint
statement refuting a key part of the Obama program, that is, the evaluation of teachers by the test scores of their students. Edward H. Haertel,
a distinguished leader in the field of educational testing, challenged the
reliability and validity of this practice; teachers, he wrote, account for
about 10 percent of the variation in their students' test scores, a proportion that is overshadowed by out-of-school factors. Daniel Koretz, an
expert on testing, questioned the efficacy of standardized testing as an
accountability tool in his book *The Testing Charade: Pretending to Make
Schools Better.* Audrey Amrein-Beardsley's research debunked the idea
that teacher effectiveness can be judged by the test scores of their students. The National Education Policy Center, led by Kevin Welner of the
University of Colorado, engaged teams of scholars to critique the shoddy
research that promoted the strategies of the Disrupters.

Finnish scholar Pasi Sahlberg's *Finnish Lessons: What Can the World
Learn from Educational Change in Finland?* challenged the Disrupters'
narrative by presenting the counterexample of Finland, a nation that
achieved international acclaim by respecting teachers as professionals,
encouraging student creativity, and minimizing standardized testing.
Sahlberg coined the term "GERM" (the Global Education Reform
Movement) to describe the spread of standardization and markets
around the globe. Yong Zhao, born and educated in China but established as a scholar in the United States, refuted the Disrupters' belief
that high-scoring Asian societies are models for America. Like Sahlberg,
he encouraged the cultivation of divergent thinking and creativity, not
conformity and standardization. Linda Darling-Hammond argued in
*The Flat World and Education: How America's Commitment to Equity Will
Determine Our Future* that the future of the nation depends on educating all students, not just those who are white or live in affluent districts.
Noliwe Rooks coined the term "segrenomics" to describe a system in

Pasi Sahlberg is a Finnish educator, researcher, and author. His book *Finnish Lessons* emphasizes the importance of teacher professionalism, student creativity, and minimizing standardized testing in Finland.

which saving the poor is a highly profitable business, in her searing history of black education, *Cutting School: Privatization, Segregation, and the End of Public Education.*

Joanne Barkan wrote carefully researched articles for *Dissent* magazine about the billionaires who were funding school privatization. In 2012, Katherine Stewart's *The Good News Club: The Christian Right's Stealth Assault on America's Children* warned about efforts to erode the secular nature of America's public schools. Jeff Bryant wrote numerous articles in *Salon, The Progressive,* and other publications about the well-funded, antidemocratic assault on public education in city after city.

Documentarians, some professional, some amateur, created films to reach a larger audience. Vicki Abeles produced *Race to Nowhere,* a stinging critique of high-stakes standardized testing, then another anti-testing film called *Beyond Measure.* Abeles took her films on the road and showed them to community groups across the country. Professional videographers Sarah Mondale, Sarah Patton, and Vera Aronow produced an award-winning four-part documentary in 2000 called *School,* which was shown nationally on PBS, but when the same team produced

Yong Zhao is a Chinese-born, Chinese-educated
scholar who is now an American citizen. He has
written extensively in opposition to standardization
and test-based accountability and in favor of
education that promotes creativity and divergent
thinking.

a searing critique of Corporate Disruption called *A Backpack Full of Cash,* narrated by Matt Damon, they struggled to find funding, and PBS declined to air it. Like Abeles, they took their film on the road to hundreds of community groups and film festivals. Brian and Cindy Malone produced *Education, Inc.,* to expose the nefarious intrusion of Dark Money (anonymous contributions) into school board races, focusing on the right-wing takeover of Douglas County, Colorado. Mark Hall's film *Killing Ed* critiqued the secretive Gulen movement, whose nearly two hundred charter schools were replacing public schools with schools run and staffed largely by Turkish men connected to an imam who lived in seclusion in the Pocono Mountains of Pennsylvania. Retired teacher Norm Scott's *The Inconvenient Truth Behind "Waiting for 'Superman'"* documented parent and teacher resistance to the chaotic reign of Michael Bloomberg and his schools' chancellor Joel Klein in New York City, which was noted for multiple reorganizations, school closings, the proliferation of small schools, charter school expansion, and firings of principals. Rocky Killian, superintendent of one of the best districts in Indiana, produced *Rise Above the Mark,* a film about the corporate assault on public education, which showed how the excellent schools of the West Lafayette school district were harmed by budget cuts following the Indiana General Assembly's embrace of charter schools and vouchers.

Champions of very young children created a Resistance organization called Defending the Early Years (DEY), whose leaders included Geralyn Bywater McLaughlin, Nancy Carlsson-Paige, Blakeley Bundy, Denisha Jones, Diane Levin, Constance Kamii, Lilian Katz, Maurice Sykes, Michelle Gunderson, and Susan Ochshorn. DEY fought state efforts to impose academic discipline, computer-based instruction, and standardized testing on little children, which they viewed as child abuse.

When Barack Obama was elected in 2008, educators expected that No Child Left Behind would be radically overhauled. But President Obama's selection of Chicago superintendent Arne Duncan over scholar Linda Darling-Hammond signaled continuity with Bush's disastrous agenda, not change. When Duncan released the Obama administration's Race to the Top program on July 25, 2009, educators realized that they had been deceived. The high-stakes testing continued. The punishment of schools that did not produce higher scores every year continued. The proliferation of charters continued. The only new idea in the Obama program was the demand that teachers be judged by student test scores, a practice that was unsupported by evidence and immediately criticized by the scholars at the National Research Council.

One of the first educators to lambaste the new administration was Anthony Cody, a Berkeley-educated science teacher in the high-poverty schools of Oakland. Cody wrote an open letter to President Obama on his widely read blog called "Living in Dialogue." Cody was a fervent supporter of Obama during the election, taking seriously the candidate's promise to put an end to "preparing students to fill in bubbles on standardized tests." He believed Obama when he said he wanted to support schools, not punish them. Cody was appalled by Race to the Top, which repudiated Obama's campaign promises. He objected to Duncan's plans to "turn around" (i.e., restructure, privatize, or close) five thousand of the nation's "worst" schools, based on test scores, even though there was no evidence that closing schools is good for students; to tie teachers' ratings to test scores, knowing full well that this practice would lead to more teaching to the test and narrowing of the curriculum; and

Anthony Cody taught middle school science for two decades
in the high-poverty schools of Oakland, California. He is a
cofounder of the Network for Public Education and a leading
activist in the Resistance movement against high-stakes testing
and privatization.

to expand charter schools. Teachers are ready to be partners in reform,
Cody wrote, but not if they are demoralized, ignored, and sidelined, as
Duncan planned to do.

Cody started a Facebook group called "Teachers' Letters to Obama."
At the end of 2009, he collected scores of letters, had them printed and
bound, and mailed them to the president. A few months later, Cody
was invited to speak to Secretary Duncan for thirty minutes. He gathered eleven other experienced educators, and they rehearsed what they
planned to tell Duncan. When the call finally happened, Secretary Duncan had six staff members on the line with him, and they spoke for fifteen
of the thirty minutes. When it came time for the educators to speak, their
voices were garbled and almost incomprehensible. Cody later described
the call as "Talking into a Tin Can on a String 3,000 Miles Long." The
educators wanted classroom assessments that were individualized and
developmentally appropriate, not NCLB-style standardized tests. After
the call ended, Cody concluded that "the funny thing about the conversation was that the whole time, they seemed to think we had questions,

and their job was to answer them. We had actually approached the conversation from a different place. We thought perhaps they might want to ask US questions, or hear our ideas about how to improve schools."

Cody learned an important lesson. Duncan was a master at appearing to listen and seeming to agree, but he never changed course. Duncan believed that American education was a disaster and that many teachers were shirkers. He often said that students had been "dummied down" by their teachers, who lied to them about how little they knew. He believed in standardized testing, high-stakes accountability, charter schools, and closing schools with low scores. Duncan enthusiastically promoted the Common Core State Standards, which was an effort to standardize instruction across the nation. Duncan loved disruption.

Jesse Turner, a teacher educator in Connecticut, joined Cody's group. He walked from Connecticut to the District of Columbia to dramatize his opposition to No Child Left Behind and Race to the Top. When he arrived in D.C., he met with about fifty other dissident educators, and they began to plan a national march on Washington for the summer of 2011. The organizing group was called the Save Our Schools steering committee, and it consisted of educators from across the nation. The SOS campaign received contributions from the national teachers' unions, but it was not led by the unions. The educators raised nearly $130,000, of which about $50,000 came from the American Federation of Teachers and the National Education Association. To the Disrupters, with their millions and billions, this was chicken feed, not even crumbs from their well-stocked tables, yet even small amounts of money would give them grounds to denounce the Resistance as union-funded, as though it were shameful to accept money raised from teachers but just swell to take money from Wall Street and billionaires.

The SOS March on July 8, 2011, was a seminal event in the formation of the Resistance. People with shared values met there for the first time and talked about starting new organizations. The major groups that emerged afterward included United Opt Out (which took an uncompromising stand against standardized testing), the Network for Public Education (which nurtured connections among disparate groups across the country and eventually grew to have a following of nearly 400,000 people), and the Badass Teachers Association, a national group of fearless teachers who spoke out at school board meetings, legislative hearings, and on social media against privatization, assaults on the teaching profession, and high-stakes testing.

The SOS March occurred on a brutally hot day in D.C. More than seven thousand people arrived by the busload from across the nation to protest disruption of their schools. The many speakers that day included author Jonathan Kozol, scholar Pedro Noguera, teacher Anthony Cody, scholar Linda Darling-Hammond, educator Deborah Meier, scholar Angela Valenzuela, Texas school superintendent John Kuhn (who gave an eloquent speech about proudly accepting all students, no matter who they are, what their disability, "bring them all to me"), and yours truly. One star of the occasion was actor Matt Damon; his mother, Nancy Carlsson-Paige, a veteran early childhood educator, persuaded him to fly in from a film assignment in the Pacific Northwest for the day. Jon Stewart, then the host of *The Daily Show,* whose mother was a teacher in New Jersey, contributed a short video in honor of teachers and public schools; he said he would have come but "the dog ate my car."

The connections made at the SOS rally in 2011 were crucial for the creation of the Resistance. Teachers, parents, and teacher educators in many states formed their own SOS groups, to protest against disruption in their home states.

United Opt Out started with six people. The founding members were teachers, teacher educators, and community activists, including Peggy Robertson (Colorado), Tim Slekar (Pennsylvania), Morna McDermott (Maryland), Shaun Johnson (Maryland), Ceresta Smith (Florida), and Laurie Murphy (Florida). The leaders met weekly by Skype and organized another mass event in D.C. in the spring of 2012, which they called Occupy the Department of Education. Their event was held not on the Mall, but directly in front of the U.S. Department of Education, where they used a bullhorn to convey their outrage to Secretary Arne Duncan. Protesters paid their own way. About the same time, on Long Island, New York, a group created by parent Jeanette Deutermann began planning their own opt out movement, which eventually challenged Governor Andrew Cuomo and his disruptive education policies.

In 2013, UOO staged another demonstration in the District of

Columbia called Occupy the DOE 2.0. Peggy Robertson, parent and teacher, denounced

> ALEC, the corporations, the politicians, the billionaire boys' clubs, Michelle Rhee, McKinsey, Pearson, President Obama, and Secretary Arne Duncan.
>
> Our president's policies are privatizing our public schools. You'd think that the dismantling of our public-school system would be the news scoop of the year, wouldn't you? But when cash is involved, when billions of dollars can be made off the backs of our children who cannot speak for themselves, and that would be OUR young CHILDREN, it seems that our message falls on deaf ears. We are here today to demand that this message be told.

The Resistance grew rapidly after the SOS March in 2011, Occupy the Department of Education in 2012 and 2013, and the Chicago teachers' strike in 2012. Having no funding, the new Resistance movement took to social media, which cost nothing. Education bloggers emerged in every state. One of them, Jonathan Pelto of Connecticut, a former state legislator, organized the Education Bloggers Network and discovered more than three hundred education blogs, most written by experienced teachers, teacher educators, public school parents, and researchers. The bloggers used social media to share their stories, spread the news about the latest assault on public education in their district and state, discover allies, and build morale. What Resisters learned from one another on social media was this: You are not alone. This insight was for many a source of hope and power. Pro-public-education bloggers dominated Facebook and Twitter.

The Disrupters, endowed with money and power, had the solid support of editorialists at the nation's most powerful newspapers—*The New York Times* and *The Washington Post*—which regularly lauded charter schools, high-stakes testing, and evaluation of teachers by their students' test scores. Among the few journalists who understood that the Disruption movement was an insidious effort to privatize public schools were Valerie Strauss, who writes an education blog called "The Answer Sheet"

An **Orlando Sentinel** investigation
SUNDAY, OCTOBER 22, 2017   PAGE M1

SCHOOLS WITHOUT RULES

How the state that pioneered public school accountability is sending 140,000 children to private schools with little oversight

"Schools Without Rules" was a well-documented series about voucher schools in Florida, which are exempted from state standards, tests, and accountability while public schools are held to strict accountability for test scores.

for *The Washington Post;* Max Brantley, senior editor of *Arkansas Times,* a journalist bold enough to criticize the Walton family in their own state; and Karen Francisco, the chief editorial writer for the Fort Wayne (Indiana) *Journal-Gazette,* who frequently reproached the Republicans in control of the state for their shameless assault on public schools and their teachers.

Four mainstream newspapers stand out for their fearless exposures of school choice scandals: the *Orlando Sentinel,* which published a series about voucher schools in 2018 called "Schools Without Rules"; *The Miami Herald,* which published a series in 2011 called "Cashing In on Kids," about charter school frauds in Florida; *The Detroit Free Press,* for its yearlong investigation of charter school frauds and exposé in 2014; and *The Arizona Republic,* which won a prestigious Polk Award in 2018 for its investigation of charter school frauds in Arizona.

One of the great strengths of the Resistance was its cohort of knowledgeable bloggers. Mercedes Schneider, a high school English teacher in Louisiana with a doctorate in statistics and research methodology, frequently skewered the Common Core, the Gates Foundation, the over-hyped New Orleans "miracle," and other Disrupter projects, institutions, and personalities; Schneider has a well-honed ability to analyze IRS statements and to decipher financial documents. In addition to blogging, she published three books in three years about the dangers of Corporate Disruption, while never missing her classes.

Gary Rubinstein, one of the original corps members of Teach for America in the early 1990s, became a career math teacher in a New York City public high school. He turned against the Disruption movement. As a blogger, he is a master at puncturing "miracle" stories with data, including the inflated claims of TFA and of the charters that boasted that 100 percent of their students graduated and went to college. In every such case, Rubinstein showed that attrition was at the root of these "miracles," since the 100 percent figure referred only to those who survived until twelfth grade, not to those who entered the charter school in earlier grades.

Mark Weber (whose blogging name is Jersey Jazzman) is a music teacher who became so incensed by the fraudulent claims about charter accomplishments in Newark, Camden, and other impoverished districts in New Jersey that he earned a doctorate in education policy at Rutgers University to deepen his ability to review and expose their statistical legerdemain. Retired journalist Bob Braun, after half a century in the newspaper business at the *Star-Ledger* in New Jersey, scored scoop after scoop on his blog, lambasting the machinations of politicians and hucksters who took advantage of Governor Chris Christie's invitation to privatize and profit from public schools.

Peter Greene, a high school teacher in Pennsylvania, is the sharpest wit of the teacher-bloggers. In his blog, called Curmudgucation, he regularly ridicules the reports and pontifications of Disrupters; he says that he reads their verbiage so no one else has to.

Steven Singer, a teacher in Pennsylvania, blogs about the disruption caused by school choice (for a time, Facebook blocked his anti-choice posts) and the Disrupters' indifference to racism and poverty. Jan Resseger, who retired as a lay minister for public education on behalf of the United Church of Christ in Ohio, blogs with profound knowledge and insight about children, poverty, and schools. Tom Ultican, a retired teacher of physics and advanced mathematics in California, documents the depredations of the "Destroy Public Education Movement" in city after city, funded by the same billionaires. Stuart Egan and Justin Parmenter are teacher-bloggers in North Carolina, where they are independent voices in opposition to the Tea Party legislature, which is intent on destroying public education in what was once the South's most progressive state. Teacher-bloggers Nancy Flanagan, a music teacher for thirty years, and Mitchell Robinson, a professor of music education, provide sharp commentary on the failings of the Disruption movement in their home state of Michigan.

Anthony Cody persuaded the Gates Foundation to engage in a series of exchanges with him, in which he exposed their shallow views about education and their adamant refusal to recognize the importance of poverty as a determinant of student academic prowess. In his blog, "Cloaking Inequity," scholar Julian Vasquez Heilig uses humor and evidence to refute the claims of Disrupters, drawing upon his meticulous research about charter schools and Teach for America; his leadership role in the California NAACP helped to inform its members about the overblown claims of the Disrupters. Jennifer Berkshire blogged as "Edushyster" (then dropped the name and changed her format to a podcast called "Have You Heard?"). She shattered one myth after another, as when she reported that charter schools in Massachusetts dominated the state's list of schools with the highest suspension rates; one "no-excuses" charter suspended 56 percent of its students in a single year. No-excuses charter schools are known for their draconian discipline rules and swift punishment.

There are many more teacher-bloggers, parent-bloggers, and citizen-bloggers—informed, passionate, and outraged by the intrusion of privatizers, entrepreneurs, corporations, billionaires, and hedge fund managers into their schools and their communities.

In some districts, brave individuals led the Resistance. In Ohio, Bill Phillis, who retired after serving as deputy state superintendent of education, keeps close watch on the transfer of public dollars from public schools to unaccountable charters. His regular posts on the Internet alert parent groups to frauds in the charter industry and call attention to the

Denisha Jones is a lawyer who is active in the Badass Teachers Association, Defending the Early Years, and the Network for Public Education.

loss of billions of dollars that were wrongly removed from public schools. Former legislator Stephen Dyer reports on the funding and performance of charters and public schools; he created a website called "Know Your Charter" where interested citizens can learn about their local charters.

In Atlanta, Edward Johnson, a quality control consultant, frequently sends blast emails to the Atlanta school board, chastising its members for their infatuation with Disruption; Johnson is an adherent of the philosophy of business guru W. Edwards Deming, who valued collaboration and steady improvement over disruptive change. Sara Stevenson, a junior high school librarian in Austin, made it her personal mission to rebut every anti-public-school editorial in *The Wall Street Journal,* where her letters have been published so often that she became friends with the letters editor. Elementary school teacher Angie Sullivan regularly sends blast emails to every member of the Nevada legislature, imploring them to fund high-poverty schools like the one in which she teaches in Clark County and to cease diverting money to failing charter schools. Reverend/ Dr. Anika Whitfield, an ordained Baptist minister, a podiatrist, and a leader of Grassroots Arkansas, forcefully lead the Resistance movement in Little Rock, battling the state takeover of the district by

allies of the powerful Walton family and demanding the return of democratic control to the public schools. Some members of the Resistance
are active on multiple fronts, like Denisha Jones, a professor of early
childhood education and a lawyer who is a leader in the Badass Teachers Association, Defending the Early Years, and the Network for Public
Education.

Teacher-bloggers have significant advantages over the Disrupters: they know children; they know teaching and learning; they know
how to assess what their students have learned without relying on a
multimillion-dollar testing program; they know that computers are no
substitute for human teachers. Collectively they use their blogs to educate the public about what is being done to them, their students, and
their schools by careless billionaires. I started my own blog in 2012 and
use it as a platform to nationalize the struggle against privatization
and high-stakes testing and to showcase the work of other bloggers in
order to enable them to reach a larger audience.

The billionaires became angry that they had so little presence on social
media. To counter the omnipresent bloggers of the Resistance, Disrupters
laid out millions of dollars to subsidize blogs to defend charter schools,
high-stakes standardized testing, and other tenets of Corporate Disruption. "Education Post," funded by billionaires Michael Bloomberg, Eli
Broad, the Walton Family Foundation, and Laurene Powell Jobs, was
launched in 2014 by Peter Cunningham after he stepped down as Arne
Duncan's assistant secretary for communications in the first term of the
Obama administration. Campbell Brown's "The 74" was funded by the
Dick and Betsy DeVos Foundation, the Eli and Edythe Broad Foundation, the Bill & Melinda Gates Foundation, Bloomberg Philanthropies,
the Walton Family Foundation, Jonathan Sackler, the Doris and Donald
Fisher Fund, the Chan-Zuckerberg Initiative, and other billionaires to
support privatization and fight teachers' rights and teachers' unions.

None of the bloggers of the Resistance is subsidized or paid, but they
continue to dominate social media, as a result of their authenticity, their
knowledge, their passion, and their sheer numbers.

In 2012, Anthony Cody and I—having met each other at the first
Save Our Schools march in 2011—decided to create a new national organization to bring together activists of all kinds. We knew that billionaires

The Reverend/Dr. Anika T. Whitfield is a minister, a podiatrist, and a fearless advocate for public schools in Little Rock, Arkansas, where she frequently challenges state and local authorities to restore democratic control of the schools.

were pouring large amounts of money into state and local races to elect pro-privatization candidates, and we wanted to create a PAC—political action committee—to support candidates who opposed privatization of public education. However, we were naive. We soon learned that every state has its own laws for launching a PAC and that gaining legal status to operate in many states is prohibitively expensive. Alas, we had no money. It is daunting, in fact impossible, to be a PAC without any money. It took a year to assemble a national board of educators from across the nation for the new Network for Public Education (NPE), which is a nonprofit charitable organization, not a PAC. Our goal was to connect pro-public-education groups from different states, and even within the same state. In time, we were able to create NPE Action to endorse candidates but not to give them any money. We consider our endorsement to be the "Good Housekeeping" award of public education, identifying candidates who support public schools. Our first executive director was Robin Hiller, a parent activist in Tucson who led a Resistance group called Voices for Education. She was succeeded by Carol Burris, a retired high school principal on Long Island in New York and a skilled writer and researcher.

With a meager budget and a staff of one, NPE built up its followers

Carol Burris was a principal
in New York who helped
to build opposition among
principals across the state
to evaluation of teachers by
their students' test scores.
After retiring as principal,
she became executive
director of the Network for
Public Education and wrote
influential reports in support
of Resistance to privatization.

to 22,000 by November 2016. When the newly elected President Trump
announced his choice of Betsy DeVos as secretary of education, NPE's
followers shot up to more than 350,000 within days. The staff grew to
one full-time executive director, Carol Burris, and a part-time assistant,
Darcie Cimarusti, a parent and school board member in New Jersey;
we have never had office space, which would waste precious resources.
With such a large following, NPE was able to implement a new, low-
cost, but highly effective strategy. We send email alerts to warn members when their state legislatures are about to enact bills that endanger
public schools and teachers or are about to authorize punitive tests.
These alerts produce thousands of emails, letters, and personal visits to
state legislators in support of public schools. NPE acts in concert with
state SOS groups and other local organizations. NPE produces a steady
flow of national reports on the dangers of privatization and uses Twitter
to report daily scandals in the charter sector (hashtag #AnotherDay-
AnotherCharterScandal). Its annual conferences bring together hundreds of Resistance leaders representing every state, who compare notes
and learn from one another. NPE focuses on building the Resistance and
educating the public with its research and reports. One report, "Hijacked
by Billionaires: How the Super Rich Buy Elections to Undermine Public Schools," named names. Another, "Charters and Consequences,"

detailed charter scandals in California and elsewhere and the need for oversight to protect students and public dollars. In 2019, Carol Burris and Jeff Bryant wrote an NPE report, "Asleep at the Wheel: How the Federal Charter Schools Program Recklessly Takes Taxpayers and Students for a Ride," which documented the waste of nearly $1 billion by the federal Charter Schools Program; this program funded nearly 1,000 charters that either never opened or closed soon after opening. Members of the House Appropriations Committee cited the report when cutting Secretary DeVos's request for additional funding for the program.

Another major force in the Resistance are the BATs (the Badass Teachers Association). The name is shocking in what is generally a genteel and female-dominated profession, but the BATs came to be a major part of the Resistance. Their purpose is clear: "This is for every teacher who refuses to be blamed for the failure of our society to erase poverty and inequality, and refuses to accept assessments, tests and evaluations imposed by those who have contempt for real teaching and learning."

The organization was founded in June 2013 by Mark Naison, a professor of African and African American Studies at Fordham University in New York City, and Priscilla Sanstead, an Oklahoma parent activist. They were joined by Marla Kilfoyle, a parent and teacher on Long Island. The BATs determined to push back against the "Billionaire Privatizers" and their allies in both political parties. Kilfoyle became the national director while continuing to teach her daily classes. The BATs posted a webpage and a Facebook page, and in less than three weeks had enlisted more than eighteen thousand members. In two years, their membership had grown to more than fifty thousand, with BAT groups in every state and the District of Columbia, all operated by volunteers, each with its own Facebook page. The BATs have their own caucuses within the two major teachers' unions. When Kilfoyle retired as national director of the BATs in 2018, she joined the staff of the Network for Public Education to coordinate grassroots activities.

The BATs strongly oppose high-stakes standardized testing, privatization, evaluating teachers by the test scores of their students, for-profit corporate intrusions into public schools, and the Common Core State Standards, which they view as a top-down, educationally unsound, unfunded federal mandate that opens public schools to for-profit entrepreneurs hawking tests, test preparation materials, textbooks, and curricula. BATs alert their members when state legislatures threaten teachers' rights and educate them about the big-money interests behind the attacks on teachers and public schools.

The BATs developed creative tactics to respond to attacks on teachers. When Arne Duncan applauded the Vergara court case in California in 2013, which sought to eliminate teacher tenure, the BATs "swarmed the phone lines of the White House," calling for Duncan's resignation. The "BAT Swarm" is an effective tool for mass action, eliciting thousands of outraged calls, emails, Facebook postings, and tweets in a single day. It costs nothing, engages thousands, and draws negative attention to the object of their wrath. When the automobile maker Subaru put Teach for America on its corporate donation list for the holidays, the BATs swarmed, protesting that TFA places unqualified people into classrooms with only five weeks of training while TFA executives are paid six-figure salaries. Subaru removed TFA from its list of charitable contributions (TFA has assets of hundreds of millions of dollars). BATs have also aided, and sometimes led, teachers' strikes by spreading the word to their members.

The BATs heard the following story from a teacher in Georgia:

> I am spending the night in my building with about 70 middle school students and 20 some faculty/staff because the ice/snow has shut down this north Georgia County. Our buses couldn't continue and the parents couldn't get through the roads. We "dismissed" early at 1:00 but it really meant nothing without buses. We have even cooked for them. Evaluate that.

The term "Evaluate that" soon became a hashtag on Twitter for the BATs, representing the dedication that can never be measured by a standardized test. Many other teachers shared their stories and added to the power of the BATs #Evaluatethat meme.

BATs fight for well-resourced schools where professionally prepared teachers are free to teach in developmentally appropriate ways and where students have a balanced and full curriculum. Their goal is an excellent public education for all students, without exception. The BATs have been

Charles Foster Johnson, a pastor and public education advocate in Texas, established Pastors for Texas Children, which has played a key role in defeating vouchers. Johnson and his fellow pastors in other states are strong believers that religious liberty depends on separation of church and state.

effective members of the Resistance, not only because of their numbers, but because of their fearlessness and their ability to mobilize thousands of their members to act in concert on short notice for protests, demonstrations, or BAT Swarms.

Religious leaders in Texas play a major role in the Resistance. Pastors for Texas Children led the successful battle to defeat vouchers in the state legislature, year after year. They forged an alliance between urban Democrats and rural Republicans to protect public schools against vouchers. The pastors in this coalition believe in the separation of church and state. They do not want religious education to be subsidized by the state. Such entanglement, they fear, would ultimately endanger religious liberty, which should be strong enough to thrive without government subsidy. The founder of the PTC is Pastor Charles Foster Johnson, allied with Pastor Charles Luke; they have organized some two thousand other religious leaders across the state, who command the respect of the elected officials in their communities. Johnson patiently but forcefully explains to elected officials why vouchers are a terrible idea, how they would harm the public schools that most children attend, and why religious leaders support public schools. The PTC message reaches rural Republicans, who understand that the local public school is the hub of their communities, the sponsors of their sports teams and debate teams, and the repositories of their towns' histories. The PTC has helped to form similar organizations in Oklahoma, Kentucky, and Tennessee and is building coalitions of pastors in other states in the South and Midwest to defend the Jeffersonian wall of separation between church and state.

When Tennessee won $500 million in Race to the Top funding, parent and teacher resistance to high-stakes testing and charter schools sprang up in groups like the Momma Bears, Tennesseans Reclaiming Educational Excellence, and a group in Knoxville called SPEAK (Students Parents Educators Across Knox County). North Carolina has Public Schools First NC. Indiana has the Northeast Indiana Friends of Public Education. Texas has multiple Resistance groups, including Friends of Texas Public Schools, Texans for Public Education, Raise Your Hand Texas, and Texas Kids Can't Wait. Among many other volunteer groups are Parents Across America; Raise Your Hand for Illinois Public Education; Ohio's Public Education Partners; Citizens for Public Schools in Massachusetts; Iowans for Public Education; Public Citizens for Children and Youth, the Keystone State Education Coalition, and Education Voters PA in Pennsylvania; SOS Nebraska; SOS Kentucky; SOS Arizona; and SOS New Jersey. Almost every state has similar groups that arose spontaneously to support public schools and their students.

Educators, parents, and students fight for a vision of schooling that does not align with that of the Corporate Disrupters. Parents do not see their children as "global competitors," but as children. Early childhood educators want education that allows young children to play and have a childhood free of the stress of standardized testing, computer-based instruction, data mining, and commercialism. Educators and parents want students to have a genuine education with a full and balanced curriculum that includes science, foreign languages, history, literature, physical education, the arts, and civics, not just prep for standardized tests in reading and mathematics. Teachers want to be free to use their professional judgment and the wisdom born of experience, not to be reduced to test monitors. They believe that tests should be written by teachers, not by corporations.

This is a concept of children and education diametrically opposed to that of the Disrupters. The sides are ill-matched: on one side are money and power; on the other are large numbers of well-informed people with passion and experience. In our society at the present time, money and power usually are sufficient to prevail. But that has not happened, and it will not happen, because the Disrupters' policies are inherently flawed, and their failures have become too evident to ignore.

The role of the Resistance is, first, to publicize the persistent failure of Disruption policies and the harm they have done to children, teachers, and public schools; and second, to put forth a vision of what good education is, one that acknowledges the individuality of each child and perceives education far more broadly than what test scores measure. Education for a democratic society addresses the needs of children and young people to grow in knowledge, character, and civic understanding, not just endless preparation to take standardized tests.

CHAPTER 5

The Beginning of the End
of Disruption

Throughout its relatively short history, essentially 1983 to the present, Corporate Disruption could count on the major media to accept its claims uncritically. The assertion that American education was "failing" was taken as a given, with no need for additional probing. The claim that the schools were staffed by incompetent, lazy teachers, protected by greedy unions, was accepted unquestioningly. Press releases from billionaire-funded organizations were treated as research studies; think tank reports underwritten by the Gates Foundation, the Broad Foundation, the Walton Foundation, and others with an agenda—papers that had never undergone peer review by independent scholars—were dutifully reported as news or as results from actual research. Gullible columnists gushed over charter schools that claimed that 100 percent of their students, regardless of race or family income, had completed high school and 100 percent had been accepted into college, but the media never checked the veracity of these claims. The alleged success of such schools was supposed to prove that every school could get the same results if only they copied the methods of the charter schools.

The Resistance kept hammering away with facts and evidence that contradicted the Disrupters' narrative. Bloggers and independent researchers worked tirelessly to refute propaganda about standards, testing, teacher evaluation systems, inexperienced teachers, and privatization. But the mainstream media loved the miracle stories and kept printing them. Eventually, however, the evidence became too overwhelming to ignore.

At a certain point, the pushback against the privatization movement began to make headway and a backlash began to form against Disruption and privatization. In time, the broken promises became so numerous that the privatization movement had a credibility problem.

Nicholas Kristof, columnist for *The New York Times,* was a longtime supporter of what was called the "reform" movement. But in the spring of 2015, he wondered whether the movement had peaked. This was the first time that a national commentator noticed that the self-proclaimed "reform" movement was floundering, despite its wealthy patrons. Kristof saw it, even as everyone else continued to pretend that nothing had changed. He wrote, "The zillionaires are bruised. The idealists are dispirited. The number of young people applying for Teach for America, after 15 years of growth, has dropped for the last two years. The Common Core curriculum is now an orphan, with politicians vigorously denying paternity. K–12 education is an exhausted, bloodsoaked battlefield. It's Agincourt, the day after." He suggested that the "reformers" should "refocus their passions" on early childhood education, an important crusade that could bring everyone together from different sides of the K–12 debates without controversy.

It was good advice, but premature.

A few years later, even Disrupters began openly to acknowledge that their movement was in trouble. Some said it was time for humility and a new start on the same old ideas. Others urged their dispirited allies not to give up but to keep pressing the same tired agenda. None said, "We failed, let's admit it. Let's devote our time and money to improving the lives of children and their families, to making sure that they have access to good medical care and decent food and shelter. Together we can rebuild our underfunded public school system."

The proximate causes of the soul-searching were as follows:

First, the scores on the National Assessment of Educational Progress (NAEP) were flat in 2015 and flat again in 2017. Even Disrupters reluctantly acknowledged that the scores were essentially unchanged since 2007. A few states or districts gained or lost a few points, but the overall conclusion was inescapable: the Disrupters' promise of higher and higher test scores did not happen. Scores did not go up, and the gaps between white and black students remained large; the scores of the lowest-performing students on the national tests were flat. This was not what the Reformers had promised. Michael Petrilli of the conservative Thomas B. Fordham Institute reacted to the 2017 scores as "bleak news" that marked "America's 'Lost Decade' of Educational Progress." Martin West of Harvard described the results as "disappointing . . . continuing a period of stagnation that's now persisted for a decade." They did not draw any connection between the unrelenting emphasis on high-stakes standardized testing and the unimpressive results of the national and state audit, often referred to as "The Nation's Report Card." All those tests, all the billions spent on test prep and interim assessments, all that narrowing of teaching and curricula, and so little to show for it.

Second, the patrons of Disruption had often pointed to Washington, D.C., as the crown jewel of their efforts; they were proud that consistent leadership, ever since Michelle Rhee became chancellor in 2007, had implemented their favorite strategies, and success was supposedly ensured. Philanthropists had poured more than $120 million into the district's radical changes, including its reliance on high-stakes testing to evaluate teachers, its bold expansion of charter schools, and its decision to put principals on one-year contracts. Arne Duncan praised the district as an example of "what can happen when schools embrace innovative reforms and do the hard work necessary to ensure that all students graduate ready for college and careers."

That bubble burst in early 2018 when a public high school claimed an improbable 100 percent graduation rate for 2017, following a year in which its graduation rate was only 57 percent. The heartwarming story was broadcast on National Public Radio. After teachers at the school blew their whistles, the local NPR station returned and found that more than 60 percent of the graduating class had been chronically absent and ineligible to graduate. The FBI launched an investigation. The city ordered an independent audit of the entire district, which determined that about one third of its graduates lacked the credits to receive a diploma. The district claimed a 2017 graduation rate of 73 percent, but the audit showed that only 42 percent were on track to graduate, with another 19 percent "moderately off-track" and still able to earn the credits needed to graduate. The district was certainly not ensuring "that all students were ready for college and careers," as Duncan had asserted. The graduation rate scandal threw cold water on the Disrupters' boasts about the dramatic transformation of a school district that they had continuously controlled since 2007.

Third, in 2016, the National Association for the Advancement of Colored People (NAACP) called for a national moratorium on new charter schools. It held hearings in urban districts across the country and listened to parents complain about the exclusionary practices of charters. The NAACP said that no new charter schools should open until such schools were "subject to the same transparency and accountability standards as public schools"; until public funds were no longer diverted to charter schools "at the expense of the public school system"; and until charter schools stopped expelling students that public schools were legally obliged to educate. The NAACP resolution pointed out that it had historically supported public schools and denounced "movements toward privatization that divert public funds to support non-public school choices."

Fourth, the Disrupters' belief that teachers should be evaluated by the test scores of their students was demolished in 2018 by a Gates-funded independent study of this Gates-funded practice. The RAND Corporation and the American Institutes for Research released their study of a teacher evaluation program implemented over six years in three districts (Hillsborough County in Florida, Memphis, and Pittsburgh) and four charter chains. The project did not improve student test scores. Nor did it weed out ineffective teachers. It failed.

Fifth, a wave of teacher walkouts and strikes dramatized widespread underinvestment in education. The strikes began in West Virginia in the spring of 2018 and spread rapidly to other states where teacher pay was low. The strikes dramatized the fact that many state legislatures had failed to restore funding that had been cut over the previous decade. The strikes continued, as teachers across the nation realized that only by mass action would legislators respond to their demands for a reduction in class sizes, a full-time nurse and librarian in every school, more counselors, and a moratorium on new charter schools. Teachers recognized that school choice was contributing to the underfunding of public schools.

Sixth, the appointment and tenure of billionaire heiress Betsy DeVos as secretary of education in the Trump administration clarified the extremist nature of advocacy for school privatization by charter schools, for-profit management corporations, and vouchers for religious schools and the danger that privatization posed to the nation's underfunded public schools. DeVos dampened Democrats' enthusiasm for school choice.

The Disrupters' responded defensively to their multiple failures. After the NAEP scores went flat, after charter studies showed uneven and often poor results, after voucher studies concurred that students who attended voucher schools got lower test scores than their public school peers, privatizers began to move the goalposts. Where once they seemed certain that the point of their disruptive tactics was to raise test scores, several key figures opined that test scores were not really the purpose of Disruption. This was a major abandonment of the central tenet of their movement, because Disrupters had insisted since the passage of No Child Left Behind that annual measurement would improve test scores, especially those of low-scoring students, and would close achievement gaps, and they had used those scores to close public schools and replace them with charter schools.

Even Disrupters began to question the value of standardized test scores. Jay P. Greene, chair of the Walton-funded "Department of Education Reform" at the University of Arkansas, warned that test scores had little or no relationship to later life success. Test scores, he wrote, do not consistently affect such outcomes as "graduating from high school, going to college, earning a good living, staying out of jail." He concluded that "the direction and magnitude of changing test scores does not correspond with changing later life outcomes." "No-excuses" charter schools, he said, produce higher test scores but have no effect on high school graduation rates or college enrollment. ("No-excuses" charter schools have harsh discipline codes and are known for high suspension rates of non-compliant students.) Greene, a champion of school choice, insisted that vouchers were unlikely to produce higher test scores but more likely to produce superior "life outcomes," like increased graduation rates and college enrollment.

When Secretary of Education Betsy DeVos learned in 2017 that the latest federal evaluation of vouchers in the District of Columbia produced negative results, she responded that test scores don't matter. She said, "When school choice policies are fully implemented, there should not be differences in achievement among the various types of schools." In other words, there was no reason to expect that students using vouchers or attending charters would get higher test scores than their peers in public schools. They would all get similar scores. Although she did not mention it, this was the case in Milwaukee, a city that had experienced three decades of school choice—public schools, charter schools, and voucher schools—whose students received similar test scores, all very low. Milwaukee is both a model of full-blown school choice and one of the nation's lowest-scoring urban districts on the National Assessment of Educational Progress.

The conservative American Enterprise Institute released a study that questioned whether test scores were the right way to measure schools and whether school choice would raise scores. Three school-choice-friendly researchers exploded the Disrupters' dogma that test scores should be the gold standard for judging the success of educational programs. Their study "Do Test Scores Even Matter? Lessons from Long-Run Outcomes in School Choice Research" began by noting that "for the past 20 years, almost every major education reform has rested on a common assumption: Standardized test scores are an accurate and appropriate measure of success and failure." The researchers concluded that "for school choice programs, there is a weak relationship between impacts on test scores and later attainment outcomes. . . . Test scores should not automatically occupy a privileged place over parental demand and satisfaction as short-term measures of school choice success or failure." Standardized test scores were poor measures of long-term student success, they said. They held that "the teachers who produce improvements in student behavior and non-cognitive skills are not particularly likely to be the same teachers who improve test scores." This admission directly refuted the claims by Arne Duncan and Bill Gates that the best way to evaluate teachers is by the test scores of their students.

So do we need to wait decades to learn how school choice affects graduation rates, college attendance, and earnings?

Not really. In Texas, two economists studied the long-term effects of attending charter schools. Roland G. Fryer Jr. of Harvard University and Will Dobbie of Princeton University studied "Charter Schools and Labor Market Outcomes." (Fryer's Education Innovation Lab at Harvard was funded primarily by the charter-mad Eli and Edythe Broad Foundation, but closed down in 2019 when Harvard suspended Fryer after multiple reports by his colleagues of sexual harassment.) Fryer and Dobbie concluded that, on average, charter schools in Texas had "no impact on test scores and a negative impact on earning." The "no-excuses" charter schools, which employ strict disciplinary rules and suspend students for infractions of those rules, "increase test scores and four-year college enrollment, but have a small and statistically insignificant impact on earnings, while other types of charter schools decrease test scores, four-year college enrollment, and earnings." In other words, the long-term effects of attending charter schools were nil.

There was one prominent dissenter from the emerging Disrupter consensus that test scores did not matter anymore, and that school choice would not produce them. Arne Duncan continued to defend all the strategies of Disruption: national standards, annual testing, punitive accountability, test-based teacher evaluation, and charter schools. This was his legacy, and he refused to admit that it was failing. In early 2018, he knew before their public release (a privilege granted to former secretaries of education) that the national test scores showed no improvement, and he wrote an op-ed in *The Washington Post* in defense of the policies he favored. He ignored the teachers' marches and protests, which were dominating the news at the time. The title of his article captured its defensive tone: "People Are Saying Education Reform Hasn't Worked. Don't Believe Them." He didn't identify who those naysayers were, other than "a lot of people in Washington." He credited current policies for the rise in NAEP scores since 1971, a good thirty years before passage of No Child Left Behind and forty years before his own Race to the Top. He praised NCLB for introducing annual testing, even though there was no evidence for its efficacy. He reiterated his support for charter schools and lamented the fact that most districts didn't have any. He lauded test-based teacher evaluation and ignored its failure wherever it was tried. He dismissed the evaluation of his Race to the Top program by

Arne Duncan was U.S. secretary of education for seven years during the Barack Obama administration. He created a program called Race to the Top, which was built on the test-based approach of George W. Bush's No Child Left Behind law. Duncan supported high-stakes testing of students, the Common Core State Standards, evaluation of teachers by their students' test scores, and charter schools. His advocacy for charter schools paved the way for the choice policies of Betsy DeVos.

his own department, which concluded that the $7 billion Duncan spent to "reform" America's schools had had no impact on test scores, graduation rates, or college enrollment rates; the study was released the day before the Obama administration left office. He preferred to cite a favorable study published six years earlier, in 2012, even though his program operated from 2010 to 2015. More of the same, he insisted, would surely work, but leaders lacked the "courage" to insist on "bold interventions," as he had done. The ship he launched was sinking, but he insisted that valiant leaders should ignore the critics (and the evidence) and make everyone row harder.

Frederick Hess, who led the education program at the conservative American Enterprise Institute, opined that the teachers' walkouts were a sign that the Bush-Obama disruptive "reforms" had run their course. Teachers, he wrote, are "immensely sympathetic actors." They are "trusted and popular." He attributed the wave of strikes in large part to the Disruption movement's negative view of teachers and its indifference to their salaries or their status as professionals, "which may be why bread-

and-butter demands from teachers are ascending as the guts of Bush-Obama school Reform are sinking to the bottom of the 'discarded school Reform' sea." He wondered whether the strikes and the new teacher militancy were "glimpses of what's ahead as the school-reform pendulum swings away from the Bush-Obama era?" His column read like an obituary for the Disruption movement by one who had been in the thick of it as both an advocate and an occasional skeptic of its nostrums.

Another frank admission of failure came from two leaders of the school choice wing of the Disruption movement, the previously mentioned Jay P. Greene and Michael Q. McShane, director of national research at the pro-voucher EdChoice in Indianapolis. They convened a group of academics to discuss what had gone wrong and what lessons could be learned. The abstract of their paper said,

> Over the last two decades, federal and state policy makers have launched a number of ambitious, large-scale education Reform initiatives—No Child Left Behind, Race to the Top, the Common Core State Standards, and others—only to see them sputter and fail. In 2017, the authors convened a number of leading scholars to explore why those initiatives failed and what can be learned from them. Participants agreed that to be more successful in the future, Reformers will need to balance ambition and urgency with humility, political acumen, and the ability to recognize when it's time to slow down or scale things back. . . . American education is littered with failed Reforms. Across the country, we see charter schools that have been shuttered, federal funding streams that have run dry, philanthropic initiatives that never panned out, and brand-new teacher evaluation systems that have already been marked for the junkyard.
>
> Of course, failure isn't necessarily a bad thing—when pursuing a goal as urgent and complex as school improvement, some amount of failure will be inevitable. The problem, though, is that policy makers, foundation officials, and pundits have strong incentives to deny that their favored initiatives have gone badly, and they rarely acknowledge and learn from those failures before moving on to the next Reform. As a result, they tend to repeat their mistakes and make much less progress than they should.

Despite the repeated failures, major new philanthropic money was committed to Disruptive Reform by the Chan Zuckerberg Initiative; by Laurene Powell Jobs's Emerson Collective; and by the Charles Koch Foundation, all intended to disrupt and reinvent American public education. This ongoing stream of funding guaranteed that there would be even more half-baked, punitive policies landing on students, teachers, and public schools, in addition to the destructive disruption policies enacted by state legislatures, centered on testing, choice, and online learning.

Greene and McShane offered this advice: Be humble. Don't try to make an end run around democracy (as the promoters of the Common Core standards did). Don't try to hide behind exaggerated claims that "research shows" or "experts agree," because issues in the real world of education are far too complicated to be reduced to a single course of action or to allow for controls on relevant variables. "Best practices" might be right in one school or district, but not in another.

The advice offered by Greene and McShane was sensible. But it did not support Duncan's rosy view that the disruptive policies of the past twenty years were swell but just needed more time and more courage to reach fruition. The two dissidents warned against the danger of searching for magic bullets or secret sauce or rushing in to break things, as the Disrupters had done so blithely with so little regard for what they were breaking and how to replace it. Greene and McShane wisely recognized that agents of the Disruption agenda can't shove their preferred ideas down the throats of teachers, principals, and parents. Policy can make a difference, but only if it has the enthusiastic support of those who are expected to implement it.

For the preceding twenty or thirty years, Disrupters had searched for sweeping policies that could be applied en masse to everyone at the same time. Greene and McShane argued for a different approach. Take time to build support. Don't pooh-pooh an innovation that works in one place but not another. Don't look down on standards developed by a community. In short, if I read them correctly, abandon the fantasy that all changes must be "scalable" for hundreds if not thousands of schools, for entire districts and states, for the nation. In contrast to the Disrupters' wholehearted embrace of standardization, Greene and McShane called for an approach that recognized the value of diversity, pluralism, and small improvements.

This is a tone of humility that is out of step with the big, bold, and failed disruptions of the past twenty years. But it makes sense.

Arne Duncan must have heard the lamentations from his allies, and as a former professional athlete, he felt it was up to him to rally the troops once more. They needed a pep talk. So, in this same sad spring of 2018, as the odor of failure clung to the Disruption movement, he enlisted Margaret Spellings to join him in writing a rousing article on behalf of their failing project. What a pair: Duncan was Obama's secretary of education and Spellings was George W. Bush's. How fitting to see them standing shoulder to shoulder, defending the ramparts against the naysayers within their own ranks. Critics had often said that there was no discernible difference between George W. Bush's top-down and intrusive No Child Left Behind Act and Barack Obama's punitive Race to the Top. The two initiatives were without doubt the least popular, most damaging federal education initiatives in American history. They lowered the quality of American education, they forced the firing of untold numbers of teachers whose only crime was to teach in impoverished districts, they forced the closure of hundreds, perhaps thousands, of public schools that operated in high-poverty areas and enrolled disproportionate numbers of students with disabilities and students who were English language learners.

Duncan and Spellings bemoaned the collapse of the bipartisan consensus that supported thirty-five years of test-based policies, from Reagan's *A Nation at Risk* report to Obama's Race to the Top. They repeated the stale mantras about "closing the achievement gap" and reaching for equal opportunity in education, which neither No Child Left Behind nor Race to the Top had achieved. They complained about the stagnant test scores on the NAEP, refusing to admit that those flat scores happened on their watch and were the result of the very policies that they had imposed on unwilling teachers and schools and had enforced with the power of federal might.

They took no responsibility for the ruinous policies they championed. Instead, they blamed the current disillusionment on "an absence of vision, a failure of will and politics that values opposition over progress."

They could not bring themselves to admit that the reason for the gloom among their allies was that their programs had failed by the very measure they valued: test scores. The scores were flat, and in many places, declining. The achievement gaps among the advantaged and the disadvantaged were not shrinking. Their plea to "stay the course" despite their having taken the nation down a path to a dead end was sad.

Veteran journalist John Merrow—once an enthusiast for Disruption (as I had been)—noted that the two former cabinet secretaries began their lament with this sentence: "We have long benefited from a broad coalition that has advanced bold action to improve America's education system." Of course, their "bold actions" had produced no evidence of success over the course of nearly two decades, a long trial period. Merrow wondered who the "we" was to whom Duncan and Spellings referred and who had "benefited" from their policies.

> It's far easier to identify those who have NOT benefited from "No Child Left Behind" and "Race to the Top." Let's start with students, because their performance on the National Assessment of Educational Progress, which everyone agrees is education's "gold standard," has basically been flat for the 20+ years of Bush and Obama. Next on the list are teachers, whose salaries and morale have declined over the years of increasing reliance on multiple-choice testing and "test-and-punish" policies. Collateral damage has been done to the occupation of teaching, which has lost prestige and now fails to attract enough candidates to fill our classrooms with qualified instructors. . . .
>
> So let's try to figure out who benefited. Here are five: Testing companies (whose profits have climbed an estimated 5000 percent), those ideologues intent on fracturing public education to satisfy their political agenda, profiteers who are riding the charter school bandwagon (whether for-profit or not-for-profit, because that's become a distinction without a difference), and—surprise—the two former United States Secretaries of Education. One now leads the University of North Carolina higher education system, and the other is one of three Managing Partners of The Emerson Collective, Laurene Powell Jobs' very wealthy and active education venture.

The vigor of the Disruption movement had dissipated. The recriminations had begun. No one except the two architects of the failed policies was predicting a victory that lay just around the corner or even off in the distance. The NAEP scores were a wet blanket on the Disrupters' PR machine. After nearly two decades of being in control of the federal government and of most states, the Disrupters had little to boast about. They had beguiled the media, the billionaires, the hedge fund managers, and the philanthropists for a long while, fooled them into thinking that more testing, more punishment, and more choice would lead to high test scores and a national resurgence of excellence and equity. It didn't happen. The monied elites loved the promise that schools could be reinvented on the cheap: No new taxes. Don't throw money at the schools. But the teachers marching on state capitols nixed that idea. A nation that is unwilling to pay a professional wage to teachers cannot expect to recruit and retain professionals. Education is expensive. A nation unwilling to pay for it in the present will pay even more in the future, and that cost will be widespread ignorance and despair.

CHAPTER 6

The Resistance to High-Stakes
Standardized Testing

George W. Bush's No Child Left Behind and Barack Obama's Race to the Top shared the assumption that annual standardized testing is a cure-all and that it would miraculously raise the achievement of all students to the point where everyone was "proficient."

This is a truly ridiculous idea.

Standardized testing is a way to measure skills and low-level knowledge. It is not a reform. It is not a substitute for instruction. In fact, it takes time away from instruction and devotes that time to test preparation, which may raise test scores in the short term but inevitably undermines the quality of education in the long term. Testing can be helpful when used diagnostically, to ascertain what students already know and what they need to learn. Teachers can use this information, if it is available soon after the test, to improve instruction. Testing is not useful when it is merely a tool to rank students, to label them, to stigmatize them, to tell them that they have "failed" in comparison to their peers in the school, the district, the state, and the nation.

Noneducators, including legislators, typically assume that tests created by major education publishers are accurate and objective. Wrong. The same student can take the same standardized test on different days and get different scores. All standardized tests—the SAT, the ACT, state tests, national tests, international tests—typically reflect family income and education.

By design, every standardized test is scored on a bell curve. Students from advantaged homes always cluster in the top half of the bell curve. Standardized tests reliably produce distributions in which children born into affluent and educated families will be certified as winners and children without those advantages will be certified as losers. The results of standardized testing tend to confirm the social structure of the status quo and make it appear to result from IQ or inherent ability rather than from the good fortune of being born to successful parents (that is, being members of what British sociologist Michael Young called "the lucky sperm club"). There are poor kids who get high scores and rich kids who get low scores, but these are outliers. Low scores on standardized tests typically identify kids from low-income homes and schools in poor communities, not "bad teachers" or "failing schools." Yet the results of those tests are used to punish students, their teachers, and their schools.

Standardized tests evolved from the intelligence tests that were first used on a mass scale during World War I to sort recruits for the army. Those who had life advantages got higher scores than those who did not. Those with higher scores became officers. Those with lower scores became foot soldiers. Psychologists wrongly assumed that men who had lower scores had lower intelligence. Those same psychologists, the leaders of their new field, wrote books about the inherent mental superiority of Aryans and Nordics, as compared to American blacks and to immigrants from southern and eastern Europe. They were wrong. Northern blacks had higher scores than Appalachian whites did. The scores on those tests measured environmental factors, such as family education, familiarity with the English language, and income, as they continue to do today. Those born into educated, English-speaking families had higher scores than did Italian, Russian, Jewish, Hungarian, and Polish immigrants. Ironically, people from many of the same groups who were labeled inferior by the test givers in the early decades of the twentieth century now receive high scores on standardized tests. The tests were not actually measuring ability but, rather, language skills and economic status, and as the language skills and economic status of those peoples improved, so did their test scores.

The Disrupters ignored this history or never learned it. They relied on the validity of annual standardized testing as both the measure and the goal of schooling. They thought that students would get smarter if tests were harder. They often said, "Raise the bar and students will get higher test scores." But testing students often, with ever more difficult tests, doesn't make them smarter.

Federal law made annual testing the linchpin of schooling. Test scores were used to identify the lowest-scoring schools, which would then be closed or turned over to private management. Entire school staffs were fired because scores were too low. Test scores were used to determine which teachers were effective or ineffective. They were used to award merit pay. They became a measure of educational quality, teacher quality, and student success or failure. Students were punished for being poor or because their parents could not read English. Their teachers and schools were punished because of the population they enrolled, not because the teachers and schools were doing a bad job.

Who benefits from the federal requirement of annual testing? Not students or teachers or schools. The information they get from the testing is not at all helpful. The students take the tests in the spring and the results are not returned until August or September, when the students have different teachers. The teachers learn the students' scores and their ranks in comparison to other students, but they get no information about what individual students know or don't know or what they can and can't do. The tests have no diagnostic value. Neither the teachers nor their students are allowed to review the questions on the tests after they are given; those are confidential and proprietary. Nor can they review the answers that the students gave, which would reveal their errors and misunderstandings and help teachers address these. State officials can say whether the state's scores went up or down and whether more or fewer students passed the tests, but this paltry information comes at a high cost in time and money, with dubious accuracy and no benefit to students. Test publishers keep the test questions and answers secret; they even monitor social media accounts of students and teachers to make sure that no test questions or answers have been revealed.

Do we need more information? Actually, we have all the information we need without annual testing of every student in the nation in grades 3–8. In the United States, the federal tests offered every other year by the National Assessment of Educational Progress (NAEP) provide an external audit function. The NAEP tests are given to national, state, and urban samples of students; no student takes an entire test, and no school is identified by NAEP scores. There are no stakes (consequences) attached to NAEP tests for any students or schools. The tests are purely informational, intended to reflect the progress (or lack thereof) of students and states and of those urban districts that choose to participate. NAEP generates enough information to compare states and participating urban districts, to measure achievement gaps in every state and many districts, and to report data by race, gender, special education status, English language learner status, poverty level, and so on.

In the immediate aftermath of the passage of No Child Left Behind, test scores on NAEP went up, probably because of additional time devoted to test preparation. But from 2007 forward, for an entire decade, *scores have been almost completely flat.* Billions of dollars were spent on testing and test preparation; untold hours, days, and weeks were spent preparing students to take the tests; and for a full decade the scores on NAEP were stagnant. The external audit demonstrated that the vast national effort devoted to annual testing of millions of students was *a massive waste of time and money.*

Even more troublesome was that Congress and the American people put their faith in a measure that is subjective. When NAEP began giving assessments in 1969–1970, the results were reported as "scale scores" on a scale of 0–500. The scale reported what students could do. It could not be translated into letter grades; all one could say was that scale scores went up or down, but it was not possible to make a headline-ready judgment about the scores.

In 1992, the governing board of the NAEP inaugurated a second way of scoring tests using "achievement levels." The achievement levels were supposed to reflect what students *should know and should be able to do.* The NAEP achievement levels are "advanced," "proficient," "basic," and "below basic." Typically, a small percentage (less than 10 percent) score in the advanced category, about one third are proficient, about one third are basic, and about one quarter are "below basic."

What few people realize is that the "cut scores," the decision about where to draw the line between advanced and proficient, between proficient and basic, are matters of human judgment. They are not arrived at objectively. Panels of people, including educators and members of the general public, sit together and decide what students in fourth grade and eighth grade *ought* to know. The process is *collective guesswork*. When the achievement levels were set in 1992, no one ever expected that someday 100 percent of American students would achieve a score of proficient. To date, in only one state—Massachusetts—have even 50 percent of students done so. Yet No Child Left Behind endorsed the absurd notion that everyone—every single student—regardless of language, poverty, or disability—would be "proficient" within twelve years of the law's passage. Not knowing this context, the media treat "proficient" as equivalent to a pass-fail mark. Those who do not score at the proficient level are treated as failures. This is simply wrong, equivalent to expecting every student to score an A in every subject. It will never happen.

When Congress finally got around to revising the No Child Left Behind Act in 2015 and wrote a new law, it did not abandon annual testing. The Every Student Succeeds Act continued to mandate annual testing of every child in grades 3–8. The members of the Senate committee who wrote the new law pretended that federal law could magically guarantee the academic success of "every student," which was as ridiculous as believing that "no child" would be "left behind." By 2015, legislators surely knew that such testing had not closed achievement gaps. Yet Congress preserved this federal mandate, whose only value is to generate reams of data and make it easier to identify schools to close and privatize.

Every year, teachers and parents complain about the time wasted on test preparation. Some schools devote weeks or months to test prep. When the annual tests are administered in the spring, they don't simply take an hour or two for each subject; each subject (reading and mathematics) requires several hours of testing over many days or weeks. Students as young as eight are subjected to grueling test sessions that take more time than college admission tests or even law school examinations. Some teachers keep "vomit bags" on hand in case the children throw up on the testing booklets; the vomit bags are not for the children but to protect the test booklets. Some teachers keep extra clothing available in case children wet their pants.

Who scores the answers to standardized test questions? Multiple-choice questions are scored by machine. Written answers, however, are scored either by computers or, in many cases, by ill-trained low-wage workers. In recent years, major testing corporations have recruited people to score tests by advertising on online websites like Craigslist. Todd Farley's book *Making the Grades* shows how capricious the scoring of test questions is. Farley spent fifteen years in the industry, working for most of the major testing corporations. His description of the hasty and arbitrary grading of five-paragraph essays by poorly trained scorers is alarming when you realize (as he did) that their snap decisions determine which students would be promoted (or not) to the next grade, which students would graduate (or not) from high school, and which would gain entry (or not) to college. He asks, why discard the informed judgment of the teacher who knows the student best and instead trust "the snap judgments of bored temps giving fleeting glances to student work"?

The wave of the future, if you listen to the testing experts, is computer scoring of essays. Let's hope the experts are wrong. Computers are worse than humans at scoring student writing. Les Perelman, a retired MIT professor of writing, has conducted studies of computer grading of essays and has learned their algorithms. Michael Winerip of *The New York Times* wrote about Perelman and his discovery that the computerized essay grading systems are easy to fool. Perelman analyzed the computer program used by the Educational Testing Service to score written answers for the SAT. The ETS e-rater can score 16,000 essays in 20 seconds. Perelman learned that the e-rater likes big words ("egregious" is better than "bad") and long sentences. But it can't tell the difference between fact and fiction or even between sense and nonsense. Winerip writes that Perelman "tells students not to waste time worrying about whether their facts are accurate, since pretty much any fact will do as long as it is incorporated into a well-structured sentence. 'E-Rater doesn't care if you say the War of 1812 started in 1945,' he said."

Perelman was interviewed by Steve Kolowich of *The Chronicle of Higher Education* about a computer program called the "BABEL Generator," which he designed with his students. The BABEL Generator could write sentences that were total nonsense but likely to receive high scores from a computer, like this one:

"Privateness has not been and undoubtedly never will be lauded, precarious, and decent . . . humankind will always subjugate privateness."

Not exactly E. B. White. Then again, Mr. Perelman wrote the essay in less than one second, using the Basic Automatic B.S. Essay Language Generator, or Babel, a new piece of weaponry in his continuing war on automated essay-grading software.

Before No Child Left Behind, there was an alternative to annual standardized testing of every student, but policymakers ignored it. In the early 1990s, a small number of progressive educators in New York City sought and received a state waiver to exempt their students from the state-mandated standardized testing at the end of high school. Led by veteran educator Ann Cook, they created the New York Performance Standards Consortium, a group of schools that demonstrated that "performance assessments" are far better measures of student skills and knowledge than are standardized tests. In New York, the state board of education is called the Board of Regents, and high school students must pass what are called "Regents' examinations" to graduate. Instead of the usual battery of five standardized tests that other students in the state must take, students in Consortium schools take only the Regents' English language arts examination. In place of the other four exams, the Consortium students "design experiments, make presentations, write reports and defend their work to outside experts." The students' tasks are approved by teachers and evaluated by external observers. During a twenty-year period, the number of schools in the Consortium grew from twenty-eight to thirty-eight, located in New York City, Rochester, and Ithaca. In New York City, the students in the Consortium schools have exactly the same demographic profile as those in the regular public schools, but they have significantly higher graduation rates, lower dropout rates, and higher persistence rates in college. Despite this impressive record of success and accountability, the state made no effort to expand the number of schools that participate in the innovative and effective work of the Consortium."

The parents and teachers who became active in the Resistance knew that the annual testing regime was warping what happened in the classroom. It was easier for parents to take the lead in opposition to standardized testing rather than teachers, because teachers could be disciplined or fired if they spoke out against the testing regime.

The resistance to abusive standardized testing was widespread. In Texas, parents created a group called Texans Advocating for Meaningful Student Assessment (TAMSA), better known in the Lone Star State as "Mothers Against Drunk Testing." This group organized against a proposal in the legislature to require students to pass fifteen tests in order to graduate; TAMSA persuaded legislators to reduce the required tests to five, not fifteen. How many of the legislators poised to pass this draconian legislation would have been able to pass the same fifteen tests that they wanted to impose on all the state's public school students? Or even the five that remained?

Almost every state has organizations of parents and teachers trying to moderate or block standardized testing. Their activism has been encouraged and tracked by FairTest, a Massachusetts-based organization that has fought the misuse of standardized testing since 1973. FairTest has compiled a list of more than one thousand colleges and universities that are "test-optional," because research has demonstrated that a student's high school grade point average is a better predictor of future academic success than a college admission test like the SAT or ACT.

In this chapter, I have chosen three examples of the Resistance to abusive standardized testing: the parents who led the opt out movement in New York; the students who fought high-stakes testing as a graduation requirement in Providence, Rhode Island; and the Seattle teachers who boycotted an unnecessary standardized test. These are inspiring models for others to follow.

The nation's most significant opt out movement began in New York State in 2011, the same year that the Common Core State Standards were first introduced into the state. New York won a $700 million grant in the Race to the Top competition, and the Board of Regents enthusiastically agreed to all of Arne Duncan's requirements: to adopt the Common Core standards, to use a test aligned with the Common Core, to increase the number of charter schools, and to evaluate teachers and principals by their students' test scores.

In January 2011, the Regents approved an overhaul of the state's curriculum and testing, aligning them to the Common Core standards and to passing marks similar to those on the federal NAEP; the state education department aggressively promoted Common Core as the apex of education reform. State officials convened training sessions for superintendents, principals, and teachers, where they were advised that "we are building the plane in the air as we fly it" and were shown a video in which engineers wearing parachutes constructed a plane in midair, filled with passengers who had no parachutes. A terrifying scenario, to be sure. Students, teachers, principals, and administrators suddenly found themselves in the grip of Disruption, faced with new standards, new tests, new curricula, and a new way to evaluate educators based on their students' test scores.

The opposition to Common Core testing and test-based evaluation of teachers began with principals, not with teachers or unions or parents. The revolt was launched in 2012 by Carol Burris and Sean Feeney, leaders of high schools on Long Island, where some of the state's best schools are located. They drafted a public letter challenging the new policy of evaluating teachers based on the test scores of their students, and one third of the principals in the state signed it. A protest of this magnitude, coming from school principals, was unprecedented. The principals objected that this approach to teacher evaluation had no research evidence behind it. They worried about the demoralization of their teaching staffs and about the harm that would be done to children by making standardized testing so important. They anticipated a narrowing of the curriculum, with less time for the arts, civics, and other nontested subjects.

In the spring of 2012, encouraged by the principals' revolt, parents in New York began to organize the nation's most significant opt out movement. Jeanette Deutermann, a parent on Long Island, became upset that her son, a fourth grade student, stopped liking school because he was inundated with dull worksheets and endless test prep. She read the principals' letter and connected her son's school phobia to ubiquitous high-stakes testing. She talked to other parents, who agreed; they did not want their children to be responsible for punishments levied against their teachers, and they did not like the Common Core State Standards or the state's efforts to standardize instruction.

Jeanette Deutermann is a parent on Long Island in New York who has been a major leader of the opt out movement in that state.

Deutermann decided that her son would not take the state tests. She started a Facebook group called Long Island Opt Out, which was joined by 1,000 parents in its first year. The next year, the number grew to 16,000, then to 23,000, and the number continued to grow. Parents had one powerful weapon: They could refuse to let their children take the mandated state tests. They could opt out. Opting out was a simple act of civil disobedience that hurts no one.

The state's powerful teachers' union initially kept its distance from the opt out movement, and the New York City teachers' union strongly supported the Common Core standards, as did the national union, the American Federation of Teachers.

But many teachers agreed with the parents and thought that the heightened emphasis on testing was a crazy idea, wrong from the start, that could have been conceived only by people who knew nothing about educating actual children. Chris Cerrone, a social studies teacher in upstate New York, announced in 2012 that his children were opting out of state testing. In an article in a Buffalo, New York, newspaper, he explained why his children would not take the tests:

I do not need a test to determine if my children are progressing with their education. By simply listening to them read regularly and checking their work, I can establish their strengths and weaknesses. My children's teachers can conclude if they need extra reading or math assistance within a few weeks from the start of the school year. We do not need the expensive testing systems to make that determination. . . .

We need to return to a system where parents and teachers are involved in educational decisions and remove the corporate reformers and politicians from our schools. My children's district is facing drastic budget cuts to vital programs in the arts, and class sizes will soar because we are spending scarce financial resources on standardized testing and expensive data systems.

In July 2013, Deutermann and Cerrone met with other concerned parents and formed a statewide organization called New York State Allies for Public Education (NYSAPE), to fight high-stakes standardized testing, the Common Core standards, and the state's test-based teacher evaluation law (called APPR, or Annual Professional Performance Review). NYSAPE founders included Deutermann; Cerrone; Lisa Rudley, a parent and community activist in Ossining; Danielle Boudet, parent; Eric Mihelberger, parent; Lori Griffin, parent and teacher; Bianca Tanis, parent and teacher; and Kris Nielsen, parent and teacher. The board expanded over time to represent parents and educators in every region of the state. Some sixty grassroots organizations joined NYSAPE, and it became a formidable political operation. Its leaders were parents, and they were not willing to compromise with politicians on what was best for their children.

NYSAPE became one of the most active parent-educator groups in the nation. It sent parents and educators to meet with state legislators and to testify at hearings. During testing season, it rented billboards on busy roads and hired roving trucks with signs urging parents to opt out. It prepared sample test-refusal letters for parents. Its members refused to be ignored by state leaders. Despite the state's threats of punishment, there was nothing the state could do to stop parents from opting their children out of the tests.

State Commissioner of Education John King (later secretary of education during Obama's last year in office) was a zealous advocate for the Common Core and the new Common Core state testing. He began a tour of communities to conduct public forums touting the changes, but King encountered parent outrage wherever he went.

The new Common Core–aligned state testing began as a trial run in 2012, after the state awarded a $32 million contract to the British megacorporation Pearson. Students and teachers pounced upon unusually ridiculous questions that were leaked by students. One question on the eighth grade English language arts test created a national and international scandal known as "Pineapplegate." The question was based on a reading passage about a race between a talking pineapple and a hare; it was posted immediately on the blog of parent activist Leonie Haimson. She discovered that the same question had appeared on Pearson exams in other states, and students everywhere thought the passage was stupid. The author of the original story, Daniel Pinkwater, ridiculed Pearson's bowdlerization of his story. Parents and students demonstrated outside the offices of Pearson in Manhattan, brandishing pineapples, and Pearson deservedly became the all-purpose punching bag for parents who hated the new testing regime.

When the Common Core testing started for real in the spring of 2013, parent opposition intensified. Some parents objected to the high stakes attached to the tests. Some worried about the pressure on their young children. Some objected to the loss of recess and the arts, sacrificed to test preparation. Some complained about the amount of time required for the testing, nearly five hours per week for two weeks; perhaps they remembered their own childhood, when a math or reading test took forty-five minutes, not four or five hours.

The opt out movement grew stronger when the results of the new Common Core tests were released in 2013. Commissioner John King had predicted that passing rates would drop precipitously across the state, and they did. Only 31 percent of the students in the state met the proficiency standard in English and mathematics (the proportion reaching proficiency in 2012 had been 55 percent in English; 65 percent in math). *The New York Times* editorialized, echoing Arne Duncan, that "most states" had "deceived the public about the dismal quality

Lisa Rudley is a parent in New York who was a leader of New York State Allies for Public Education, a coalition of sixty parent and educator groups that encouraged parents to opt their children out of state testing to protest the harmful emphasis on standardized testing whose only purpose was to rank students, teachers, and schools, but not to inform instruction.

of public schools by adopting pathetically weak learning standards that made children appear better educated than they actually were." It never occurred to the *Times*'s editorial writer to question the validity of the tests or the arbitrariness of the passing mark. The testing organizations administering Common Core tests had decided to use NAEP's definition of proficiency as the passing mark, a decision that was ridiculous on its face. What the editorial writer for *The New York Times* did not know and what the public did not know was that the testing consortia had chosen a "passing mark" that they knew was beyond the reach of most students. The test-makers deliberately chose a goal—like expecting all students to run a five-minute mile—that was impossible for most students, thus dooming most students to failure.

Thanks to the grassroots organizing work of NYSAPE, led by Lisa Rudley, opt outs continued to grow. This was no easy feat, since every year the eighth grade students moved out of the testing pool and new students entered the third grade. The opt out movement had to replenish its ranks every year.

New York state officials, especially Governor Andrew Cuomo, were perplexed by the opt out movement. Although he didn't know much about it, Cuomo loved Common Core and especially the test-based teacher evaluation part, which he thought would expose large numbers of "bad teachers." He believed the Disrupter propaganda that the key to success was to find and fire "bad teachers." He wanted the teacher evaluation component to be as tough as possible. He was disappointed when fewer than 1 percent of teachers in the state were rated "ineffective."

By 2015, about 20 percent of all eligible test-takers in New York State opted out, which was 200,000 students. The opt out movement could no longer be ignored, not even by Cuomo. Most opt outs occurred on Long Island and in rural upstate counties, where parents (and even principals and superintendents) strongly opposed the tests. In some schools and districts, more than 80 percent of students refused the tests. The numbers were lowest in New York City, where officials warned students, teachers, and parents that opting out might cause students to be held back or prevent them from gaining admission to the middle school or high school of their choice (during the administration of Mayor Michael Bloomberg, the number of selective public schools increased).

Faced with parent resistance, Governor Cuomo blinked. He appointed a commission to review the state's standards and tests, and at the commission's suggestion the state Board of Regents suspended implementation of the educator evaluation law until 2019, at which time it was revised.

It was by no means a complete victory, but it showed the power of parent protest. In 2018, the hard-line state commissioner, MaryEllen Elia, threatened to compel schools with high opt out numbers to use their federal Title 1 funding (meant for disadvantaged students) to "teach" parents the value of standardized testing. But parent leaders continued to resist state compulsion, and the opt outs continued, and the state commissioner dropped her threats. She resigned in 2019.

Why should children be forced to take tests that have no diagnostic value? Why does no high-performing nation in the world require annual testing? If annual testing improves performance, why have New York State's scores on the National Assessment of Educational Progress remained flat since 2003? Why have national scores on NAEP flat-lined since 2007 despite annual testing? Don't expect answers from the New York State Education Department or the U.S. Department of Education or the U.S. Congress, which mandated the testing.

Like the parents in New York, teachers at Garfield High School in Seattle were upset by the pressure to impose unnecessary tests.

On January 10, 2013, they called a press conference in Adam Gish's second-floor English language arts classroom to announce that they intended to boycott the state-mandated MAP examinations for their students. The MAP tests are computer tests of reading and mathematics that students were required to take three times a year. The tests supposedly measured student improvement from one test to the next and were also used to evaluate the effectiveness of their teachers. The teachers complained that the tests were stealing time from instruction and were not testing the curriculum that they were teaching.

At the press conference, history teacher Jesse Hagopian announced, "The teachers at Garfield High School have voted unanimously to refuse to administer the MAP test."

Jesse Hagopian was a fierce critic of high-stakes testing and privatization and a determined activist. He had debated Arne Duncan about charter schools and had even been arrested while trying to execute a citizen's arrest of the Washington legislature for failing to fund public schools adequately. In 2010, Hagopian and another Seattle teacher, Noam Gundle from Ballard High School, had endorsed a resolution condemning MAP testing, which was adopted by their union, the Seattle Education Association.

Teachers at Garfield High decided to take action against the MAP test. Teachers read articles and books about standardized testing and informed themselves about its uses and misuses. One of the articles was written by Sue Peters, a Seattle parent activist (who was later elected to the school board). The article, "15 Reasons Why the Seattle School District Should Shelve the MAP Test," lambasted the value, accuracy, and validity of the test. Peters estimated that the test cost the district as much as $10 million and called it "an unfunded mandate." She complained that the test was required of all students in kindergarten through ninth grade but was completely inappropriate for children in grades K–2. The kindergartners, she said, did not know how to use a computer or how to read. Furthermore, the test narrows the curriculum, encourages test prep instead of instruction, and did not reflect what Seattle teachers were expected to teach.

Garfield teachers had their own stories about the MAP. Kit McCormick, an experienced English language arts teacher, told the other teach-

Jesse Hagopian is a high school
history teacher in Seattle,
Washington, who led the
Garfield teachers' strike against
unnecessary testing.

ers about a freshman who asked her what the word *enjambment* meant,
because it appeared on the MAP test; she explained that it was a word
referring to "a poetic technique . . . wherein a line of poetry travels to
the next line without a pause in thought or punctuation, usually indi-
cating either an inevitability of action or a stream-of-consciousness state
of mind." This concept might appropriately be taught at the eleventh or
twelfth grade Advanced Placement level, not to freshmen. A teacher of
mathematics, Mario Shaunette, said that he peered over the shoulder of
his ninth grade algebra students and spotted a geometry question, which
he likened to a Spanish teacher seeing a question in French on the exam.
Those who taught English language learners and students with disabilities said that the MAP test humiliated their students because the test was
"neither linguistically nor culturally appropriate." Teachers of nontested
subjects, like Hagopian, who taught history, complained that the school
library was shut down three times a year for weeks at a time while the
MAP test was administered, meaning that students could neither check
out books nor use the school computers for research. This hurt low-
income students most, since they did not have home computers.

The MAP test was used to evaluate teachers, even though the test
publisher (the Northwest Evaluation Association) said it was neither
valid nor reliable for that purpose.

The teachers in the tested subjects won the support of the teachers in the nontested subjects, who shared their view that students were over-tested and that teachers had a responsibility to find better ways to assess their students' progress. They were not opposed to testing on principle, and some were not opposed to standardized testing. But they were united in their opposition to the MAP. They knew that they were risking their jobs and careers by taking a stand, but they believed that if they all stood together, they would not be punished. It is easy to fire a single dissenter, but not so easy to punish an entire school's staff. All ninety teachers agreed to launch what may well have been the nation's first all-school boycott of a district-mandated test.

Some teachers were shaken when their MAP boycott immediately elicited a negative response from the Seattle superintendent, José Banda, who warned every teacher in the district that the MAP was mandatory, not optional. The Garfield teachers feared that this was a precursor to declaring them insubordinate, a first step toward termination.

Only minutes after receiving the superintendent's warning, a boycott leader announced on the intercom that all staff were invited to the conference room at lunchtime to enjoy pizza sent to them by a school in Florida. The greetings and salutations from teachers across the country began to pour in. Hagopian wrote that "our determination was buoyed over the coming days as the chocolates, flowers, cards, books, donations, emails, photos of teachers holding 'Scrap the MAP' signs, and resolutions of support came streaming in from around the country—and later from around the world."

Then something remarkable happened: the boycott won the support of the Garfield High School Parent Teacher Student Association. Other high schools and even elementary schools in Seattle joined the MAP boycott. To be sure, not everyone was happy about the boycott. *The Seattle Times,* the major newspaper in the city, railed against the teachers and urged the superintendent to stand firm. Hagopian felt sure that Gates-funded groups were pressuring the superintendent to block any resistance to standardized testing. In an effort to stop the boycott, Superintendent Banda told all the district principals to convene mandatory staff meetings and warn teachers that anyone who refused to give the MAP test would receive a ten-day suspension without pay. He directed school principals to give the test themselves if teachers refused to do so.

Buoyed by the national and even international support for their boycott, the teachers at Garfield remained united. The superintendent came to meet with the boycott leaders at Garfield High School and promised to form a task force to reevaluate the MAP *after* they gave the test that spring. The boycott leaders explained their reasons for refusing the MAP. The superintendent was not persuaded.

Hagopian gave the superintendent a short lecture, which he hoped would win him over. He said:

> You are new to this district and the decision you make in the next twenty-four hours will have a profound effect on your legacy in this school district. If you decide to carry out your plan to require administrators to remove students from our classrooms and take them to the computer lab, you will have made your choice to side with the corporate education reformers, some of the wealthiest people the world has ever known. They want the public schools to use standardized testing to evaluate teachers. Or you can cancel that plan and decide to stand with the unanimous vote of the teachers of Garfield High School, the unanimous vote of the student body government of Garfield High School, and the unanimous vote of the PTSA of Garfield High School.

Sensing that Superintendent Banda was not impressed by what he hoped was a powerful offer, Hagopian promised that when CNN came to the school, he would tell them that Banda was a "real educational leader." That didn't work either.

The teachers were afraid that the administrators, fearful for their jobs, would undermine the boycott, and they did. They called students out of their classrooms to come to the library to take the test. The students, however, were prepared. Juniors and seniors handed out flyers to younger students, informing them of their right to refuse to take the test. The PTSA sent out emails informing parents of their right to opt their children out of the MAP. When administrators announced which students were supposed to report for the MAP, some students stayed in their seats.

They exercised their right to say no. "Other students marched off to the computer lab, only to express their creative defiance by repeatedly hitting the 'A' key, completing the test in mere seconds and thus rendering their test scores invalid."

As the impasse continued, the Garfield leaders organized "a national day of action" on February 6, 2013, to support their boycott. The Seattle NAACP called a press conference to denounce the MAP as a racially discriminatory test that kept black students out of AP courses. Teachers at Berkeley High School in California rallied at their lunchtime to express solidarity. Chicago parents who belonged to a group called More Than a Score endorsed the boycott. The Portland (Oregon) Student Union announced their support for their peers in Seattle. Randi Weingarten of the American Federation of Teachers and Dennis Van Roekel of the National Education Association endorsed the boycott. The boycotters had used the slogan "Scrap the MAP." The boycotters added a new slogan, "Suspend the Test, Not the Teachers."

On May 13, 2013, Superintendent Banda gave in. He sent out a blast email to all employees of the Seattle School District that contained this single sentence, buried under other verbiage: "MAP will be optional for high schools for the 2013–2014 school year." Jesse Hagopian jumped to his feet in the middle of a lesson and told the students, "We won! We scrapped the MAP!" The students erupted in cheers.

The victory was incomplete. Students in elementary and middle schools were still required to continue taking a test that educators agreed was useless, invalid, unreliable, and actually harmful. However, some students in the early grades opted out, including Jesse Hagopian's young son.

High schools in Seattle no longer are required to administer the MAP but they still give plenty of other tests, including end-of-course exams, the Smarter Balanced Assessment (a Common Core standardized test), Advanced Placement tests, and SATs for the college bound.

Not only did parents and teachers oppose high-stakes testing. Students did as well.

High school students in Providence, Rhode Island, joined the Resistance with bravado and creativity. In 2010, they formed the Providence Student Union (PSU) to fight budget cuts and to demand adequate resources and a voice for students in decisions about their schools. Their activism escalated in 2013 when the Rhode Island State Board of Education decided that students could not graduate from high school unless they first passed a standardized test called NECAP (pronounced "knee-cap"), an acronym for the New England Common Assessment Program. The students understood, as the adults did not, that standardized test results are represented on a bell curve. They understood, as the adults did not, that as many as 40 percent of their classmates would never receive a high school diploma, and that most of those students would be low-income, would have disabilities, or would be English language learners. The PSU launched a sustained campaign to persuade the State Board of Education to reverse its decision.

To educate the public, the PSU developed a strategy of flamboyant actions and political theater. They were far more creative than were adult protesters elsewhere. They began with sit-ins at the Providence school board, demanding an end to high-stakes testing. The school board, of course, ignored the students.

PSU called on Governor Lincoln Chafee to reject the test. They said that the 40 percent who had failed NECAP included 71 percent of black students, 70 percent of Latino students, 86 percent of students with disabilities, and 94 percent of students whose English skills were limited. They said it was unconscionable that these students would be denied a diploma based on a single test whose value was not proven. Kelvis Hernandez, a member of PSU, said,

> We believe that we should graduate with a high-quality education. But this policy is not the right way. Punishing students—particularly those who haven't had the opportunity to receive the great education we deserve—is neither effective nor just. It is ineffective because we have spent 10, 11, or 12 years in schools that are underfunded, under-resourced, and unable to give us the support we need to do well on the NECAP. And it is unjust because the students who have received this inadequate support are the ones being put on trial.

Another PSU member, Tamargeiae Paris, a high school junior, said, "the NECAP was not designed to be used as a high-stakes test. The makers of the NECAP themselves have said that the test should not be used as a graduation requirement." What the students said was true. It was irrefutable. The adults didn't listen.

In February 2013, PSU staged a "Zombie March" in front of the state education department headquarters. They covered their faces, hair, and shirts with catsup to signify that their lives would be ruined without a high school diploma. They chanted, "No education, no life!" At their rally, the students spoke out. High school student Claudierre McKay declared, "To take away our diploma is to take away our life," and was answered by moaning and shrieking from the crowd of "undead" students.

The PSU's next demonstration was brilliant. The students created an event called "Take the Test" and invited accomplished professionals to spend a Saturday morning taking a mock test composed of questions used on previous NECAP mathematics exams. Fifty people volunteered to do so, including elected officials, architects, scientists, engineers, col-

The student-led Providence Student Union engaged in spirited and creative resistance to the state's policy of using a standardized test (the New England Common Assessment Program) as a high school graduation requirement.

lege professors, reporters, directors of nonprofit organizations, and lawyers. When their tests were scored, 60 percent did not score high enough to qualify for a diploma.

Priscilla Rivera, a high school junior, said:

Of course, it is true that many of these professionals who participated in our event had not been prepared to take the test. But our point is, neither have we. For 10, 11, or 12 years we have been taught to different standards. We have not been following a curriculum aligned with this test, and we are trapped in an education system that is failing to give us the education we deserve. If it does not make sense to punish adults for not being prepared to take this particular test, we believe it does not make sense to punish us for not having been effectively taught this material over a period of years. Give us a good education, not a test!

The superintendent of schools in Providence, Susan Lusi, agreed with the students. The Providence City Council agreed with the students. But the responsible authorities—the State Board of Education and State Commissioner Deborah Gist—did not back down. Gist called the event "deeply irresponsible on the part of the adults" because they were sending a message that the tests don't matter.

Much to their surprise, the Student Union received an endorsement from the editorial board of *The Boston Globe,* which is widely read in neighboring Rhode Island. The editorial noted that the high school students had outscored the "accomplished professionals." Forty percent of the students had failed to meet the threshold to graduate, but 60 percent of the adults had also failed. The editorial said:

The fundamental problem, though, is that the test wasn't originally designed to be a graduation requirement and isn't suited for that purpose. Schools need more high standards and accountability, and the NECAP was designed not to evaluate individual students' proficiency, but to rank the quality of the schools they attend. Unlike tests meant primarily for student assessment, such as the MCAS in

Massachusetts, the NECAP expects a certain portion of test-takers to fail. Research suggests that percentage will likely come from low-income, working-class neighborhoods—the students who are least likely to return for a fifth year of high school, even if skipping it means going without a diploma.

Plus, as the adults' mock exam suggests, the NECAP may not even be testing the right skills. The Rhode Island Department of Education should reconsider its graduation requirement—and not only to salve the embarrassment of so many high-salaried professionals.

Of course, the NECAP was also not a good measure of school quality because it inevitably measured the demographics of the students enrolled in the schools.

When State Commissioner Gist scheduled her annual "State of Education" speech in April 2013, the PSU countered her message on the same day by giving their own "First Annual State of the Student Address" at the Rhode Island State House. The students put out a press release summarizing their proposals to improve education.

Claudierre McKay, a junior at Classical High School, said,

We should look for inspiration at successful systems like the New York Performance Standards Consortium. These schools require a student to complete four performance-based assessments that show oral and written skill, including an analytic literary essay, a social studies research paper with valid arguments and evidence, a science experiment that shows understanding of the scientific method and an applied math problem. These schools outperform New York schools using high-stakes testing—and we can see why.

Leexammarie Nieves, a sophomore at Central High School, said,

We're told to sit and listen, to do our test prep so we can pass our NECAP and move on. But that's not how we learn. That's certainly not how I learn. We need an education that is as creative as we are. We need projects, hands-on learning, debates, and conversations. We need opportunities to do arts and technology and to work in groups. And we need small enough classes where teachers have the flexibility to teach us like individuals.

Neither the State Board of Education nor Commissioner Gist was moved by the students' pleas.

In the fall of 2013, PSU staged a student talent show to draw a contrast between what they could do and the narrow scope of the multiple-choice tests. A small part of the show was captured in a few minutes of video, in which a student playing a bagpipe is interrupted by other students saying it was time to take the test. They hand him a giant #2 pencil and show multiple-choice questions. He refuses, tosses the pencil to the floor, and leads the audience in a chant, "NECAP is not right! That is why we have to fight!"

In January 2014, PSU launched "Operation Guinea Pig," in which students dressed as guinea pigs and lab rats crowded into the rotunda of the State House. Students wore mouse ears, whiskers, and guinea pig masks. Jose Serrano, a sophomore at the Met School, said, "The reason we are dressed like guinea pigs and lab rats is simple—that is how we are being treated."

The students had one more trick up their sleeve. In April 2014, there was a mayoral election under way, and the PSU joined with the Nellie Mae Education Foundation and a local group called Young Voices to sponsor a mayoral forum conducted by young people. Every mayoral candidate declared their opposition to using NECAP as a graduation requirement. Every one of them agreed to fight for student-centered education, hands-on education, support for the arts, and fair disciplinary policies rather than punishment.

The students won a huge victory when the Rhode Island House of Representatives passed a three-year moratorium on the use of NECAP by a vote of 63–3. The students made their voices heard. They won!

Behind the scenes, however, the state's policymakers had already decided to phase out the hated NECAP and to replace it with a new standardized test called PARCC (Partnership for Assessment of Readiness for College and Careers). PARCC was a federally funded test aligned with the Common Core standards. It was even more difficult than NECAP was. Rhode Island was one of twenty-six states that agreed to adopt PARCC, while thirty-one (there was overlap) agreed to use another federally funded test, called the Smarter Balanced Assessment Consortium (SBAC).

The students didn't realize that state officials were playing along with them, while planning to drop NECAP and launch PARCC.

Rhode Island first administered the controversial PARCC exam in 2015, and the results were a disaster. Only one in three students in grades 3–10 met the exam's unrealistic expectations in English, and only one in four met them in math. The pass rates were even lower for the students who were most at risk of failing, such as students with disabilities and English-language learners. In the spring of 2016, the new state commissioner of education, Ken Wagner, announced that the PARCC test would not be used as a graduation requirement. That headed off a renewal of student protests and also avoided the calamity of denying a high school diploma to a majority of students in the state. If passing PARCC had been a graduation requirement, nearly two thirds of students in the state would have been denied a diploma, including 78 percent of black and Latino students, 91 percent of English learners, and 94 percent of students with disabilities.

Perhaps the testing officials clung to the myth that students would score higher if the tests were made more difficult, or "rigorous," as the Disrupters liked to say. Nonsense. There is no evidence that constant failure produces higher test scores. But in the meanwhile, states using the new Common Core exams had to tell most students that they had not met expectations, or in common parlance, had "failed," which was the common refrain in newspapers. Almost every state agreed to use one of the two tests but to take a "wait-and-see" approach before using them for high-stakes decisions about promotion or graduation. What they did not tell students or parents or even teachers was that the "passing mark" was not objective; it was an arbitrary construct that could be set higher or lower to raise or lower passing rates.

The startlingly high failure rates produced by PARCC and SBAC made parents angry and caused many of them to oppose the Common Core standards and the tests aligned with them. Arne Duncan chided the critics of Common Core and the tests and referred to them as a "fringe element" of "extremists" who didn't want to admit how poorly prepared American students are. Duncan believed that the dismal results of the Common Core tests would wake communities up and get them to take education as seriously as students and families in Asian nations did.

As state after state learned that most of their students had "failed" exams whose passing marks were wildly unrealistic, they began withdrawing from the federal consortia. When PARCC began in 2010, twenty-six states (including the District of Columbia) signed on as partners. By 2019, PARCC was almost extinct, as only the District of Columbia and New Jersey remained committed to using it, and New Jersey threatened to drop out. Membership in the Smarter Balanced Assessment Consortium had shrunk from thirty-one states to only fifteen (or fewer). With each passing year, the number of states using the federally funded Common Core tests declined.

The students in the Providence Student Union were wiser than our national education leaders were. They understood that students have many talents and skills, and that standardized tests don't measure the full range of those talents and skills. These young people sought to save their fellow students from the dead, cold hands of the robots currently in charge of the nation's education policy and testing industry. The students have heart. They have creativity. They have wit. They are innovative. They are alive with spirit. They have the qualities that made America great. None of our Founding Fathers ever passed a standardized test.

Those students know this great secret: We are not Singapore; we are not South Korea; we are not China. We are America. We should cultivate the wit of Ben Franklin, the thoughtfulness of Abraham Lincoln, the ingenuity of Thomas Alva Edison, the spirit of the Wright brothers, the eloquence of Dr. Martin Luther King Jr. Were they good test-takers? Who knows? Who cares? I bet that the financial wizard Bernie Madoff (now in jail for his crimes) and the guys at Enron had great test scores.

CHAPTER 7

Rewards and Punishments Are
Not Good Motivators

No Child Left Behind and Race to the Top wrongly assumed that threats, punishments, and rewards would produce better education, which they defined solely as higher test scores. It was time to get *tough,* the Disrupters believed, to demand accountability from "lazy" students and teachers. Students, they thought, would surely try harder if they were tested frequently and threatened with failure. Teachers and principals, they believed, would surely get students to produce higher test scores if they were worried about losing their jobs or were offered a bonus based on their students' test scores. Best of all, from the perspective of Disrupters, was to threaten their schools with closure. Living in fear of losing one's job, career, and reputation would surely motivate everyone, they thought, as would the hope of winning extra money.

The Resistance did not agree. If there was one belief that united the parents, teachers, students, and scholars of the Resistance, it was their conviction that threats, punishments, and rewards are poor motivators. The Resistance hated disruption, because they knew that children, families, teachers, and schools need encouragement, support, and stability, not constant upheaval.

Maybe incentives and fear of punishment work in the corporate world (and there are management gurus who disagree), but they do not work in education. Those government officials and legislators who designed No Child Left Behind and Race to the Top thought that they were working on the cutting edge of innovation, but in fact they were unknowingly applying ideas that had been popular a century earlier. They believed in top-down management that tightly controlled the workforce. They believed in standardization and compliance. The Common Core standards were supposed to align every part of the education system and to create a common curriculum, common textbooks, common tests, and a common means for preparing and evaluating teachers (and a national marketplace for vendors to schools).

The Disrupters believed that standardization would make everyone smart, would reduce inequality, and would end poverty. They often proclaimed that the way to end poverty was to "fix" schools, despite the lack of any evidence that this was the case. And the best way to "fix" schools, they thought, was to disrupt them with external mandates and force them to improve. Their love of disruption was borrowed from the business world, where the concept of blowing things up was considered to be cutting-edge thinking.

Historian Jill Lepore demolished the peculiar corporate love of disruption in a brilliant article in *The New Yorker*. She wrote about the origins of "disruptive innovation," which she attributed to Harvard professor Clayton M. Christensen. Anyone who criticized disruption, Lepore wrote, risked being seen as a defender of the status quo, an old fogey. But Lepore was unimpressed by Christensen's theory of disruptive innovation. She pointed out that it was built on case studies and proceeded to take apart each of them, showing that successful companies built upon prior successes. Incremental improvement, she suggested, was more successful than disruption. The entire thesis of disruptive innovation, she wrote, was a circular argument:

> If an established company doesn't disrupt, it will fail, and if it fails it must be because it didn't disrupt. When a startup fails, that's a success, since epidemic failure is a hallmark of disruptive innovation. . . . When an established company succeeds, that's only because

it hasn't yet failed. And, when any of these things happen, all of them are further evidence of disruption.

The gospel of disruptive innovation certainly does not make sense in every sphere of activity, she wrote, because human relations are not the same as industrial relations:

> Innovation and disruption are ideas that originated in the arena of business but which have since been applied to arenas whose values and goals are remote from the values and goals of business. People aren't disk drives. Public schools, colleges and universities, churches, museums, and many hospitals, all of which have been subjected to disruptive innovation, have revenues and expenses and infrastructures, but they aren't industries in the same way that manufacturers of hard-disk drives or truck engines or drygoods are industries. . . . Doctors have obligations to their patients, teachers to their students, pastors to their congregations, curators to the public, and journalists to their readers—-obligations that lie outside the realm of earnings, and are fundamentally different from the obligations that a business executive has to employees, partners, and investors.

The ideology of the Disruption movement in the education world relies on two dogmas: first, the benefits of standardization, and second, the power of markets, at scale, to drive innovation and results. Their blind adherence to these principles has been disastrous in education. These principles don't work in schools for the same reasons that they don't work for families, churches, and other institutions that function primarily on the basis of human interactions, not profits and losses.

Disruptive leaders (like those trained by Eli Broad's unaccredited Broad Academy) are trained to be top-down managers who crack down on teachers, reduce their autonomy, and require them to organize their classrooms and their lessons according to prescribed protocols. Teachers are expected to recognize that they will be judged by the test scores of their students. If they are not teaching math or reading in grades 3–8 (about 70 percent of teachers do not teach these subjects in these grades),

Eli Broad made his fortune in home building and insurance. He used his fortune to promote charter schools and to establish an unaccredited training program, the Broad Academy for urban superintendents, which teaches his belief in top-down management and closing public schools with low test scores.

they will be judged by the scores of students they never taught in subjects they never taught. If this seems crazy, that's because it is.

"No-excuses" charter schools are an extreme form of Disruption, where demands for compliance are taken to chilling extremes. Lengthy guidelines prescribe how students should dress and act, where they should sit, where they should look ("track the teacher") and how they should behave when walking in the halls. Any slight sign of resistance—a shirttail sticking out, failure to walk in a straight line, daring to whisper in the hallway—is swiftly punished with demerits, even suspension. If students feel the urge to speak to other students while walking in the hallways, they are told to "blow an air bubble" (that is, to puff up their cheeks without speaking). Students in these schools are called "scholars," even though that term usually refers to someone who has spent many years becoming expert in their field of study. The "scholars," as even the youngest of them are called, are taught to obey without hesitation or question. Far from being innovative, such schools resemble the regimented schools of the nineteenth century.

The current regime of command and control that dominates federal and state policy echoes two movements that were popular in American society and American education in the late-nineteenth and early-twentieth centuries: Taylorism and behaviorism.

Frederick Winslow Taylor (1856–1915) was an engineer who believed that there was a single best way to organize every line of work. Just as Clayton Christensen is lauded as the "thought leader" of "disruptive innovation," Frederick Winslow Taylor was widely praised as the pioneer of "social engineering." His ideas were hailed by manufacturers, legislators, policymakers, and journalists as the greatest revelation of the age. He developed the Taylor System, a way of "rationalizing" the workplace to maximize efficiency and productivity. He conducted experiments to demonstrate that factories could be reorganized by using his time and motion studies with a stopwatch to become more efficient, less wasteful. The Taylor System "involved the establishment of many rules, laws, and formulae to replace the judgment of the individual workman."

Those workers who complied with his schema would be rewarded with higher pay and bonuses, while those who were recalcitrant would be punished with lower pay and eventually lose their jobs. Defiance of instructions from the workers' superiors was unthinkable. Taylor's most famous experiment was commissioned by Bethlehem Steel in the late 1890s. It was hailed as a breakthrough that ushered in a new era of "scientific management." The steel company asked him to devise a way to increase the number of tons of pig iron that a manual laborer could carry from one place to another in a single day. Historian Raymond Callahan recounted Taylor's plan of action. When Taylor began his experiment, Bethlehem had some 75 men whose job was to carry a "pig of iron which weighed 92 pounds, carrying it some 30 or 40 feet and then up an inclined plank into a railway car, and depositing the pig of iron on the floor of the car." The men were loading an average of 12½ tons of pig iron per day, or 304 pigs in a ten-hour day, or about 30 pigs an hour, or one every two minutes. Taylor engaged "an intelligent, college-educated man" to conduct a time and motion study, and he predicted that "a first-class man should be able to handle 48 tons of pig iron per day instead of 12½." This meant that each worker would load 106,400 pounds of pig iron each day compared with the 28,000 pounds they were accustomed to. Each would load 115 pigs per hour instead of 30 pigs per hour.

Taylor had to figure out how to nearly quadruple the men's workload without causing a strike or quarrels with the men. He and his team picked out one industrious workman, a fellow named Schmidt, and asked him if he was "a high-priced man" who was willing to work for $1.85 an hour instead of $1.15. Schmidt said in his broken English that he was a high-priced man, and he did indeed want to make more money.

Taylor instructed Schmidt as follows:

"Well, if you are a high-priced man, you will do exactly as this man tells you tomorrow, from morning till night. When he tells you to pick up a pig and walk, you pick up a pig and walk, and when he tells you to sit down and rest, you sit down. You do that right straight through the day. And what's more, no back talk. Now a high-priced man does just what he's told to do, and no back talk. Do you understand that? When this man tells you to walk, you walk; when he tells you to sit down, you sit down, and you don't talk back at him. Now you come on to work tomorrow morning and I'll know before night whether you are really a high-priced man or not."

Schmidt did exactly as he was told, and by the end of the next day, he had loaded 47½ tons of pig iron onto the car. That became the expectation for the entire crew.

Taylor's well-publicized work was widely discussed and admired. He said that his system of scientific management was applicable to any social institution, including homes, farms, businesses, churches, philanthropies, universities, and government agencies. All one had to do was set goals, measure how quickly workers were accomplishing them, and brook no dissent. Setting high expectations, measuring output, and standardizing the process were the keys to scientific management.

Taylor's pronouncements launched a national movement on behalf of "social efficiency." In the blink of an eye, acolytes of Taylorism descended on public schools to root out waste and inefficiency (at the time, many urban school districts were overflowing with immigrant students and had as many as one hundred students in a single classroom). Almost every large school district hired efficiency experts to determine how to make the schools more efficient. Popular magazines complained that the schools were out of touch with the times and wasted time and money on "medieval" studies like Latin, Greek, literature, and history when they should be preparing students for "real life," to prepare for vocations such as farming, factory labor, homemaking, blacksmithing, and other trades.

Behaviorism was another craze that captured popular attention in the late nineteenth century and early twenty-first century. Behaviorist psychologists believed that animals (including humans) can and should be conditioned by repetitive training and discipline to behave as others want them to behave. Behaviorists taught that employers and teachers should be concerned only with observable behaviors that would be rewarded or punished. It didn't matter what employees or students thought or felt, only what they did. Disrupters today, like the behaviorists Edward Thorndike and B. F. Skinner, believe that students can be trained by rigidly prescribed conditioning via punishments and rewards to respond and behave as their superiors prefer.

The Disrupters' insistence on conformity and standardization is at odds with the world of variation in which we live. Innovation and creativity stem from diversity of thought and action, not conformity and standardization. Our success as a society is built on our variety, not our sameness and unquestioning obedience to authority. We live in a diverse, pluralistic society that should welcome nonconformity and human variation—filmmakers *and* accountants, cosmetologists *and* cosmologists, disrupters *and* consensus builders, dreamers *and* builders, masters of routine *and* visionaries, and so on. Behaviorists, and the Disrupters who mimic them today, lack appreciation for the value of divergent thinking and for the creative potential of variety. And they emphatically discount mere "feelings." What mattered to the behaviorists, and what matters to Disrupters today, is the data derived from standardized testing and the measurement of behavior. But it is precisely this obsession that leads Disrupters astray, as it did the now discredited behaviorist psychologists. What really matters, in the long run, for students and for everyone else, is intrinsic motivation, the drive to accomplish something for its own sake, not by order or command.

Had they been alive in the opening years of the twenty-first century, Frederick Winslow Taylor, Edward Thorndike, and B. F. Skinner would no doubt have looked approvingly upon the mass social experiment now

conducted on the nation's students and teachers. Thanks to No Child
Left Behind, what had once been a highly decentralized system with
thousands of districts in fifty states and territories, each deciding upon
its own standards and tests, each granted the flexibility to meet local
needs and conditions, staffed by teachers free to meet the unique needs
of their unique students, was increasingly welded into a national system
controlled by federal law. The fact that this law was introduced by a
conservative Republican president, George W. Bush, was the height of
irony, since Republicans had traditionally defended local control and
resisted federal intrusions. In their newfound devotion to privatization,
Republicans became outspoken opponents of local control, seeking to
pry public schools away from local school boards and hand them over
to entrepreneurs, corporate chains, mayors, emergency managers, and
governors.

This new era of federal control relied on sanctions and incentives to
produce higher test scores. We now know that the testing regime about
which Bush boasted failed to produce a miracle in Texas and that NCLB
failed to produce a miracle in the nation. We also know that Race to
the Top copied NCLB, with similar lackluster results. Yet the farce was
prolonged when Congress replaced NCLB with the Every Student Succeeds Act, which retained many of the failed assumptions and policies
of its predecessors.

Social scientists have studied the issue of motivation for decades.
Modern cognitive psychology no longer relies on threats and rewards to
produce long-term benefits. Leading figures in the field of cognitive psychology have found that for cognitive tasks, threats and rewards actually
suppress outcomes because they undermine intrinsic motivation.

Edward Deci, professor of psychology at the University of Rochester, has studied motivation for many decades. He and his colleague
Richard Ryan developed what they called "Self-Determination Theory,"
which refuted the dominant belief that people perform best when given
rewards. In their books, Deci and Ryan describe experiments they devised
to demonstrate that people who receive tangible rewards for tasks are *less*
motivated than those who do the same work because they want to do it.

In his book *Why We Do What We Do: Understanding Self-Motivation*,
Deci explains that people work at their best when they do so with a sense

of autonomy and authenticity, not when they work in a spirit of compliance. Rewards may produce desired behaviors, he writes, but when the rewards end, the desired behaviors also end. He gives the example of seals in the Central Park Zoo, who entertain the crowds as long as the trainers throw them fish. Stop throwing fish, and the seals stop entertaining.

Children, he says, are naturally inquisitive. They "explore, manipulate, and question; they pick things up, shake them, taste them, throw them, and ask 'What's this?' Every bit as interested in a cardboard box as in a gleaming new plastic marvel, they try things, bend things, and transform one thing into another. They seek the novel and they are eager to learn." Children are born learning and wanting to learn. They are intrinsically motivated to learn. Deci wondered, why do so many children lose that motivation as they grow older? At the start of his career as a psychologist, Deci was indoctrinated into behaviorism, the dominant theory of the time, but then he had the "blasphemous" thought that "maybe all the rewards, rules, and regimentation that were so widely used to motivate schoolchildren were themselves the villains, promoting not an excited state of learning, but a sad state of apathy."

Throughout his career, he explored this question: "What happens to people's intrinsic motivation for an activity when they receive an extrinsic reward for doing the activity that they had previously been quite willing to do without the reward?"

He created an experiment using a Soma cube, produced by the toy manufacturer Parker Brothers and described as "The World's Finest Cube Puzzle Game." The puzzle had seven pieces of different shapes. The pieces could be fitted together to create thousands of different cubes. One is called "Sam's Sitting Dog," another is "The Couch," and a third is "The Airplane." He wrote, "Some of the shapes were easy, others were very difficult. The fun came in using the various pieces to reproduce the designs, and when that happened the feeling of accomplishment was quite palpable. Once someone gets started with the puzzles, it is tough to stop." Deci himself became entranced by the game and imagined different possibilities in his head.

Deci assembled two groups of students in an experimental laboratory. One group was invited to solve a series of tasks using the Soma cube. They were offered no compensation. The other group was offered a monetary reward for solving the same puzzles. The subjects were given a half hour or so to solve the puzzles; then the experimenter told them that the time was up, and he had to leave the room to enter their data into a computer. The experimenter left the room for eight minutes exactly. Some popular magazines were lying on a table in the room with the students. Deci was interested in this question: Would the experimental subjects continue solving the puzzles, or would they read the magazines, or daydream? "As it turned out, those students who had been rewarded monetarily for doing the puzzles were far less likely to play with them 'just for fun' in the free-choice period. Stop the pay, and stop the play." Introducing rewards made the subjects dependent on the rewards for motivation.

Deci repeated the experiment in other settings and each time he got the same result: "Monetary rewards undermined people's intrinsic motivations." The rewards brought temporary success, but the students' motivation lasted only as long as the rewards were offered for the task.

Deci tells a story that he heard from a colleague:

> It seems that bigots were eager to rid their town of a Jewish man who had opened a tailor shop on Main Street, so they sent a group of rowdies to harass the tailor. Each day, the ruffians would show up to jeer. The situation was grim, but the tailor was ingenious. One day when the hoodlums arrived, he gave each of them a dime for their efforts. Delighted, they shouted their insults and moved on. The next day they returned to shout, expecting their dime. But the tailor said he could afford only a nickel and proceeded to hand a nickel to each of them. Well, they were a bit disappointed, but a nickel is after all a nickel, so they took it, did their jeering, and left. The next day, they returned once again, and the tailor said he had only a penny for them and held out his hand. Indignant, the young toughs sneered and proclaimed that they would certainly not spend their time jeering at him for a measly penny. So they didn't. And all was well for the tailor.

Based on many experiments, Deci concluded that "intrinsic motivation is associated with richer experience, better conceptual understanding, greater creativity, and improved problem solving, relative to external controls. Not only do controls undermine intrinsic motivation and engagement with activities but—and here is a bit of bad news for people focused on the bottom line—they have clearly detrimental effects on performance of any tasks that require creativity, conceptual understanding, or flexible problem solving."

Echoing the certainties that are a century old, the Disrupters of our day are sure that people do their best when offered extrinsic rewards. After all, don't businesses incentivize their workers and executives with bonuses? But the evidence has not supported their claims. When Michael Bloomberg was mayor of New York City, he repeatedly tried merit pay plans. None of them made a difference. The biggest controlled experiment with merit pay happened in Nashville, where economists at the National Center on Performance Incentives at Vanderbilt University tried a three-year plan, offering a $15,000 bonus to fifth grade math teachers whose students increased their test scores.

The conclusion: with minor variations, teachers eligible for bonuses did not get different results from those teachers not eligible for bonuses. Soon after the release of the negative results of the Vanderbilt study, the Obama administration announced that it intended to spend $1 billion on a national merit pay program.

Merit pay is a zombie idea. It never works, and it never dies.

Dan Ariely, a behavioral economist at Duke University, conducted studies that demonstrated the difference between doing a task willingly and doing it for pay. Like Deci, he found that those driven by intrinsic motivation consistently outperform those promised rewards. Ariely made a distinction between social norms (doing a task willingly) and market norms (doing a task for pay).

He observed that people will work harder for a cause than they will for cash. He wrote, "A few years ago, for instance, the AARP asked some lawyers if they would offer less expensive services to needy retirees, at something like $30 an hour. The lawyers said no. Then the program manager from AARP had a brilliant idea: he asked the lawyers if they would offer free services to needy retirees. Overwhelmingly, the lawyers said yes." Market norms made them refuse the offer of pay that was far below their usual hourly rate. But social norms made them willing volunteers. Ariely noted that market norms are powerful. Once they are applied, the social norms disappear, seldom to return.

Ariely noted that people in service professions are typically not driven by market norms. Police officers, firefighters, and soldiers do not risk their lives for money. They are usually motivated by a desire to help or to serve or to protect the public. The same may be said of teachers. Teachers do not go into the teaching profession expecting to get rich. They are drawn by a desire to make a difference in the lives of students. If asked, that is the answer that the great majority of teachers give. They became teachers to educate and to serve and to protect their charges.

Ariely worried that standardized testing and performance-based salaries were likely "to push education from social norms to market norms." He observed that:

> Cash will take you only so far—social norms are the forces that can make a difference in the long run. Instead of focusing the attention of the teachers, parents, and kids on test scores, salaries, and competition, it might be better to instill in all of us a sense of purpose, mission, and pride in education. To do this, we certainly can't take the path of market reforms. The Beatles proclaimed some time ago, "Can't Buy Me Love," and this also applies to the love of learning— you can't buy it, and if you try, you might chase it away.

Ariely and Deci were invited to serve on a prestigious panel of seventeen social scientists assembled by the National Academy of Sciences to study the value of test-based initiatives and accountability. Called the Committee on Incentives and Test-Based Accountability, it spent a decade studying No Child Left Behind, incentive pay systems in several cities and states, high school exit exams, teacher incentive pay in other nations, and pay-for-scores programs in New York City and in Coshocton, Ohio.

The committee's report, started in 2002, was released in 2011, and it found that these programs had little to no positive effects overall on learning and provided inadequate protection against gaming the system. Its major conclusion was that "test-based incentive programs . . . have not increased student achievement enough to bring the United States close to the levels of the highest achieving countries. When evaluated using relevant low-stakes tests, which are less likely to be inflated by the incentives themselves, the overall effects on achievement tend to be small and are effectively zero for a number of programs." The panel was sharply critical of the common practice of using tests tied to incentives as the "marker of progress."

The committee pointed out that performance measures become distorted when they are used as incentives. They cited the famous axiom known as Campbell's Law, for Donald Campbell, the eminent social scientist who wrote in 1975: "The more any quantitative social indicator is used for social decision making, the more subject it will be to corruption pressures and the more apt it will be to distort and corrupt the social processes it is intended to monitor."

With specific reference to education tests, Campbell wrote: "Achievement tests may well be valuable indicators of general school achievement under conditions of normal teaching aimed at general competence. But when test scores become the goal of the teaching process, they both lose their value as indicators of educational status and distort the educational process in undesirable ways."

Campbell's Law predicts that the overemphasis on tests leads to gaming the system, score inflation, narrowing of the curriculum only to what is tested, cheating, and other efforts to reach the goal and satisfy the measure without actually improving student performance. The committee noted, "When goals are set so high that people do not believe they can achieve them, the goals are demotivating and set the stage for feelings of helplessness, reduced effort, withdrawal and lower self-esteem." This explains how No Child Left Behind's unreachable goal of 100 percent proficiency caused many teachers to lose heart and abandon their careers.

When the committee's report was released in 2011, Ariely spoke about its findings. "It raises a red flag for education," Ariely said. "These policies are treating humans like rats in a maze. We keep thinking about how to reorganize the cheese to get the rats to do what we want. People do so much more than that."

Ariely went on to point out that this reductive thinking is responsible for spreading the notion that teachers are in the profession for the money. "That's one of the worst ideas out there," he said. "In the process of creating No Child Left Behind, as people thought about these strategies and rewards, they actually undermined teachers' motivations. They got teachers to care less, rather than more," he added, because "they took away a sense of personal achievement and autonomy."

When the committee published its long-awaited report in 2011, Congress ignored its findings. This was surprising because it was produced by the nation's most prestigious research institution and written by a panel described as "a veritable who's who of national experts in education law, economics and social sciences." Its findings undercut the assumptions behind NCLB, but Congress was not interested in rethinking NCLB. It remained infatuated with the testing, punishments, and rewards attached to NCLB and Race to the Top. When Congress did finally get around to reauthorizing NCLB in 2015, it kept intact nearly all the flaws that the committee report had criticized as ineffective and counterproductive. It continued the stale and failed tradition of treating students and teachers like "rats in a maze."

Surprisingly, the best advice about running a better organization, that is, one that respects the individuality and autonomy of people who work in organizations, can be found in the writings of business guru W. Edwards Deming. Deming is often credited for the revival of the modern Japanese economy. Some American corporations have taken his advice to heart as well. One of his biographers, Andrea Gabor, called Deming "the man who discovered quality" and wrote a book, *After the Education Wars,* to propose a Deming-style approach to reform, instead of the failed policies of Disruption.

Deming, she writes, opposed the corporate evaluation systems that produced a few winners and many losers. These rankings were at odds with efforts to build teamwork, she wrote, "which smart companies recognize as a key to long-term success." Rating people on a bell curve, in relation to one another, guarantees that some few will be winners and most will be losers, even though the "incremental differences" from best to worst are insignificant. Deming said, "A merit rating is alluring. The sound of the words captivates the imagination: pay for what you get; get what you pay for; motivate people to do their best, for their own good. The effect is exactly the opposite of what the words promise. Everyone propels himself forward, or tries to, for his own good, on his own life preserver. The organization is the loser. The merit rating rewards people [who] conform to the system. It does not reward attempts to improve the system."

Based on Deming's ideas, Gabor writes, "if management is doing its job in terms of hiring, developing employees, and keeping the system stable, most employees will perform well. . . . Deming believed that ranking employees is a cop-out for inadequate leadership." Deming excoriated top executives who insisted on grading employees. He wrote, "The merit rating nourishes short-term performance, annihilates long-term planning, builds fear, demolishes teamwork, [and] nourishes rivalry and politics." Gabor summarized Deming's view "that most people want, and deserve, to take joy in their work. It is management's moral obligation to create a system that enables them to do so. . . . Given a chance by management and the system, most people will seek fulfillment in their work by doing the best they can."

No Child Left Behind and Race to the Top borrowed the wrong lessons from corporate America. They relied on carrots and sticks to motivate teachers. They set goals that were unattainable. They disrespected the people who did the daily work of education. They discounted the importance of teamwork. They forced teachers to compete with one another for ratings. They treated children as interchangeable widgets whose sole purpose was to generate high scores on standardized tests that were designed to produce winners and losers. Neither the NCLB law nor Race to the Top valued education as an end in itself, worthy of pursuing for the joy it imparts. They valued data, not education.

If No Child Left Behind and Race to the Top had been business plans, the businesses would have quickly gone bankrupt because of their shabby treatment of their workers (teachers and principals). They failed because these were political attempts to remake education without any sense of what education is or should be. Politics and a failure of imagination kept these two bankrupt interventions on life support long after their failure was evident to everyone except the political establishment in Washington, D.C.

CHAPTER 8

Bait and Switch

How Liberals Were Duped into Embracing School Choice

I n early 1988, I attended a conference about testing at the leafy campus of the Educational Testing Service in Princeton, New Jersey. I don't remember the formal presentations, but I vividly recall a private conversation with Albert Shanker, president of the American Federation of Teachers. I had known Al since 1975, when my first book, *The Great School Wars: A History of the New York City Public Schools*, was published. Back then, I received a phone call from him while I was at my desk at Teachers College at Columbia University. He said, gruffly, "I just read your new book. I like it. I am going to write about it in my column in *The New York Times*. Do you want me to praise it or slam it?" You can guess what I said. Subsequently, we became friends and enjoyed dinners a few times a year with our spouses.

On that day in Princeton, he shared an idea that intrigued him. He had recently returned from Germany, where he visited the Holweide School in Cologne. The school was organized so that students stayed with the same team of teachers for three or four years, getting to know them well and building strong relationships. He wanted to encourage the same spirit of innovation in American public schools, and he sketched out his idea on a napkin.

Suppose, he said, that a group of teachers within a large school sought the permission of their colleagues to form a school-within-a-school. Suppose they got the endorsement of the local school board for this semiautonomous school, which would be free of most regulations, except those affecting health, safety, and civil rights. Suppose they were allowed to try experimental methods, pedagogy, and curricula, with the goal of reaching the kids who were unmotivated, the ones who were bored, the ones who slept through class, the ones who had dropped out of school. Suppose that this commitment to trying out new approaches was encouraged in districts across the country. The new schools would be akin to research-and-development laboratories within schools, with permission to operate for, say, five or ten years to see what they could accomplish. When their trial period ended, the teachers would be reabsorbed into the school, along with their students and their best ideas. Some of them might try the Holweide model; some might dream up other models that no one else had imagined. But whatever their plan, the teachers would have to win the consent of their colleagues and the school board to try out their ideas to motivate the kids who were turned off by traditional schools. Whatever they learned, through trial and error, would be shared with their school and other schools.

I thought it was an exciting idea, and I was interested to see what he did with it.

A few months later, he introduced his proposal at a press conference at the National Press Club in Washington, D.C. He said that a group of six or more teachers could set up a school within their own school to try out different ways "of reaching the kids that are now not being reached by what the school is doing." Their proposals would be reviewed by panels run jointly by districts and the local teachers' union affiliates. If approved, the new schools would be schools of choice for both students and teachers. Before the new schools were allowed to open within a school, they would have to get the consent of the teachers already there, so they would not be operating in hostile environments. Shanker said he did not want to be "shoving things down people's throats, but enlisting them in a movement and a cause."

At his union's national convention in July 1988, Shanker shared his idea for teacher-led autonomous schools-within-schools with the AFT

delegates. He hoped that these research programs would solve important problems of pedagogy. He did not want anyone "to go off and do
his own thing." He originally called the new schools "opt-for schools"
but changed the name to "charter schools" after reading an essay by
Ray Budde, a professor at the University of Massachusetts who suggested "charter schools" as a way for teams of teachers to create their own
schools, thus restructuring school districts by "flattening" the management. Shanker promoted the idea of charter schools in his weekly *New
York Times* paid column and in meetings with union locals.

But at the very beginning of the charter school movement, Shanker's
idea was sabotaged. Paul Peterson, professor of government at Harvard
University and a zealous supporter of charter schools and vouchers, later
explained that Budde and Shanker's idea was transformed by school
choice advocates in Minnesota who wanted charter schools to break free
of all constraints:

> Charters only took off because others radicalized the charter concept
> Budde had devised. Reading Shanker's column, Joe Nathan and Ted
> Kolderie, at work on educational reform in Minnesota, saw potential
> in the charter idea. Delighted that the powerful Al Shanker had given
> it his blessing, they invited him to the Twin Cities to help peddle it
> to Governor Rudy Perpich and the state's legislature.

While writing Minnesota's charter law, "Nathan and Kolderie fundamentally altered the charter concept." Budde and Shanker wanted
charter schools that were authorized by the district, run by teachers,
and subject to collective bargaining. But Nathan and Kolderie wanted
schools that were authorized by state agencies and not subject to local
district control. As Peterson put it, "That opened charter doors not only
to teachers but also to outside entrepreneurs. Competition between charters and districts was to be encouraged. All of a sudden, charter schools
were free of the constraints imposed by collective bargaining contracts
districts negotiated with unions."

Minnesota passed the first charter law in the nation in 1991, and the
first charter school opened in 1992. The Minnesota law set the national
pattern, putting charters into competition with public schools instead

of making them the collaborative R&D labs that Shanker envisioned. In 1994, Shanker realized that his idea had been hijacked. As he watched the charter movement evolve into the charter industry, as he saw new charters launched by entrepreneurs and corporations, he turned into a vociferous critic of his own proposal. He realized that charters would not be research programs run by teams of teachers, they would not be unionized, and they would not be designed to collaborate with public schools. The new charter model, he understood to his horror, would compete with public schools for funds and students. Instead of helping public schools, they would become a mechanism for privatizing public schools. He was outraged to learn that the first charter school in Michigan would be the "Noah Webster Academy," whose target enrollment was Christian homeschoolers. He worried that the "real aim" of some charter supporters was not to innovate, but "to smash the public schools." In future columns, he warned about the "risky business" of letting charter schools operate as "free market" schools without any connection to local districts.

As the charter idea was beginning to catch on, John Chubb and Terry Moe published their influential book *Politics, Markets, and America's Schools* (1990), which asserted that the solution to the nation's educational problems was school choice. The biggest obstacle to improvement, they argued, was democratic politics. Vested interests—school boards, teachers' unions, superintendents, and professional educators—blocked "reform," they argued. Democratic institutions needed to be pushed aside. Just let parents choose, and all would be well. They proposed universal vouchers, with minimal regulation. Their paradigm worked as well for charter schools as for vouchers. They boldly claimed that "reformers would do well to entertain the notion that choice *is* a panacea."

Disrupters took the advice of Chubb and Moe to heart, putting their faith in mayoral control, state takeovers, governor-appointed commissions, and other mechanisms to eliminate democratic participation in school governance. The self-styled "reformers" agreed that the enemy of "reform" was democracy!

At its inception, the charter movement had bipartisan support. In 1994, Jeanne Allen, the chief education analyst at the ultraconservative Heritage Foundation, created the Center for Education Reform (CER) to lead the battle for charter schools. Allen supported school choice, both vouchers and charters, but the latter were an easier sell. Her center kept count of the growing number of charters and urged states to give charters the same funding as public schools. The Center judged state charter laws by the degree to which they kept hands off their charter schools, with the least regulation, oversight, and accountability considered best.

The Clinton administration embraced the charter school idea as a "Third Way" policy that was neither left nor right. In 1994, as part of the Clinton education program, Congress passed legislation to create the federal Charter Schools Program, which would award federal dollars for new charter schools. By 2000, when Clinton left office, there were about 500,000 students in charter schools. The George W. Bush administration enthusiastically endorsed charter schools, which was in keeping with the Republican preference for school choice. By the time Bush left office in 2009, the CER reported some 4,600 charter schools with 1.4 million students in forty states and the District of Columbia. The Obama administration energetically promoted charter schools and added more federal funding to open new ones. By 2018, a Republican-controlled Congress awarded $440 million each year to expand the charter sector, adding to the hundreds of millions that foundations and wealthy individuals annually gave to charter schools. Under Secretary of Education Betsy DeVos, most of the federal money for charter schools went not to small start-ups, but to established corporate chains like KIPP and a Texas-based chain called IDEA.

By 2018, there were about 7,000 charter schools with 3 million or so students, about 6 percent of the 50.7 million students in K–12 schools. The states that had no charter law then were Montana, North Dakota, South Dakota, Vermont, West Virginia, and Nebraska (in 2019, the Republican legislature in West Virginia passed a law authorizing charters). These are largely rural states where the public and the legislature see little need to turn their community public schools over to entrepreneurs and corporations, although right-wing groups in these states continually promote the passage of school choice laws.

Disrupters prefer state laws that permit multiple authorizers of charter schools, not just local districts. The more authorizers, the more charter schools. Since the authorizers usually get a commission (a set percentage of the state tuition) for every student who enrolls in the charters they authorize, they have a financial incentive to keep the numbers growing and no incentive to close low-performing charters. Local school districts are slow to authorize charters, because they have no incentive to encourage competition for state funding. In Wyoming, only districts can authorize charters, and there are only four in the state. In Virginia, only districts can authorize charters, and there are only nine in the state. Kansas charter law allows only charters approved by districts, and there are ten in the state.

The states with the largest numbers of charter school students and the loosest regulations are Arizona, Florida, Indiana, California, Ohio, Texas, Michigan, and the District of Columbia. California has some 1,300 charter schools, more than any other state.

Democrats never figured out that they had been taken to the cleaners by Republicans and their right-wing billionaire patrons like the DeVos family, the Walton family, and the Koch brothers. Many Republican-dominated states adopted the model charter legislation written by ALEC, the American Legislative Exchange Council, called the "Next Generation Charter Schools Act."

How in the world did Democrats find themselves advocating for the same education policies as billionaires, evangelicals, Republican governors, corporations, ALEC, and fringe groups on the far right? Some became charter supporters because billionaires and financiers gave them handsome campaign contributions. Others were taken in by the oft-repeated claim that charter schools would "save poor kids from failing public schools." They ignored the fact that most of the charter hype was coming from conservatives who had always supported school choice but were not known for their commitment to helping poor children of color.

Most Democrats drew the line at vouchers, but they hoped that charters would generate innovation, cost savings, and higher test scores for poor children.

None of those promises came to pass. The biggest innovation in the charter sector was the invention of "no-excuses" schools, which resurrected early-twentieth-century behaviorist models and strict discipline. Black and brown children, said charter advocates, needed "boot-camp" discipline, sternly administered, to learn the values of the white middle class to prepare them to join it. If they were unwilling to comply with the strict rules about behavior and dress, they would be suspended repeatedly until they left or were expelled.

When the charter industry was first launched, its boosters promised that charter schools would produce better results with less money. But in time, charters demanded the same amount of public money as public schools, and studies show that they typically spend more on administration than public schools do.

Charters have been funded not only by right-wing billionaires like the Walton family, but also by hedge fund multimillionaires and billionaires. Eva Moskowitz's Success Academy charter chain in New York City is munificently funded; her students get very high test scores. The chain has often received multimillion-dollar gifts from hedge fund tycoons, which enabled it to rent Radio City Music Hall in Manhattan for a test-prep rally ("Slam the Exam") in 2017 and the massive Barclays arena in Brooklyn in 2018 (at a cost of $60,000). With the help of its ally, the billionaire-funded group called Families for Excellent Schools, the chain spent more than $700,000 to bus students, staff, and parents to a political rally in Albany in 2015 to demand more funding for charters (a tactic that would be illegal if done by public schools) and spent more than $68 million to buy classroom space in a luxury building in Manhattan. Whoever says that money doesn't matter is not familiar with the fabulous funding of Success Academy charters. The "secret sauce" in its success appears to be a combination of intense test preparation and high levels of attrition. The chain manages to exclude students it does not want (those with severe disabilities and behavior problems) and to push out students who don't conform to its regimen; it does not accept new students after fourth grade. Of the seventy-two students who started first grade in the chain's first year, only sixteen graduated in 2018 at a posh ceremony in Lincoln Center's Alice Tully Hall.

In Ohio, the state spends $1 billion each year on charter schools, which collectively have a dismal academic record. In 2017, Ohio's charters had a graduation rate of 45 percent, half the rate in the state's traditional public schools and 28 percentage points behind the state's urban districts. Two thirds of Ohio's charter schools were given grades of D or F by the state in 2018. In Nevada, charter schools dominate the list of the state's worst-performing schools. Andre Agassi's richly funded charter school, which was supposed to prepare students for the nation's best colleges, was one of the state's lowest-performing schools and was handed over to a New York charter chain, Democracy Prep. How bad were the charters in Nevada? In 2015, after completing a national survey of charter schools, Margaret Raymond, director of Stanford University's CREDO (the Center for Research on Education Outcomes), told a national conference of education journalists that Ohioans should "be very glad that you have Nevada, so you are not the worst."

Charter schools on average get about the same results when they enroll the same demographic groups of students. Those charter schools that report outstanding test scores typically have high rates of attrition and do not enroll the most difficult to educate students, such as English language learners and students with disabilities. Charters have the freedom to write their own rules about suspensions and discipline, and some have used this freedom to push out the students they don't want, those who are discipline problems and those who can't meet the school's academic demands, who then return to public schools.

The Center for Education Reform, the nation's premier cheerleader for charter schools, issued a study of charter school closures to demonstrate that charters are held accountable. The report said that more than 15 percent of charter schools that had opened since 1992 had closed. But a task force of the National Education Association reviewed federal data and found that 40 percent of all the charter schools opened since 1992 had closed. As private entities, charter schools are as likely to close as are any other businesses, such as shoe stores, bookstores, and restaurants.

In Washington State, charters have confronted determined opposition from public school parents and civil rights groups. Public referendums aimed at authorizing charter schools failed in 1996, 2000, and 2004. After three consecutive losses, Bill Gates and his fellow billionaires decided that 2012 was finally the time to get charter schools approved. Unable to persuade the legislature to pass charter legislation, Gates launched another referendum, called Measure No. 1240. Nothing was left to chance. He and his allies outspent the opponents of charter schools by a margin of sixteen to one. Just ten donors contributed 90 percent of the money for the "YES on 1240" campaign. Some of the largest contributors were Bill and Melinda Gates ($3.3 million); Paul Allen, former CEO of Microsoft ($1.6 million); financier Nick Hanauer ($1 million); Eli Broad of California ($200,000); the parents of Jeff Bezos ($1.1 million); Doris Fisher of California ($100,000); Reed Hastings ($100,000); Connie Ballmer, wife of former Microsoft CEO Steve Ballmer ($500,000); Alice Walton of Texas ($1.7 million); and a New York–based group called Education Reform Now Advocacy, which contributed Dark Money funds from anonymous sources. On the other side, supporting public schools, were the League of Women Voters, the NAACP, the Washington Education Association, the Washington State PTA, elected school boards, the Washington Association of School Administrators, and local Democratic Party groups. Bill Gates and his friends spent about $12 million. Supporters of public schools spent $727,400. Money won. The billionaires' referendum passed by 50.7 percent to 49.3 percent.

But the story did not end there.

Once the referendum passed, the Gates Foundation handed out $31 million in three years to charter organizations to "give public charter schools in Washington State a strong start." As journalist Joanne Barkan recounted, Bill Gates used his resources to shape the new charter sector to his liking:

> The Gates Foundation spent more than $13.5 million to set up and run the Washington State Charter Schools Association—a private group whose work includes awarding "fellowships" to educators who want to open schools. Green Dot Public Schools, a charter management organization founded in Los Angeles, received $8 million in 2013 to expand into Washington. Green Dot has received about $24 million from Gates since 2006. Another charter management organization, the Bay Area's Summit Public Schools, also received $8 million in 2013 to branch into Washington. Charter Board Partners, a D.C.-based nonprofit consultancy for charter school governance, received more than $1.2 million to open a Washington office. The Gates Foundation gave California's Seneca Family of Agencies almost $1 million to develop support for at-risk students in Washington's charter schools.

The battle in Washington State over charter schools occurred at the same time that the state was embroiled in an extended legal struggle over the state's obligation to fund its public schools. In 2012, as the charter referendum commanded public attention, the Washington State Supreme Court ruled that the legislature had violated the state constitution by underfunding K–12 education (a ruling known as the McCleary decision). Two years later, in response to the legislature's failure to act, the Supreme Court ordered the legislature to pay a fine of $100,000 a day for contempt of court.

Education funding is a perennial issue in Washington State because the state has no personal or corporate income taxes. The state relies primarily on local taxes and sales taxes for its revenues. Activist parents and civil rights groups recognized that the introduction of charter schools would divert funding from the state's underfunded public schools.

The first charter school in Washington opened in 2014, and more were expected to open in the following years. But on September 4, 2015, the State Supreme Court ruled in a 6–3 decision that the law authorizing charter schools was unconstitutional because privately managed charter schools are not public schools. The lawsuit was brought by the League of Women Voters, the Washington Education Association, El Centro de la Raza, and others. In a decision written by Chief Justice Barbara Madsen, the court held that charter schools are not "public schools" as defined in the state constitution because they are not governed by elected school boards. As such, they do not meet the state's definition of "common schools" and cannot receive public funds.

What was a poor billionaire to do when his pet project was declared "unconstitutional" by the state's highest court? Gates briefly funded the new charter schools while he and his allies sought a new source of public revenue. The legislature agreed to fund charter schools from the state lottery. The Democratic governor, Jay Inslee, allowed the bill to pass without his signature or veto.

In an especially vindictive move, Stand for Children (a Gates Foundation grantee) created a political action committee to try to defeat Judge Madsen and other judges who had signed the charter school decision when they stood for reelection in 2016. Friends of the charter industry contributed about $650,000 to unseat Judge Madsen in what was usually a nonpartisan election, and about $900,000 to defeat her colleague Judge Charles Wiggins. Despite their limited resources, Judge Madsen, Judge Mary Yu, and Judge Charles Wiggin won reelection easily.

In 2018, the Washington Supreme Court ruled unanimously that the state had fully implemented a new school-funding plan, thus bringing the McCleary case to a close. Later that year, it ruled that the legislature could assign lottery money to support the charter schools so eagerly sought by Bill Gates and his allies. This created a revenue stream for the 3,500 students already in charter schools, a tiny percentage of the more than 1.1 million students enrolled in the state's public schools.

The first evaluation of Washington State's charter schools was published in 2019 by the Center for Research on Education Outcomes (CREDO). The bottom line was that "the typical charter student in Washington demonstrates no statistically different academic growth in reading and math when compared to their exact-match counterpart in nearby district schools."

Even more embarrassing for Bill Gates and his allies was the lack of demand for the new charter schools. In 2019, *The Seattle Times* reported that three of the state's charter schools were closing, due to "dwindling enrollment" and financial difficulties. Two charters affiliated with the California-based Green Dot charter chain were unable to meet their enrollment goals of 600 students; fewer than 200 students enrolled in each of them. The state's charter school association bravely insisted that all was well and new charters were on the way. But the charter sector was down to 3,300 students, or about three-tenths of 1 percent of the students in the state, hardly worth the time, energy, and millions poured into creating it.

Why were the billionaires so eager to open charter schools whose results were no different from those of public schools and for which there was very little demand? Why not put their millions into fighting for better funding for public schools, where the vast majority of students are?

In 2017, Carol Burris, executive director of the Network for Public Education, conducted a yearlong investigation of charter schools, beginning with those in California, which has the largest number of charter schools and students in the nation. Democratic governor Jerry Brown was a strong supporter of charter schools, having started two of them himself when he was mayor of Oakland. Brown opposed charter school regulation and vetoed efforts by the legislature to hold charters accountable. The state has 6.3 million students, of whom 10 percent (or 630,000) are in some 1,300 charter schools. Anyone can apply to open a charter school, without any previous experience as an educator. If would-be charter school operators are turned down by the local school board, they can apply to the county school board. If the county school board rejects them, they can appeal to the state school board, where they are likely to win approval without any consideration of the fiscal impact on the district where the charter chooses to open for business. Efforts to regulate the charter industry have been stymied in the legislature by the powerful California Charter Schools Association (CCSA), whose annual income exceeds $20 million, donated by some of the wealthiest people in the nation, including billionaires Reed Hastings and Eli Broad. The CCSA operates a PAC and a Super PAC that fund charter-friendly candidates in state and local elections.

Reed Hastings, founder of Netflix, is opposed to elected school boards; he is a major donor to the California Charter Schools Association and to other organizations that promote school privatization.

Carol Burris found charter schools operating in storefronts in strip malls, where young students meet their teacher "on demand," and online or partially online schools where students meet a teacher only once every twenty days. Twenty percent of the state's charters, she reported, are "independent learning centers," where students rarely, if ever, interact with a teacher or fellow students. In some of these "independent learning centers," the graduation rate is 0 percent. She identified one chain of "independent learning centers" that listed eight not-for-profit corporations at a single address; this chain enrolled eleven thousand students and collectively received more than $61.4 million in 2013–14. The chain's average graduation rate for 2015 was 13.7 percent. One man served as CEO of six different corporations, which also employed his wife and his son-in-law.

California allows tiny districts to open charters that are not located within its boundaries and to launch charters in districts where they are not wanted. One district with three hundred students collected $1.5 million in oversight fees for authorizing distant charters enrolling three thousand students in dozens of "learning centers." In 2017, Steve Van Zandt, the superintendent of the small Mountain Empire Unified School District, was charged with felony conflict of interest "after it was discovered that he was personally receiving 5 percent of the revenue generated from oversight fees from the thirteen charter schools his district authorized beyond its boundaries." Van Zandt, known as the "charter school king," pleaded guilty and was sentenced to thirty days of home confinement, three years of probation, and forfeiture of his pension after 2012.

After Governor Brown was succeeded by Gavin Newsom, the legislature revised the state charter law, which had remained unchanged for twenty-seven years. When the charter law was written in 1992, legislators expected that the public would fund a small number of charters created by teachers and parents; what emerged instead over nearly three decades was an unaccountable and aggressive sector of more than 1,300 schools and 630,000 students, backed by the political power of a billionaire-funded lobbying organization. In 2019, Governor Newsom forged a settlement between the charter lobby and supporters of public schools. The legislature passed a reform bill that curbed the reckless expansion of the charter industry and restored a measure of local district control, allowing districts to reject charters if they threatened the district's fiscal stability and restricting charters' ability to locate wherever they wanted.

The five biggest charter chains in the nation, Burris wrote, are KIPP, the Gulen schools, IDEA, Aspire, and Uncommon Schools. This corporate takeover, via large charter chains, of what once were local public schools is in itself remarkable and, frankly, abhorrent. It represents the "Walmartization" of American education. Institutions serving the common good are replaced by private ones, operating outside the purview of many state laws and controlled by distant entities. The replacement of local institutions by corporate-controlled ones is a loss for civil society.

The most controversial of the charter chains are the Gulen charter schools, consisting of nearly two hundred schools located in twenty-six states and the District of Columbia. Gulen schools are associated with the Imam Fethullah Gülen, a Turkish exile who lives in seclusion in the Pocono Mountains of Pennsylvania. Gulen schools usually deny that they are Gulen schools, but they share similar characteristics, which include "founding boards and school leadership composed of nearly all Turkish men; curriculum that includes the Turkish language and Turkish cultural instruction; extensive use of the H-1B visa program to employ Turkish and Turkic nationals, and an emphasis on teaching math and science." The Gulen schools operate under a variety of names (for example, Harmony, Magnolia, Horizon, and Sonoran). Until Imam Gülen was banned from Turkey by its autocratic leader, President Recep Erdogan, the Gulenists curried favor with politicians by offering them free trips to Turkey and campaign contributions. Liz Essley Whyte of The Center for Public Integrity published an investigative report in *USA Today*, in which she said that "152 state legislators from 29 states . . . toured Turkey between 2006 and 2015 thanks to more than two dozen nonprofits associated with the Gulen movement." Those who accepted these Gulen-sponsored trips to Turkey included Illinois's powerful speaker of the house, Democrat Mike Madigan, who traveled four times to Turkey, as well as several legislators from Idaho and Texas who were on education committees. The Gulen-sponsored junkets to Turkey came to an abrupt end in 2016, after Turkey's leader blamed Fethullah Gülen for an abortive coup. It is incomprehensible that American public schools, which are expected to teach and model democratic citizenship, would be outsourced to foreign nationals.

Despite the high rate of charter closures and recurrent scandals, the charter industry enjoyed the support of both parties in Congress, Republican governors, many Democratic governors, multiple billionaires, and most state governments. Until the arrival of the Trump administration and Secretary of Education Betsy DeVos, the charter industry appeared to be unstoppable.

CHAPTER 9

School Choice, Deregulation, and Corruption

Any organization that receives millions of dollars in public funds should be subject to public oversight and accountability. Lobbyists for the charter industry have fought against oversight and accountability, claiming that any regulation would hinder innovation. The unregulated charter industry is riddled with self-dealing, conflicts of interest, and embezzlement. Some canny charter operators enrich themselves in ways that George Washington Plunkitt, a Tammany Hall politician in the nineteenth century, called "honest graft," by engaging in real estate deals and other transactions that allow them to pocket millions of dollars intended for students, teachers, and schools.

Starting in 2014, the Center for Media and Democracy, the Center for Popular Democracy, Integrity in Education, and the Alliance to Reclaim Our Schools—all public interest organizations—wrote well-documented exposés of the waste, fraud, and abuse in the charter industry, but their publications did not get much attention. The first report in 2014 warned that at least $100 million had been wasted by charters due to lack of oversight. The second report in 2015 determined that the losses due to waste, fraud, and mismanagement were at least $200 million and possibly in excess of $1 billion. Reports in 2015 and 2016 upped the cost of charter fraud. The Network for Public Education's 2019 report "Asleep at the

Wheel" calculated that the federal government had wasted about $1 billion on charter schools that never opened or closed soon after opening.

In its 2015 report, the Center for Media and Democracy charged that the systemic lack of transparency and accountability for public funds in the charter sector had created "an epidemic of fraud, waste, and mismanagement that would not be tolerated in public schools." To the extent that charter schools were "policed," it was done by charter proponents, not by independent public officials.

> Unlike truly public schools that have to account for prospective and past spending in public budgets provided to democratically elected school boards, charter spending of tax monies is too often a black hole.
>
> This is largely due to the way the charter industry has been built by proponents favoring "flexibility" over rules. That flexibility has allowed an epidemic of fraud, waste, and mismanagement that would not be tolerated in public schools. Charters are often policed—if they are really policed at all—by charter proponents, both within government agencies and within private entities tasked with oversight as "authorizers" of charters.

Fortunately, there are courageous individuals and groups who insist on holding privately managed charter schools accountable.

One of them is Curtis J. Cardine, a former superintendent of both public and charter schools, who created the Grand Canyon Institute to study charter school improprieties in Arizona. Three quarters of the state's charter schools, he found, engaged in "related-party transactions," in which the charter was doing business with its owners, their family members, or board members. "Gaming the system is often done through contractual transactions with subsidiary for-profit companies owned by the charter school holder and overseen by the same corporate board as the nonprofit charter school." He reported that 42 percent of the charters authorized in the state since 1994 had closed due to financial shenanigans.

Cardine demonstrated that state oversight in Arizona is a bad joke played on taxpayers. For example, the Arizona State Board for Charter

Schools renewed the charter of Discovery Creemos Academy in Good-year, Arizona, for a twenty-year period, despite its debt of $3.3 million and its D rating for academics (only 13 percent of its students passed the state English test and only 7 percent passed the math test). Cardine wrote, "Its members might not have been aware that the charter holder had increased administration charges by $1.4 million in 2016 and pur-chased $575,000 in goods and services from four for-profit companies he founded to conduct business with his school." Seven months after the charter was renewed, the school abruptly closed its doors, abandoning its students in midyear.

Cardine wrote that the finances of the schools were rigged in 77 per-cent of the charters that he studied. As a result of the debt load of these charters, he wrote, "the bulk of educational funding is going to manage-ment and debt rather than children."

In Arizona, charter schools are lightly regulated, if at all. Nepotism and conflicts of interest are not prohibited. For-profit charters are not audited.

Eddie Farnsworth opened a for-profit charter chain in 1996, before he was elected to the legislature in 2001. His four-campus Benjamin Frank-lin Charter Schools were profitable. Farnsworth owned LBE Investments, the company that owned the real estate where the schools were located and leased his property to his schools at rates well above the mortgage payments and taxes due. In 2018, Farnsworth sold his for-profit charter chain to a nonprofit corporation for a price between $11.9 million and $29.9 million. The amount was not disclosed because for-profit charter operators in Arizona are not required to reveal their finances or to hold open meetings. Farnsworth said he would retain $3.8 million in "share-holder equity" in the for-profit company and expected to get a contract to manage the schools since he recruited the members of the new board. The new structure enabled Farnsworth to avoid property taxes and to qualify for new federal funding. The deal ensured that Arizona taxpayers "will have paid for the same schools twice," making legislator Farnsworth a very wealthy man. Laurie Roberts, a columnist for *The Arizona Repub-lic,* wrote that Farnsworth was one among many charter operators who were using charter schools "as a personal ATM."

Another charter operator, Glenn Way, moved to Arizona in 2009 from Utah; at the time, he was deeply in debt to the IRS, "had sought bankruptcy protection, and had recently resigned from the Utah legislature after his wife filed a protective order against him," according to public records. Way made a new start in Arizona, founding the American Leadership Academy charter chain, which featured a patriotic theme—red, white, and blue student apparel—in a conservative area. In nine years, he grew a chain of a dozen campuses with more than eight thousand students. His development and finance companies bought the land, built most of the buildings, and then sold or leased them to his schools. An investigation by *The Arizona Republic* determined that Glenn Way's businesses made about $37 million on real estate deals, "funded largely by the Arizona tax dollars allocated to his charter schools." Way countered that his profit was "only" $18.4 million. He also received management fees of $6 million a year to operate the schools. Then there was the Primavera Online High School, whose CEO was paid nearly $9 million per year, even though its test scores were abysmal (fewer than a quarter of the students passed the state math test), and its dropout rates were sky-high (49 percent). But in addition to its high CEO salary, the company was shifting public funds away from instruction and into its investment portfolio in stocks, bonds, mortgage-backed securities, and real estate.

In response to the investigations reported by *The Arizona Republic*, the legislature promised to rewrite the charter law. However, charter industry lobbyists took control of the task of revising the law, and there was no chance that the malfeasance would end.

Voucher payouts in Arizona are even less regulated than the charter industry. The president of the state senate, Steve Yarbrough, is also executive director of the Arizona Christian School Tuition Organization (ACSTO), which received $72.9 million from the state for vouchers. ACSTO keeps 10 percent of that money and pays Senator Yarbrough a salary of $125,000 (in addition to his public salary). The group "outsources data entry, computer hardware, customer service, information processing" and other functions to a private, for-profit company called HY Processing. It paid HY Processing $636,000 in 2014, and millions over the past decade. The owners of HY Processing are Steve Yarbrough, his wife, and another couple. ACSTO pays $52,000 a year in rent to its landlord, Steve Yarbrough. When Yarbrough bought a car, ACSTO paid the bill.

The BASIS schools in Arizona regularly top the rankings of the "best high schools in America" compiled by *U.S. News & World Report* and *Newsweek*. Charter advocates frequently cite these rankings as "proof" that charter schools are superior to public schools. In 2017, five of the nation's ten "best high schools" were BASIS schools in Arizona, according to *U.S. News*. BASIS schools enroll anyone who completes an application and wins a random lottery, but the academic requirements are so demanding that only the strongest students apply and survive. There are eighteen BASIS charters in Arizona, three in Texas, and one in the District of Columbia; all are run by the same for-profit firm, owned by Michael and Olga Block, who are paid $10 million annually by taxpayers to manage the BASIS chain. In order to graduate, students at BASIS must take at least six Advanced Placement courses and pass at least one of them with a score of 3 or more out of 5. Students begin taking high school-level AP courses in middle school. The students enrolled in the eighteen BASIS charters in Arizona are very different from those in the state's public schools. The BASIS charters in Arizona are 32 percent Asian and 51 percent white in a state where these groups comprise only 42 percent of students. Only 10 percent of BASIS students are Hispanic in a state where the Hispanic student enrollment is 44 percent. In the 2015–16 school year, only 1.2 percent of students at the BASIS schools had a disability as compared to 11.3 percent in the public schools; BASIS had no English language learners, no free transportation, and no free lunch for needy students. It asks parents to make a $1,500 contribution to fund teacher bonuses. Most students who enroll in BASIS don't make it to graduation. At BASIS Tucson, 130 students were enrolled in seventh grade, but only 54 in that grade graduated in 2015–16. The nation's number one high school, BASIS in Scottsdale, doesn't look like Arizona, wrote Laurie Roberts of *The Arizona Republic*. White and Asian students comprised 87 percent of the school's enrollment.

The most celebrated "no-excuses" charter school chain in the nation was the American Indian Model Schools (AIMS) of Oakland, California. Founded in 1996 as a middle school dedicated to educating students of

American Indian heritage, AIMS later opened a K–8 school and a high school, with a total enrollment of seven hundred students. In 2000, the board of AIMS hired Ben Chavis as its executive director and soon boasted the highest test scores in the state. Governor Arnold Schwarzenegger visited and hailed its success. Journalist David Whitman published a book in 2008 praising "no-excuses" charters as exemplars of "the new paternalism." Whitman called AIMS "one of the great educational turnaround stories in recent history." In 2009, Whitman became Secretary of Education Arne Duncan's chief speechwriter.

George Will praised Chavis, and the *National Review* called him "undeniably one of the country's finest educators." When Chavis recruited new teachers on Craigslist, the advertisement said, "We are looking for hard-working people who believe in free-market capitalism. . . . Multicultural specialists, ultra liberal zealots and college-tainted oppression liberators need not apply." Chavis said that iron discipline and exclusion of unionized teachers were the keys to AIMS's success.

But there was more to the AIMS story. Chavis quietly changed the schools' demographics. He replaced almost all the American Indian students with Asian American students. He kept the students who were most compliant and most likely to earn high test scores. His charters got spectacular scores on state tests by careful selection of students and equally careful deselection of those unlikely to succeed, relentless test preparation, and tough discipline.

AIMS's reputation was severely damaged, however, when a state audit in 2012 disclosed that the charter chain paid $3.8 million to businesses owned by Chavis and his wife. Chavis resigned and was charged in 2017 by federal authorities with mail fraud and money laundering for using federal grants to lease facilities in buildings he owned. In 2019, federal authorities reduced the charges and sentenced him to a year's probation, crediting him for his good work as an educator.

In Georgia, a charter school founder named Christopher Clemons founded the Latin Academy charter school chain, ostensibly to serve disadvantaged youth and give them an elite education. A graduate of the University of Pennsylvania with an MBA from MIT, Clemons was a rising star in the charter movement. But he stole more than $1 million from his schools to support his taste for strip clubs and luxury cars. After he pleaded guilty, he was required to pay restitution of $810,000 and received a sentence of twenty years, divided into ten years in prison and ten years of probation.

In January 2017, federal agents raided the headquarters of the Celerity Charter Network in Los Angeles, which ran seven schools in the district and wanted more. The district turned down the charter chain's request for two more schools because of questions about its financial practices, but the state board overruled the district and allowed Celerity to open two more charters. In March 2017, the *Los Angeles Times* reported that Celerity's founder, Vielka McFarlane, used the schools' credit card to pay for her luxurious lifestyle. Her salary was $471,842, more than that of the superintendent of the Los Angeles public school system, the second largest in the nation. She wore designer suits, ate at fancy restaurants, used a limousine service, and patronized expensive hotels and hair salons—all on the charter schools' credit card. Meanwhile, her chain expanded into other states, hired her relatives, and grew new related organizations that received millions of dollars. After the exposé appeared, the state board reversed its approval of new charters for Celerity. In 2019, McFarlane was sentenced to thirty months in federal prison for misspending $3.2 million in public funds.

In 2017, after the most expensive local school board election in American history—nearly $15 million spent, most of it by a small number of billionaire charter supporters—voters in Los Angeles elected a pro-charter majority to their school board. However, shortly after the election, Ref Rodriguez, one of the pro-charter members of the board majority, was indicted and convicted of money laundering in his campaign for the board. He did not resign, however, until the board had selected Austin Beutner, a former financier and former publisher of the *Los Angeles Times,* as the district's new superintendent, despite his lack of any experience in education. In 2019, voters in Rodriguez's district elected pro-public-education firebrand Jackie Goldberg—an experienced teacher and legislator—to fill his empty seat, which eliminated the billionares' control of it.

Chicago's leaders welcomed charter schools as replacements for low-scoring public schools. The city's charter-friendly officials, all Democrats, were Mayor Richard Daley, Mayor Rahm Emanuel, Superintendent Paul

Vallas, Superintendent Arne Duncan, and every other superintendent selected under mayoral control by either Daley or Emanuel. In this atmosphere, Juan Rangel, a politically connected leader of the Hispanic community, launched what soon became one of the city's largest charter chains, called UNO, which eventually grew to sixteen charter schools. In the five years preceding Rangel's downfall in 2014, his chain collected $280 million in public money to operate and expand his network. UNO received additional funding from the anti-union, right-wing Walton Family Foundation and the Dell Foundation. Rangel hired an outside management company, then fired it so that UNO could collect the 10 percent management fee; in 2012, the management fees generated $5 million, which could be used at the discretion of UNO's leaders. In 2009, UNO received a grant of $98 million from the state to construct new schools. After he won that grant, he violated state law by engaging in nepotism and conflicts of interest, awarding contracts to his relatives, relatives of board members, and relatives of his allies.

After the *Chicago Sun-Times* published a list of UNO's insider contracts, Rangel's charter school empire began to fall apart. Governor Pat Quinn suspended the last $15 million of the state's $98 million construction grant. Rangel stepped down from the UNO board and set rules to bar nepotism and conflicts of interest. He even agreed to allow the teachers at UNO schools to unionize, a move that certainly did not please his funders in the philanthropic world, especially the anti-union Walton family. The SEC announced an investigation into UNO's financial practices, and Rangel resigned at the end of 2014.

Juan Rangel assumed that there were no controls in the charter industry and that he could do whatever he wished with public money. He was wrong. But today, operators of thousands of charter schools continue to run their businesses with no public oversight or accountability.

The stench of charter corruption became so noticeable that the inspector general of the U.S. Department of Education launched an investigation of federal funding of charter schools and released an audit report, which held: "We concluded that these examples of internal control weaknesses represent the following significant risks to Department program objectives: (1) financial risk, which is the risk of waste, fraud, and abuse; (2) lack of accountability over Federal funds . . . and (3) performance risk."

Despite these warnings by the inspector general, the U.S. Department of Education did nothing to heighten scrutiny of charter schools that applied to the federal Charter Schools Program and received federal funding. Arne Duncan was a fan of charter schools, as was his successor, John King (who founded Roxbury Prep, a "no-excuses" charter school in Massachusetts known for the highest suspension rates in the state), as was his successor, Betsy DeVos.

The online charter industry is especially vulnerable to fraud due to absence of oversight. Online charter schools are known for high attrition, low test scores, and low graduation rates. In Tennessee, the virtual charter school is the lowest-performing school in the state. Pennsylvania has more than a dozen online charter schools, none of which has ever met state academic standards. These schools receive full tuition for every student who enrolls, so they compete to draw students away from public schools, even from other charter schools. But unlike brick-and-mortar schools, the online schools do not need custodians, groundskeepers, lunchroom staff, librarians, social workers, and security guards; nor do they pay for water and heat and electricity. Because of their low costs, the virtual charter schools are immensely profitable. Online schools spend large amounts of public money advertising on television and online. They set up enrollment booths at large malls. The name of the game is enrollment because enrollment keeps the money rolling in.

Nicholas Trombetta, the chief executive officer and founder of the Pennsylvania Cyber Charter School, was convicted of tax fraud and conspiracy after he admitted stealing $8 million from the school and using the money to purchase personal luxury goods, including multiple homes and an airplane. In 2018, Trombetta pleaded guilty to tax fraud and was sentenced to twenty months in prison and three years' probation. He was convicted of tax evasion, not of stealing $8 million from the Commonwealth of Pennsylvania. Apparently, stealing money from the state is not a crime, but tax evasion is. The school had more than 11,000 students, each generating state tuition of $10,000. So the school had more than $100 million rolling in every year. This much money was too tempting, especially when state oversight was lax, a situation established by charter lobbyists and a charter-friendly Republican governor and majority in the legislature. Trombetta, like some other charter operators, set up "related companies" to supply goods and services to his booming online charter business. Another cyber charter operator in Pennsylvania, Dorothy June Brown, was charged with the theft of $6.5 million by federal authorities, but the case ended in a hung jury, and the judge decided that she could not be retried due to her age and dementia. Some parents complained about the questionable practices at her school ("phantom charter school board members, fabricated documents, and forged signatures on contracts that benefited Brown or her management firms"), but they were bankrupted by lawyers' fees after she filed a defamation suit against them. Evidently her age and dementia did not prevent her from filing a lawsuit against disgruntled parents.

The largest online charter school in the nation collapsed in 2018. The Electronic Classroom of Tomorrow (ECOT) in Ohio started as a for-profit business in 2000. Its founder, software executive William Lager, made generous campaign contributions to elected officials in the state, mostly Republicans, who often appeared as commencement speakers at the school's graduation ceremonies. Jeb Bush, an enthusiastic promoter of online learning, was ECOT's commencement speaker in 2010; Ohio governor John Kasich was its commencement speaker in 2011. Over the eighteen years of its existence, ECOT collected at least $1 billion from the taxpayers of Ohio.

In 2016, *The New York Times* published an investigation of ECOT. Its enrollment was then 17,000 students, mostly in high school. It had a graduating class of 2,300 students. But it also had the lowest graduation rate of any high school in the nation. Only twenty of every 100 high school students enrolled in ECOT received a diploma. One of every twenty-six high school students in the state was enrolled in an online school, yet the graduation rates at these "e-schools" were worse than those of the public schools in the state's most impoverished districts, Cleveland and Youngstown. Although the school was not performing well, Lager profited handsomely. In 2014 alone, the companies associated with Lager were paid "nearly $23 million, or about one-fifth of the nearly $115 million in government funds it took in."

After the *Times*'s exposé appeared, the state began to investigate ECOT. The state auditor Dave Yost determined that a significant number of students on ECOT's register were not actually engaged in learning. Some were phantom students; others registered but never participated in classes. ECOT claimed that it should be paid even for students who did not participate in classes. The auditor tried to force ECOT to return $60 million to the state. ECOT fought in court and lost, then declared bankruptcy in 2018 rather than pay back any of its undeserved millions.

Other states, including Oklahoma, Indiana, and California, have had large online charter scandals. The biggest scandal occurred in 2019 in California, where a grand jury indicted eleven people for participating in an online charter scam that cost the state more than $50 million. At the center of the indictment were Sean McManus and Jason Shrock, who founded the A3 charter organization, which ran nineteen online charter schools and multiple summer athletic programs, with multiple boards and corporations. Its charters were authorized by tiny rural school districts to operate in other districts or to operate cyber charters, none of which was supervised. State law was written to block accountability or oversight for charter operators. The profits from this sprawling operation ended up in the private bank accounts of its founders. The result was the biggest financial scandal in charter history.

In Ohio, the for-profit Imagine charter chain spent more than $7.7 million of taxpayers' money renovating a property whose value was $2.4 million. The actual cost of the renovation was $3.3 million. One of Imagine's corporate arms, Schoolhouse Finance, rented the property, then leased it back to Imagine's charter school, which paid nearly $1 million a year in rent. Schoolhouse Finance also financed the renovations. It was a win-win for Imagine. Real estate deals like this enriched unscrupulous charter operators.

Michigan became a playground for the charter industry, thanks in large part to the billionaire DeVos family, which funded pro-choice organizations like the Mackinac Center for Public Policy and the Great Lakes Education Project, as well as the American Federation for Children, a political group that funds pro-voucher and pro-charter candidates. About 80 percent of the charter schools in Michigan are managed by for-profit corporations. State law forbids for-profit ownership of charter schools but not for-profit management. Arizona is the only state that does not prohibit for-profit charters. Nationally, many nonprofits are operated by for-profit education management organizations, making the distinction between "for-profit"and "nonprofit" meaningless. In 2014, the *Detroit Free Press* published the results of a yearlong investigation of the charter industry and blasted it for its lack of accountability:

The newspaper reported:

Michigan taxpayers pour nearly $1 billion a year into charter schools—but state laws regulating charters are among the nation's weakest, and the state demands little accountability in how taxpayer dollars are spent and how well children are educated. . . .

In reviewing two decades of charter school records, the Free Press found:

Wasteful spending and double-dipping. Board members, school founders and employees steering lucrative deals to themselves or insiders. Schools allowed to operate for years despite poor academic records. No state standards for who operates charter schools or how to oversee them.

And a record number of charter schools run by for-profit companies that rake in taxpayer money and refuse to detail how they spend it, saying they're private and not subject to disclosure laws. . . .

According to the Free Press' review, 38 percent of charter schools that received state academic rankings during the 2012–13 school year fell below the 25th percentile, meaning at least 75 percent of all schools in the state performed better. Only 23 percent of traditional public schools fell below the 25th percentile.

As it handed out public money to entrepreneurs without exercising any oversight, Michigan became the poster state for charter school waste, fraud, and abuse. As the *Free Press* put it, "Anyone and everyone can apply to open a charter school. There are no state guidelines for screening applicants." The organizations that authorize charter schools get 3 percent of the revenue of the charters. Only the authorizers have the power to close down a failing charter school. And they don't. Why should they?

They make money by keeping them open. Most charter schools in the state perform below the state average in reading and math.

The *Free Press* investigation uncovered numerous examples of egregious waste of public money, including a quarter million dollars for a Dale Carnegie confidence-building class, a million dollars for swampland, millions of dollars for excessive rents, and lucrative business deals awarded to family members.

After embracing school choice, Michigan saw significant declines in its standing on the federal test, the National Assessment of Educational Progress (NAEP). In little more than a decade, Michigan went from being an average state on national tests to the bottom ten. In 2003, Michigan was 28th in the nation in fourth grade reading; by 2015, it was 41st. In fourth grade math, the state had dropped from 27th to 42nd in the nation. The declines occurred among all students including white students, black students, and upper-income students. On tests offered in 11 states from 2015 to 2017, third graders in Michigan were the lowest performing in every demographic group.

The New York Times Magazine published a story about Michigan's ill-fated gamble on charter schools:

> Charters continue to be sold in Michigan as a means of unwinding the inequality of a public-school system in which districts across the state, overwhelmingly African-American—Detroit, Highland Park, Benton Harbor, Muskegon Heights, Flint—grapple with steep population declines, towering financial obligations, deindustrialization and the legacy of segregation. By allowing experimentation, proponents argue, and by breaking the power of teachers' unions, districts will somehow be able to innovate their way past the crushing underfunding that afflicts majority-minority school districts all around the country. In reality, however, a 2017 Stanford University analysis found that increasing charter-school enrollment in a school district does little to improve achievement gaps.

Detroit is a test case for the efficacy of charter schools as a means of "saving" the poorest children from "bad" public schools. According to theory, competition with charters is supposed to "force" the pub-

lic schools to improve. That didn't happen. The city suffers from high
poverty, intense segregation, deindustrialization, urban blight, and
every other ill that could afflict a once-thriving city where entry-level
and blue-collar jobs have nearly disappeared. Instead of developing an
economic policy to revive Detroit, state and civic leaders invested in
charter schools. More than half the students in the city attend charter
schools, and at least half of the charters performed worse or no better than the public schools. Kate Zernike wrote in *The New York Times*
that the introduction of choice and competition into Detroit had produced chaos. The "unchecked growth of charters" had spawned "a glut
of schools competing for some of the nation's poorest students" and
"produced a public education fiasco that is perhaps unparalleled in the
United States." Scott Romney, the leader of a civic group called New
Detroit, told Zernike: "The point was to raise all schools. Instead, we've
had a total and complete collapse of education in this city." Douglas N.
Harris of Tulane University (the same researcher who later praised Disruptive reform policies in New Orleans) described Detroit as "the biggest
school reform disaster in the country." Of the urban districts tested by
NAEP, Detroit ranks lowest. Charters did not cure the economic and
political abandonment that ails Detroit, nor did charters cause the public
schools to improve.

Charter school advocates like to wear the mantle of progressivism,
but it is ill-fitting. About 90 percent of charter schools in the nation
are nonunion, reflecting the anti-union views of major funders like the
right-wing Walton Family Foundation. As a rule, progressives are not
anti-union.

Charter schools are more segregated than public schools are, even in
school districts with high levels of segregation. The Civil Rights Project
at the University of California called charter schools "a major political
success" but "a civil rights failure." Choice advocates ignore segregation,
on the assumption that high test scores matter more than racial integra-
tion does. As a rule, progressives do not endorse school segregation.

Charters are the gateway to vouchers because they are the entering
wedge for school choice and consumerism. School choice, it should be
remembered, was the goal of Southern governors in the decade after
the U.S. Supreme Court's *Brown v. Board of Education of Topeka* deci-

sion of 1954. For many years, the term "school choice" was stigmatized because most people, familiar with the backlash to the *Brown* decision, understood that "choice" was a strategy devised by Southern governors to preserve racial segregation. The racist origins of school choice are well documented.

In the late 1960s and early 1970s, some liberals—like Christopher Jencks, Ted Sizer, and Deborah Meier—supported some form of choice, though it is unlikely that they would have endorsed the current version of free market privatization. The only surviving member of that group is Deborah Meier, who opposes private management of public schools; her own schools of choice, in New York City and Boston, were part of the public school system.

Half a century after school choice was championed by white Southern politicians, it returned in the supposedly benign guise of consumerism, marketed to appeal to parents' right to choose, just as they choose their brand of automobile or milk or cereal. The logic of consumerism eases the transition from charters to vouchers. Right-wingers and libertarians have pursued this goal for decades. They derisively refer to the schools that have educated 90 percent of the American people as "government schools," and they hate anything government-related except defense expenditures and government contracts directed to their businesses.

As voucher programs became established, independent studies converged on the conclusion that students who use vouchers to enroll in private and religious schools do not fare as well as do their peers who are eligible for vouchers but remain in public schools. Independent evaluations of voucher programs in Ohio, Louisiana, Indiana, and the District of Columbia agreed that students who used vouchers to attend religious or private schools actually lost ground academically. The Ohio study, funded by the conservative Thomas B. Fordham Institute, found that "the students who use vouchers to attend private schools have fared worse academically compared to their closely matched peers attending public schools. The study finds negative effects that are greater in math than in English language arts. Such impacts also appear to persist over time, suggesting that the results are not driven simply by the setbacks that typically accompany any change of school."

Voucher advocates usually assert that poor kids should have the same choices as rich kids, but voucher programs never offer a voucher large enough for a student to enroll in an elite private academy, where tuition may be $25,000 to $50,000 a year, and many elite schools do not accept vouchers. Red state legislators want vouchers to cut costs, which guarantees that the stipend will remain low. The size of the individual voucher is usually equal to or less than the average amount of money spent on each student in public schools. In North Carolina and Indiana, for example, it is less than $5,000. Voucher students are able to enroll in low-cost religious and private schools, which typically employ uncertified teachers and use textbooks that teach Bible-based religious doctrine in place of modern science or history. The United States is not a theocratic society, and we have a long tradition of separation of church and state that is violated by using public funds to pay tuition to religious schools. That tradition, however, is under serious challenge today.

At present, about half the states offer some form of voucher program for private and religious schools. The most expansive program is offered by the state of Indiana, even though its state constitution forbids spending public dollars in religious schools. The Indiana state constitution states simply and clearly: "No money shall be drawn from the treasury, for the benefit of any religious or theological institution." The legislature and the governors of Indiana (Mitch Daniels and Mike Pence) decided to ignore the state constitution, as did the State Supreme Court, which creatively ruled that the voucher went to the family, not to the religious school where it paid the tuition. Half of the state's one million students are eligible for a voucher; yet only 3.5 percent use a voucher, and nearly 60 percent of those never attended public schools. The program is simply a giveaway of public funds to families that prefer religious schools. Vouchers for a tiny number of students subtract $153 million from the schooling of the vast majority of students in Indiana.

The main effect of school choice is to drain funds from the public schools, forcing them to lay off teachers, cut programs, and increase class sizes. Vouchers are a "lose-lose": the small number of kids who take vouchers go to schools with less qualified teachers and learn less, and the great majority of kids in public schools are subject to budget cuts, which cause them to lose teachers and programs.

What are the voucher schools teaching? In 2017, *The Huffington Post* created a database of the more than seven thousand schools that receive public money through voucher programs. Education editor Rebecca Klein summarized the findings: about three quarters of the voucher schools are religious. Thirty-one percent are Catholic schools. Most of the other Christian schools are evangelical. These schools teach whatever they want, and many use curricula that teach "racist, sexist, and intolerant views of the world." Some evangelical schools teach, for example, that other religions, especially Catholicism, are evil. Why should taxpayer dollars fund religious bigotry?

In Florida, Klein found, voucher dollars pay tuition for students to attend five schools that teach the ideas of the Church of Scientology. Between 2012 and 2016, these schools collected $500,000 in taxpayer dollars.

At least 14 percent of the religious schools in the *Huffington Post* database openly discriminated against students and staff based on suspicion that they might be LGBTQX. Klein described a Christian school in Virginia that expelled an eight-year-old girl because she "wasn't acting 'Christlike' by wearing her hair short and preferring pants to skirts." How did the school know that Christ preferred skirts to pants and long hair to short hair? Should boys do the same?

The public has never demanded school choice. In no state has a majority of students enrolled in charter schools or sought vouchers. Charter advocates boast about long waiting lists, but such claims are a marketing ploy. Charters in Los Angeles and New York City have empty seats. If long waiting lists actually existed, the charters would not seek access to the names and addresses of public school students for recruitment purposes. Only in New Orleans, where every public school was closed by Hurricane Katrina and politicians imposed charters on the victims of the storm, did all students enroll in charter schools. This was coercion, not choice.

Whenever vouchers have been put to a vote in state referendums, they have lost by large majorities. Even when they lose, politicians, religious zealots, and billionaire ideologues perform a "workaround" and find ways to offer them anyway, despite the will of the public.

The urban district that has had full-blown school choice the longest is Milwaukee. That city has had charters since 1994 (the Wisconsin charter law was passed in 1993) and vouchers since 1990 (the city's voucher program won court approval to include religious schools in 1998). All three sectors—public, charter, and voucher—are fully developed. In 1999, before the choice movement took off, the Milwaukee public schools enrolled 96,000 students. By 2018, that number had dropped to about 66,000, or about 56 percent of school-age children. Nearly 29,000 attend voucher schools, and another 15,000 are in charter schools. According to Milwaukee journalist Alan Borsuk, the three sectors seem to have stabilized, and all three sectors get the same poor academic results. Competition has not improved the public schools. On the National Assessment of Educational Progress (NAEP), Milwaukee is one of the lowest-scoring districts in the nation. The only district that scored significantly below Milwaukee was Detroit. What is the rationale for taking taxpayer money to pay for private and religious schools that get similar or worse results than public schools?

Private choices, we now know, come at the expense of public schools, which enroll 85 to 90 percent of America's students. Every dollar that goes to a charter or a voucher school is a dollar subtracted from the public schools where the overwhelming majority of students are enrolled.

Furthermore, vouchers exist not because of parental demand but because of the campaign cash that libertarians and religious zealots have donated to state legislators. The proportion of students who use vouchers is tiny in every state, and voters have never approved vouchers in any state referendum.

Charters exist not because they are more effective or more innovative than public schools but because the federal government and the Walton Family Foundation together spend at least $600 million every year to open new charters, a staggering amount of money that is supplemented by hundreds of millions more from other foundations, hedge fund managers, financiers, entrepreneurs, corporations, state governments, and free market ideologues. Without that powerhouse funding, there would be few charters, and the ones that exist might embody the brilliant idea that Albert Shanker proposed in 1988: teacher-led schools-within-schools that collaborate with their host schools, welcome unions, and act as R&D centers for new ideas that can be adopted by the public schools in which they operate.

CHAPTER 10

The Resistance Fights Back

How does a David beat a Goliath? How can parents and teachers with no significant backing other than occasional support from the two national teachers' unions defeat the financiers, billionaires, and tech titans who are closely allied with the U.S. Department of Education, the United States Congress, and the president of the United States? From Ronald Reagan to Donald Trump, six successive administrations in Washington, D.C., actively encouraged and funded Corporate Disruption.

As each year passed, as each new indignity was heaped on public schools and teachers, the Resistance grew. Randi Weingarten of the American Federation of Teachers and Lily Eskelsen García of the National Education Association funded lawsuits to stop unfair teacher evaluation programs in individual districts and states. But their resources were never equivalent to the hundreds of millions or more spent each year by the Disrupters and the federal government, nor were their voices strong enough to counter the force of federal law.

Most of the media, whether national or local, assumed that "Reform" is good and that resistance to "Reform" is driven entirely by self-interested teachers' unions. They could not have been more wrong. The Disrupters are led by a cabal of self-centered billionaires who love to exercise their power over others, and the Resistance is led by tireless parents, students, grandparents, public school graduates, teachers, retired teachers, com-

Lily Eskelsen García began her career as a cafeteria worker in an elementary school in Utah, then as an aide in a classroom for students with disabilities. She returned to college to earn her degrees and became a classroom teacher as well as being active in the National Education Association, first as president of the Utah Education Association, then, rising through the ranks to win election in 2008, as president of the NEA, the nation's largest union, with three million members. The NEA has given organizational and financial support to teachers who resisted privatization and underinvestment in public schools.

Randi Weingarten grew up in a union family; her mother was a public school teacher. She became a lawyer with a specialty in labor relations. She represented the United Federation of Teachers, then left the law to teach social studies at a public high school in Brooklyn. She was elected president of the New York City United Federation of Teachers in 1998. Ten years later, she was elected president of the American Federation of Teachers, whose membership is 1.7 million, including teachers, paraprofessionals, nurses, higher education faculty, and early childhood educators. Weingarten has been on the front lines with striking teachers and has helped them organize, even in states that banned collective bargaining.

munity leaders, and religious leaders who are devoted to the principle of separation of church and state.

The challenge for the Resistance is to break the beneficent mask that conceals the true face of Corporate Disruption and to reveal its actual goals: privatization and profits. It takes many voices, many organizations, many individuals, many bloggers, and many scholars to pierce that mask of deception. The mask is carefully constructed by the marketing and branding teams hired by billionaires like the Walton family, the DeVos family, the Koch brothers, Bill and Melinda Gates, Eli Broad, Reed Hastings, John Arnold, and Michael Bloomberg. "Students First," they say. "Children First," they say. "Students Matter," they say. "Kids First," they say. All their slogans are designed to deceive. Ultimately the ruse failed. Not even the billionaires and their hired mouthpieces could overcome the grassroots volunteers of the Resistance, who proved that democracy can be a powerful weapon when wielded on behalf of the common good.

Amy Frogge is a lawyer and a parent of children who attended Gower Elementary School in Nashville, Tennessee. In 2010, the city suffered a devastating flood, and people came together from across the city and even from out of state to help rebuild the damaged neighborhoods. Frogge was impressed by the energy that is generated when people coalesce behind a common goal. Aware that the Parent Teacher Organization at Gower Elementary was moribund, she and another parent decided to rebuild it. Over a year, they enhanced parent engagement, developed new community partnerships, and helped to bring about major improvements in the school's performance, atmosphere, and culture.

Determined to "give back to her community," Frogge decided to run for the Metro Nashville school board in 2012. With the help of many volunteers, she rang doorbells across her district. She raised $25,000. Her opponent was endorsed by Nashville mayor Karl Dean, the Chamber of Commerce, the local teachers' union, and the Gates-funded group called Stand for Children. Her opponent spent $125,000, five times what Frogge spent. But Frogge won by a two-to-one landslide. When she ran, she was unaware of the national debates about privatization. She just wanted to do her part as a citizen. She quickly learned about the efforts by national charter chains to gain a foothold in Nashville and decided that this was not good for the local public schools.

When Amy Frogge was elected, the Metro Nashville school board was in the midst of a battle with the state over whether to allow a charter school managed by Great Hearts Academies, an Arizona-based charter chain, to open in Nashville. The Metro Nashville board rejected its application because Great Hearts wanted to locate in a mostly white neighborhood with no plans to transport black students from other parts of the city. The board insisted that the charter must serve a diverse enrollment. The board's refusal to authorize the Great Hearts proposal infuriated

Amy Frogge, a parent and lawyer,
was twice elected to the Metro
Nashville Board of Education,
despite being outspent by opponents
who favored charter schools.

the state commissioner of education, Kevin Huffman, who was determined to increase the number of charter schools in Tennessee. Huffman
(the ex-husband of Michelle Rhee) had previously worked for Teach for
America. He had the backing of Republican governor Bill Haslam and
Nashville mayor Karl Dean, a Democrat.

Commissioner Huffman punished the recalcitrant Metro Nashville
school board by withholding $3.4 million from its public schools (but
not its charter schools).

The day after Amy Frogge's election to her local school board, she got
a call from *The Wall Street Journal,* and that was her first inkling that she
had stepped into a national brawl. She ran for the school board to make
the public schools better but soon realized that debates over charters
completely dominated the board's agenda. Out-of-state charters were
competing with the public schools for money and students, and she
didn't see how that helped to improve the public schools. She provided
the deciding vote, and a 5–4 majority on the board again voted against
allowing Great Hearts to open a charter. Only five months after her election, she addressed the education committee of the state legislature and
urged it not to give the state the power to impose charters against the

will of local boards, which would have been a dream come true for the Disrupters, who oppose democratic control by local school boards. She pointed out that the existing charters had empty seats, and the city did not need more charters. What it truly needed was more funding for its existing public schools.

Frogge emerged as an articulate critic of privatization and Corporate Disruption. In her role as a board member, she wanted expanded recess time, more time for art and music, less time devoted to testing, and increased funding for the schools, but these issues were overshadowed by the persistent struggle between the school board and the state over charter expansion. She courageously stood up to the right-wing governor, the legislature, the state commissioner, and Mayor Dean, who were all pushing for more charters in Nashville. The local newspapers criticized her as "divisive" and "shrill" for taking a stand (these are the words applied to women who speak out but not to men, who are seen as "forceful" and "strong"). The newspapers grew tired of her complaints about the large amounts of outside money that poured into school board races.

In 2014, Frogge asked for time to deliver her thoughts to the board about charter schools. She asked her colleagues to consider the "endgame" in the drive for more charters. She spoke of profiteering, corporate intrusion, the exclusion of low-scoring students, and increased segregation in charters. And she worried about the disruptive effect of charters on communities.

In this excerpt, Frogge summarizes the risk that charters pose to school districts:

Last year, I voted against charter schools because of fiscal impact, and I'm inclined to do the same this year unless we come up with a plan. If we are going to pay more for charter schools, we need to figure out what else to cut from the budget. . . .

Although there are many involved in the charter school movement who have excellent motives, the charter school movement overall has become increasingly tied to profit motives as corporations interfere with education. I have watched organizations with shadowy motives exploit our Tennessee legislature. They operate like vultures, feeding hefty campaign donations and bad information to legislators through their plentiful lobbyists. They do not operate in good faith.

The charter movement is nationally funded and driven by organizations like ALEC (the American Legislative Exchange Council), which promotes and protects corporate interests and works to pass legislation that allows corporations access to more profits. The state charter authorizer came from ALEC, by the way. The Waltons, owners of Walmart, which is notorious for paying its employees such low wages that they must rely on government assistance to eat, are driving charter legislation. Hedge funders, banks and the wealthiest Americans can double their investments through generous tax credits in just seven years by investing in charters. Surely groups like these are not primarily interested in helping low income children.

The goal at the legislative level is to gain access to a steady stream of tax dollars with limited public accountability. That's why these special interest groups contend that there should be no democratically elected school boards. The desired result is to squelch the democratic process in favor of appointed bureaucracy, to take away local control of schools, and to promote less accountability and transparency for charter schools.

In 2016, Frogge ran again for the school board, and she was now Enemy Number One for the Disrupters. In hopes of ousting her, they funneled over $200,000 into the race, most of it directed through the Gates-funded Stand for Children. She won again, receiving 65 percent of the vote. Voters liked the principled stand that she took supporting public schools and demanding accountability and transparency for charters.

Amy Frogge recalled in an interview with T. C. Weber, a Nashville parent-blogger, that her husband had given her a clip of the Reverend William Barber, the charismatic leader of the Resistance in North Carolina who has often been compared to Dr. Martin Luther King Jr. Reverend Barber has championed progressive causes of every kind, including public education. Frogge remembered this message:

When you're called to service it's often not convenient. It's often very difficult and it is exhausting, but we are not allowed to give up. We don't get to determine when it's done. I think many of us have made huge sacrifices to continue to try to advocate for students and our teachers and our families. . . . I feel that I've been given a unique opportunity to make an impact, and not many people have that opportunity. I'm not allowed to squander it even though I often would like to just move to an island, buy a tiny house, and be done with the controversy because I hate controversy. I don't like conflict at all, and I've been in the midst of the worst sort of conflict for four years. But the work's not done, though I think we have made a lot of headway. We're ready now to have positive conversations and shift the focus on the work that I think will make the greatest impact on the greatest number of children.

After the Disrupters were thrashed in the second round of school board elections, the climate around school issues changed. The conversation no longer was dominated by discussion of where, how, and whether to authorize charters but about how to improve the education of all the children of Nashville. It wasn't money that made the difference. The conversation changed because of the courage and persistence of volunteers and of leaders like Amy Frogge.

Amy Frogge did not realize that she was on the receiving end of a national campaign to disrupt public education, led by groups like the hedge fund managers' Democrats for Education Reform, Stand for Children, and billionaires like the Waltons, Bill Gates, and Michael Bloomberg, who are intent on gaining control of local and state school boards. Big money flowed into school board races in Louisiana, Los Angeles, Indiana, Ohio, Texas, Newark, Denver, Rhode Island, Minneapolis, Washington State, New York, Rhode Island, and other locales. The Network for Public Education Action Fund documented the targeting of districts and states by super-rich elites, led by billionaires. What chance did ordinary citizens have to run for their school board when out-of-state organizations bundled twice as much, three times as much, five times as much money from contributors across the nation and funded their opponents?

It is fundamentally antidemocratic when billionaires who live in New York City, Seattle, Connecticut, Los Angeles, and Silicon Valley conspire to overwhelm candidates in school board races in other cities and states with their limitless funding. This is not a partisan issue; the billionaires include both Republicans and Democrats determined to promote privatization. What appears to local citizens as a contest between two candidates is all too often a struggle between local parent groups and national organizations ready to spend whatever it takes to win control. The deck is stacked because of the money advantage of the Disrupters. Fortunately, they do not always win. Amy Frogge proved that grassroots resistance, when it is sufficiently alert, determined, and organized, can beat Big Money.

Parent activists play a major role in the Resistance. No one can fire parents. They are the best advocates for children and their public schools. Among the many parents who spoke out on behalf of public schools, none was more forceful than New York City parent activist Leonie Haimson. She founded Class Size Matters to advocate for class size reduction, which she insists—with the evidence to back it up—is the single most effective reform to improve school climate and student outcomes (I serve as an unpaid member on her small board of directors, and she in turn is an unpaid member of the board of the Network for Public Education). Haimson is a fearless advocate and dedicated researcher who understands statistics and arcane legal language. She frequently testifies at city and state legislative hearings, presents research on the effectiveness of class size reduction, and challenges the misuse of public funds.

Haimson and her ally Rachael Stickland of Colorado organized the successful fight to block inBloom, a massive data-collection effort funded with $100 million from the Bill & Melinda Gates Foundation and the Carnegie Corporation of New York. InBloom planned to partner with nine states and school districts to collect personally identifiable student data, including names, addresses, family relationships, race, behavior, "character strengths (such as 'actively participates,' 'shows enthusiasm,' 'resists distractions')," economic status, test scores, grades, disability status, and disciplinary records. This information was to be collected in a database system designed by technology company Amplify (formerly Wireless Generation, a division of Rupert Murdoch's News Corporation), stored on the cloud by Amazon, and made available to third-party vendors. What could possibly go wrong?

Leonie Haimson, a parent activist in New York City who advocates on behalf of reduced class size and student privacy, is one of the most effective activists in the nation on issues that affect the well-being of students.

The backers of inBloom said that this massive collection of personally identifiable student data would enable the development and marketing of effective online learning tools. Haimson, Stickland, and other concerned parents, however, saw inBloom as a dangerous threat to student privacy, for the benefit of commercial interests.

Haimson and Stickland helped mobilize hundreds of parent activists in the affected states and districts to join the battle against inBloom. They had no resources with which to fight the $100 million behemoth, but they had the support of parents from all ends of the political spectrum whose only interest was their children's privacy.

On their website, Haimson and Stickland wrote:

The backers of inBloom pitched the project as an effort to help students by providing more personalized learning tools, yet there are no proven benefits to online learning and there are huge risks involved in commercializing this data and storing it on a vulnerable data cloud. In fact, inBloom's privacy policy originally stated that it "cannot guarantee the security of the information stored in inBloom

or that the information will not be intercepted when it is being trans-
mitted," though it has now taken that statement off its website.

There are several federal laws to protect student privacy. The main
one is called FERPA—or Family Educational Rights and Privacy Act.
FERPA was weakened in 2008 under President George W. Bush and
again in 2011 under President Barack Obama to allow the outsourcing of
personal student data without parental consent. Obama's Race to the Top
program required states to build longitudinal data systems comprised of
student information, which could be fed into inBloom's database and
then handed off to corporations to develop new software. The Gates
Foundation and the D.C.-based advocacy organizations it funds insisted
that mining big data would provide positive benefits if every student
were tracked from cradle to career.

The New York Times noted that inBloom was a natural outgrowth of
the Common Core standards, in which online testing would produce
reams of data about millions of students. *Times* reporter Natasha Singer
wrote that inBloom was part of a vision of a "techno-utopia" of "continuously quantified students and seamlessly connected teachers."

Education technology software for prekindergarten to 12th grade is
an $8 billion market, according to estimates from the Software and
Information Industry Association. One major reason is the Common
Core State Standards Initiative, a program to standardize English
and math curriculums nationally. To prepare for assessment tests for
those standards, many districts across the country are investing in
software to analyze individual student performance in more detail.

Services like inBloom want to speed the introduction and lower
the cost of these assessment tools by standardizing data storage and
security. The idea is that inBloom's open-source code could spur
developers to create apps for all its clients, reducing the need for
them to customize software to each school district. In theory, that
would make the products cheaper for schools.

Recent changes in the regulation of a federal education privacy
law have also helped the industry. That law, the Family Educational
Rights and Privacy Act, required schools to obtain parental per-

mission before sharing information in their children's educational records. The updated rules permit schools to share student data, without notifying parents, with companies to which they have outsourced core functions like scheduling or data management.

To Bill Gates and Arne Duncan, the prospect of generating continually analyzed student data was a boon to product developers, marketing firms, and educators. To parents, it was a techno-nightmare, in which their children's private information would be widely shared among vendors, without their knowledge or consent and without rigorous security to protect against data breaches.

In Colorado, Louisiana, New York, and other states, parents attended legislative hearings, badgered elected officials, and spoke out against inBloom. State after state canceled their plans to share data with the new enterprise. Last to drop out was New York, at the end of 2013, because of the intransigence of State Commissioner John B. King. In March 2014, the New York State Legislature passed a law banning the state from handing over state data to inBloom. By April 2014, having lost every state and district customer, inBloom closed down. Against all odds, the parents won.

After leading the fight to vanquish Bill Gates and inBloom, Haimson and Stickland formed the Parent Coalition for Student Privacy and were twice invited to testify before Congress. As a result of their activism, nearly a hundred state laws to protect student privacy have been passed since 2013. Haimson continues to press state and local authorities for reduced class sizes and is frustrated that school districts are willing to spend billions on new technology but nothing to reduce class size, which would enable genuinely "personalized" learning. Her home base, New York City, is a leader in funding technology instead of reducing class size. She is one of the very few people in New York City who habitually reads the details of contracts pending before the New York City Board of Education (which former mayor Michael Bloomberg renamed the Panel on Educational Policy to reduce its significance, after he gained mayoral control of the schools in 2002). In February 2015, she discovered that the board was about to award a contract worth $1.1 billion over five years, extendable for another four years at $2 billion, for "networking hardware and installation services" to the same company that had been involved in a massive "kickback" scandal just a few years earlier, while working for the same Department of Education. She shared this information with the city's Public Advocate, the head of the City Council's contract committee, and investigative journalist Juan Gonzalez of the New York *Daily News*. The board approved the contract, then hastily rescinded its approval after Haimson's information was publicized by Gonzalez. Leonie Haimson's sharp eye and quick intervention saved the city nearly $700 million.

Chicago presented a challenge to parents and community members trying to save public schools. Mayor Richard Daley and Mayor Rahm Emanuel gave free rein to Disrupters and privatizers. Since 1995, the public schools had been under mayoral control, in which the mayor selected the board members without anyone's approval. Daley's first "chief executive officer" for the school system was Paul Vallas, a noneducator who had served previously as Daley's budget director. Vallas was a devotee of privatization, as he later proved in his tenure as leader of the Philadelphia school district, where he launched a massive experiment in privatization of public schools (which failed), and in the New Orleans Recovery School District, where privatization became the norm. When Vallas left, Daley appointed Vallas's chief of staff Arne Duncan as the school system's "chief executive officer." Like Vallas, Duncan was a noneducator and a fervent believer in privately managed charter schools.

In 2004, Duncan announced Renaissance 2010, his program to "reform" the public schools by closing low-scoring schools and opening new schools. Most of the schools that he closed were in African American communities. A month after his election in 2008, President Barack Obama selected Duncan as secretary of education. Two years later, Rahm Emanuel was elected mayor of Chicago and followed Duncan's policy of closing public schools with low test scores and opening charter schools.

The Chicago Teachers Union was outraged by the city's preferential treatment of privately managed charter schools, which were overwhelmingly nonunion. In 2010, angry teachers ousted the leadership of the CTU and elected Karen Lewis, an articulate opponent of school privatization. Lewis, a high school chemistry teacher for more than two decades, was the daughter of schoolteachers and a graduate of the Chicago public schools and of Dartmouth College, where she was the only African American woman in the class of 1974. Lewis and Rahm Emanuel had a contentious relationship; he was famous for vitriol, and she was equally famous for her earthy wit and her fearlessness. She was not impressed by the mayor nor by any of his billionaire friends, especially not by venture capitalist Bruce Rauner, who was a devotee of charter schools (one of them bore his name) and was elected governor of Illinois in 2014. Rauner was also a graduate of Dartmouth College. According to Lewis's telling, she snapped at Rauner, "I wore the green jacket, too, bub!" Dartmouth's school color is green. In 2012, the Chicago Teachers Union voted to strike. Led by Lewis, the teachers remained on strike for ten days, seeking better conditions for teaching and learning. The strike had strong community support due to the union's careful attention to building strong ties with community organizations and persuading parents that the teachers were striking not just for themselves but for their children. The teachers won a pay raise and blocked merit pay, among

Karen Lewis (*right*), president of the Chicago Teachers Union from 2010 to 2014, led a strike that later became a national model for aligning the interests of teachers, communities, and parents.

other concessions by Emanuel. Karen Lewis was a hero of the Resistance and might well have defeated Rahm Emanuel in the mayoral election of 2014 but was tragically disabled by a brain tumor.

The year after the strike, the mayor took his revenge against the union by announcing the closure of fifty schools, all of them located in communities of color. Never in American history had a public official closed fifty public schools in a single day. According to Disrupter dogma, the children would surely end up in better schools. But they didn't. Studies by the University of Chicago Consortium on School Research found few gains for the students who left the closed schools. Instead what they discovered was a profound sense of loss: lost schools, lost communities, lost relationships. These were losses that Disrupters never understood. Test scores were all that mattered to them. And those were not impressive. The Consortium concluded: "Closing under-enrolled schools may seem like a viable solution to policymakers who seek to address fiscal deficits and declining enrollments, but our findings show that closing schools caused large disruptions without clear benefits for students."

The researchers found:

When schools closed, it severed the longstanding social connections that families and staff had with their schools and with one another, resulting in a period of mourning. Those impacted by school closures expressed feelings of grief in multiple ways, often referring to their closed school peers and colleagues as "like a family." The intensity of the feelings of loss were amplified in cases where schools had been open for decades, with generations of families attending the same neighborhood school. Losing their closed schools was not easy and the majority of interviewees spoke about the difficulty they had integrating and socializing into the welcoming schools. Even though welcoming school staff and students did not lose their schools per se, many also expressed feelings of loss because incorporating a large number of new students required adjustments. Staff said they wished that they had more training and support on what it meant to welcome staff and students who just lost their schools. Interviewees wished that their grief and loss had been acknowledged and validated.

Some critics blamed Chicago's school-closing policy for youth violence. The displacement of students meant the disruption of neighborhoods and communities, requiring young people to cross unfamiliar territory to get to school. This upheaval and turmoil hurt students and communities but was celebrated by Disrupters, who thought of their actions as "brave" and "bold."

Curtis Black of *The Chicago Reporter* wrote about community organizer Jitu Brown, who fought the closings:

> In 2007, CPS decided to take two Bronzeville elementary schools and redistribute their students: Jackie Robinson at 4225 S. Lake Park would take students from the entire area through third grade, and Price at 4351 S. Drexel would become a grade 4–8 school. Parents consistently warned of a rivalry between kids from the two neighborhoods, but CPS went ahead.
>
> The parents were right. Arguments and fights became common at Price. Suspensions and expulsions increased at the school, according to Jitu Brown, then education organizer for the Kenwood Oakland Community Organization, now national director of Journey for Justice, an education equity organization.

The students at the merged schools organized into gangs that did not exist before the schools were combined. A few years later, Price, one of the "welcoming schools," was closed for "chronic academic failure."

Two of the gangs got into a fight, and fifteen-year-old Hadiya Pendleton was killed in the crossfire between them in 2013. She had returned only a week earlier from performing in the inaugural ceremonies for President Barack Obama.

Brown sees school closings as a tool for gentrification of valuable properties in black neighborhoods. The school closings accelerated a significant exodus of black families from Chicago, as they have in other cities. Chicago lost over 200,000 black residents between 2000 and 2016. He told an interviewer:

> In Chicago, when we were hit with the notion of school closings in 2003–2004, we knew this was not about public education. Because

while they were branding our schools as failing and trying to close our schools, affordable housing was also disappearing. Grocery stores for our constituents were disappearing. So what we were really looking at was manufactured state-sanctioned elimination of black families from neighborhoods.

School closings are really a gentrification issue. It is an issue of disinvesting in our basic quality-of-life institutions. School choice is an illusion in black and brown communities. We don't have the choice of a great neighborhood school in safe walking distance of our homes. And in different cities, we campaign to stop schools from closing.

In 2012, the Chicago Public Schools board (acting at the behest of Mayor Emanuel) voted to close the Walter H. Dyett High School. Dyett

A native of Chicago and a graduate of its public schools, Jitu Brown heads the Journey for Justice Alliance, a civil rights group that is active in more than thirty cities, fighting school closings and the privatization of public schools. Brown has spent his professional life as a community organizer, training parents, youth, and community leaders to demand seats at the table when decisions are made about their lives. He successfully led a thirty-four-day hunger strike in Chicago to block the closure of the last open-admission high school in Bronzeville, the heart of the city's black community.

Rahm Emanuel was a congressman, chief of staff to President Obama, and mayor of Chicago. As mayor, Emanuel was devoted to closing public schools and replacing them with charter schools. In 2013, he closed fifty public schools in a single day.

was the last open-admissions public high school in Bronzeville, a historic African American community in Chicago. Jitu Brown and local parents were determined to save Dyett. They knew they had to get Rahm Emanuel's attention, since he alone controlled the school system. They protested wherever Emanuel appeared, with big signs reading "SAVE DYETT." In August 2015, they launched a hunger strike, and eleven protesters joined Jitu Brown to fight the school's closure. The twelve hunger strikers sat on lawn chairs in front of the school, surrounded by supporters. Day after day they sat there with their protest signs. When one of the hunger strikers was taken away by ambulance, they got national attention. Finally, on the thirty-fourth day of the hunger strike, Mayor Emanuel gave up. He declared that Dyett would not be closed but would receive a multimillion-dollar renovation and then reopen as an arts-focused high school. Instead of closing at the end of the 2014–15 school year, the new Walter H. Dyett School for the Arts opened in September 2016, with great fanfare, in a ceremony attended by the city's top school officials. The *Chicago Tribune* reporters wrote that "parents no longer have to worry about their children taking buses or trains to far-off schools. And they don't have to send their kids to privately run charter schools if they want to take honors or advanced placement classes." Jitu Brown was there to help cut the ribbons opening the new high school.

Eve L. Ewing, who was a teacher at one of the schools that were closed in 2013, left Chicago to earn a doctorate in sociology at Harvard and to become a novelist, poet, and playwright. She wrote a book about the school closings called *Ghosts in the Schoolyard: Racism and School Closings on Chicago's South Side*. In it, she answers the questions: Why do parents, students, grandparents, and teachers fight for schools that the authorities have labeled as failures? Why do so-called "reformers" celebrate "choice" but refuse to allow parents to choose their neighborhood school? She described the history of racism and segregation in Chicago and how deeply the public schools were interwoven into the lives of the people of Bronzeville. The local school is part of their community, their history, their memories, their traditions, their lives. The bureaucrats and technocrats had their data, but they never understood what Ewing called "institutional mourning," the loss of an institution that is embedded in one's sense of identity, regardless of test scores. The real goal of the closings, she argues, is to break up African American communities and make room for gentrification.

In another part of the country, parents in an affluent district proved the power of sustained grassroots activism. Douglas County, Colorado, was an unlikely setting for a monumental battle over school choice. Known locally as DougCo, the county is an affluent suburb of Denver. The county has little poverty and is 92 percent white. Nearly half the voters are Republicans, 20 percent are Democrats, and the rest are independents. Its schools are among the best in the state with high test scores and graduation rates. As of 2018, the district had 68,000 students, 3,300 teachers, and eighty-nine schools, including eighteen charter schools.

There was not much controversy in Douglas County before 2009. The nine members of the school board traditionally ran in nonpartisan elections for four-year terms on a staggered basis, with part of the board standing for election in alternate years. But in 2009, the Republican Party decided that the school board was insufficiently committed to school choice (in 2009, the district had thirteen charter schools). The party fielded a slate of four candidates, who ran against a slate endorsed by the local teachers' union, the Douglas County Federation (DCF). The Republican slate won handily, promising to increase charter schools and choice. The superintendent resigned, and the board hired Elizabeth Celania-Fagen, who previously had served as superintendent in Tucson. She pledged to advance a new agenda of school choice, "world class education," and a "cutting-edge System Performance Framework" that would "measure student, educator, school, leader, and District performance." The pro-voucher Milton and Rose D. Friedman Foundation listed Fagen as a speaker on the subject of education. At a salary of $280,000, she was one of the highest paid public officials in the state.

Early in 2010, after the victory of the four new members, which was a majority of the seven-member board, the board began planning to introduce vouchers. The plan was rolled out in March 2011 and was called the Douglas County Choice Scholarship Program (CSP). The district would provide three quarters of the state per-pupil expenditure (worth $4,650 in 2013) to five hundred students, who could use the money to attend any private school, including religious schools. The board was excited to be the first school board in the United States to authorize and fund a voucher program that would allow its students to use public funds to attend religious schools.

Cindy Barnard, a parent activist whose children attended DougCo public schools, was outraged by the voucher plan. A Republican with a background in corporate finance, she opposed diverting public funds to nonpublic schools. She began meeting with friends and discussing what was happening to their schools. In 2011, she and five other parents formed a group called Taxpayers for Public Education. They found a lawyer, Michael McCarthy of Faegre Baker and Daniels, willing to work pro bono. With the support of the American Civil Liberties Union, Americans United for Separation of Church and State, and the Interfaith Alliance of Colorado, they filed a lawsuit against the district's voucher plan. The American Federation of Teachers submitted an amicus brief, which infuriated the DougCo school board because it believed that the local teachers' union had agreed to take a wait-and-see approach toward vouchers.

When another school board election was held in 2011, the Republi-

Cindy Barnard was one of the key parent leaders in Douglas County, Colorado, who worked for years to organize parents and community leaders to oust an elected school board that supported vouchers.

cans again swept to victory, and now all seven board members favored vouchers. In 2012, still angry at the union's lack of enthusiasm for its reforms, the board ended its collective bargaining agreement. Thus, the board immediately accomplished one of its goals, which was to crush the teachers' union.

In the spring of 2012, another group of parents formed the Strong Schools Coalition, which was concerned about the board's budget cuts and about the accuracy of data released to the public. The school board's claims about student achievement, for example, did not match state data. SSC was organized by parent activists Laura Mutton, Susan Meek, and a dozen other parents and eventually grew to five hundred members.

The following year, 2013, the board spent $50,000 from its foundation to bring former secretary of education William Bennett to address local business leaders. Bennett, a staunch supporter of vouchers, was enthralled by what he saw. He returned to D.C. and praised DougCo as a national model for school reform.

The district and its foundation also paid $35,000 to Frederick Hess of the conservative American Enterprise Institute to write a paper about the district's reforms. Hess wrote an informative history and summary of the district's agenda. He said he was neither evaluating nor endorsing the reforms, but he titled his paper "The Most Interesting School District in America?" He expressed admiration for the district's "unconventional, bold leadership," describing its disruptive program as "a remarkable effort to rethink a high-performing suburban system." He called the DougCo plans "one of the nation's most fascinating efforts at system reform." He was impressed by the district's deep commitment to market-based decision making, its business approach to evaluating employees based on performance and the district's needs, rather than on their experience, and the board's surprising determination to introduce a "constructivist" approach to pedagogy rather than the skills-driven standards and testing usually found in struggling urban districts. The board rejected the Common Core standards as insufficiently challenging for the high-performing students of DougCo. Superintendent Fagen decided that the district would develop its own standards and district-made assessments, which she pledged would be better than the Common Core standards or the state's standards and tests.

The school board distributed the paper by Hess and his associate Max Eden to the 85,000 residents of the district on the eve of the 2013 election. As if the district needed any more huzzas from conservatives, the right-wing Independence Institute of Colorado issued a paper called "Douglas County: Building a Better Education Model," praising the disruptive changes. Suddenly, the eyes of the national media were on DougCo. *The Wall Street Journal, National Review,* and NPR featured the amazing school district that was determined to upend tradition and go all-in for school choice, performance pay, and other conservative market-based strategies.

All this publicity preceded the 2013 school board elections. William Bennett told the local DougCo radio station that its schools "are almost a laboratory for every serious thoughtful education reform on the conservative side." Colorado Public Radio reported that students and parents were holding rallies in opposition to the changes. National groups that admired market-based approaches to public education were excited by the changes in DougCo. The Koch brothers' Americans for Prosperity funded television ads praising the school board and condemning its critics, claiming that "the unions are fighting Douglas County's plan to pay teachers based on performance."

Opponents of the board's disruptive reforms spoke out against them.

Grassroots groups like Taxpayers for Public Education and the Strong Schools Coalition voiced their opposition to the upheaval in the district. They were upset by the voucher plans and by the number of teachers who quit and moved to other districts. Groups of parents and students lined key highways urging passersby to vote for the opposition slate and waved signs of support for teachers. These scenes were captured by documentary filmmakers Brian and Cindy Malone, residents of Douglas County and parents of children in the public schools, who made a video called *Education, Inc.* It portrayed the takeover of the school board by right-wing ideologues and documented the large sums of money coming into the district from out-of-state billionaires (including the Koch brothers and former New York City mayor Michael Bloomberg) to fund the school board's reelection campaign and its privatization agenda. They filmed board meetings where board members smugly ignored parents, students, and teachers who questioned them. *Education, Inc.* was shown to parent groups, and it was a powerful tool in helping to build the nascent Resistance.

Despite the growing opposition, when the votes were counted in 2013, voters in Douglas County returned control of the schools to the pro-voucher board.

Dissension was seldom absent at board meetings during the tenure of the far-right school board. Its meetings featured angry crowds, impassioned speakers, and police ousting parents and members of the media. The board reduced the time allowed to speakers from five minutes to two minutes. The two-minute limit was strictly enforced, and security in the meetings was tight.

Julie Keim, one of the candidates defeated in 2013, joined with two other DougCo residents to sue the school board and its educational foundation for violating the state's Fair Campaign Practices Act by using district funds to pay for Frederick Hess's paper, which they considered propaganda intended to sway the 2013 election. The board paid half his $35,000 fee, and its foundation paid the other half. In December 2013, a Denver judge in the Office of Administrative Courts ruled that the district had violated the Fair Campaign Practices Act. She said that "the Hess report was commissioned and published as a means to support the reform agenda and any candidates who would further that agenda."

Two years later, the Colorado Court of Appeals overturned the decision and ruled that the district did not violate the campaign law because "there was no evidence" that the report benefited "any candidate committee, issue committee, political committee, small donor committee, or political party." One of the three judges dissented and found it "undisputed that the dissemination of a report shortly before the election praising the reform agenda to 85,000 residents in Douglas County would benefit the school board's reform candidates."

As lawsuits swirled around the district, the board continued to pursue its sweeping goals. Superintendent Fagen hired Brian Cesare, a former human resources director at General Electric and Microsoft, to design a market-based pay-for-performance system for teachers. He created a system of five bands, based on the district's ease or difficulty in filling jobs. Teachers' salaries were based on the need they filled as well as their performance (mainly, their students' test scores). In the lowest band, because they were readily available in the market, were second grade teachers, third grade teachers, fourth grade teachers, fifth grade teachers, librarians, and teachers of art and drama in middle school. In the second lowest of the five bands were art teachers for elementary school, music teachers for middle and secondary schools, business teachers, deans for middle and secondary schools, drama teachers for secondary schools, and social studies teachers for seniors. Kindergarten and first grade teachers were in the third band. Foreign language teachers were in the fourth band, along with teachers of mathematics and science for the middle and secondary schools. In the highest band, because of their scarcity, were teachers of students with disabilities, like audiologists, teachers of the hearing impaired, and speech pathologists.

In addition, the district created a teacher evaluation program called CITE (Continuous Improvement of Teacher Effectiveness), which contained six components: "Outcomes, Assessment, Instruction, Culture and Climate, Professionalism, and Student Data. Each of those categories contain[ed] a number of standards with a subset of criteria—31 in all—against which teachers are evaluated." Every teacher was to be rated either "highly effective," "effective," "partially effective," or "ineffective." Teachers opposed this time-wasting, complex system. Many who left the district pointed to the paperwork and workload imposed on them by the evaluation process, which made it more difficult for them to do their jobs and take care of their own families.

Having no union to express their views, most teachers remained silent. But they hated the bands and the convoluted system that determined pay for performance. They couldn't understand the logic behind the bands, and they felt insulted. DougCo had lower salaries than the neighboring districts of Cherry Creek and Littleton did. In 2015, the average teacher's salary in DougCo was $51,274, considerably less than Cherry Creek ($67,940) and Littleton ($64,739). Even more galling than the low pay was the arbitrary way in which pay was awarded by the county's peculiar bands. A high school English teacher told a reporter from Reuters that she didn't understand why a teacher of physical education was paid less than she was. "He has more kids than I do. And he may be the one who's keeping some kids in school so they'll sit through my class. You need so many different kinds of teachers to reach all kids." A parent said, "To say that elementary teachers are of less value than middle or high school teachers—that's just unacceptable."

Meanwhile, dissident teachers and parents continued to organize against the school board's disruptive changes. One teacher-led group, Voices for Public Education, brought in speakers whose views differed from those of the school board. Parents organized a group called Douglas County Parents to prepare for the 2015 school board election.

Meanwhile, the board's voucher plan was blocked by the courts. The first case was tried in a district court in Colorado, and the judge said that the plan was unconstitutional. The board appealed, and the case went to the Colorado Supreme Court, which agreed with the lower court that the DougCo voucher plan violated the state constitution, which forbade spending public money on religious schools. The DougCo board appealed to the U.S. Supreme Court, which returned the case to the Colorado courts for reconsideration. While the legal battle continued, the voucher program was put on hold.

The legal bills for the district kept rising, eventually reaching close to $2 million, but this was not a problem, because the costs were covered by the conservative Colorado-based Daniels Foundation and the Walton Family Foundation in Arkansas.

The board approached the 2015 election with an understandable nonchalance, as it had been in the majority since 2009 and had exercised unanimous control since 2011. Besides, only three incumbents were up for reelection, so the conservative majority would still be the majority in the unlikely event that any or all incumbents were defeated. It came as a shock, therefore, when all three incumbents were decisively beaten by newcomers, each of whom won nearly 60 percent of the vote. The victorious challengers were concerned about low teacher morale, high teacher turnover, and the lack of differences of opinion on the board.

After winning three of the seven board seats in 2015, parents and teachers increased their protests against the board's policies. Teachers opposed the bizarre market-based bands that made some teachers more valuable than others. Parents were upset because so many respected teachers were leaving for other districts, not just for better salaries but to escape the chaotic and corporate-like demands of the board and its staff. When parents asked about the ongoing exodus of experienced teachers, the board and Superintendent Fagen insisted that only the "ineffective" teachers were leaving. Good riddance, they said. But parents and students knew that some of their best teachers had left the district for higher pay and better working conditions in other districts, where they were free from the oppressive atmosphere in DougCo schools.

As an affluent and high-performing district, DougCo had long been a place that teachers flocked to, despite its low salaries. But after the Disruption-minded board took office, the teacher turnover rate spiked. When that board was first elected in 2009, the teacher turnover rate (those who resigned or retired) was 10.2 percent. By the 2014–15 year, it was 16.7 percent. Of the 3,361 teachers in the district that year, 561 left their jobs. The teacher turnover rate in Douglas County was slightly less than the statewide average of 17.3 percent, but nearly double that of nearby, similar districts like Cherry Creek and Littleton, where turnover was less than 10 percent. When teachers were interviewed, they complained not about low and stagnant wages, but about the market-based pay bands and the new and time-consuming teacher evaluation methods.

When the state administered its annual anonymous survey of educators called TELL (Colorado's Teaching, Empowering, Learning and Leading survey), the report stated that "71 percent of Douglas County teachers said they don't believe that CITE accurately measure[d] their

effectiveness—a response considerably higher than the state average of
55 percent." One teacher left Douglas County after twenty-one years
to take a job in the neighboring Cherry Creek district. She said, "The
amount of stress that I had and the low morale of teachers throughout
the district affected my decision. Although I was rated highly effective,
it was because I worked countless hours beyond my time at school to
jump through hoops and prove my value as an educator." A twenty-year
veteran teacher of foreign language departed to teach in Cherry Creek
because "I'm against the way that they are trying to run schools like a
corporation. It created a really bad work environment. I didn't feel like I
could be myself as a teacher, as a mentor or as a person. I didn't feel valued." A parent of two third graders told the interviewer that the district
was trying to run the schools like a business and that it was "moving in
the direction of central control of teaching at all levels and commoditiza-
tion of the teaching profession. The pay-for-performance fad needs to be
understood against the background of a very wealthy county that simply
doesn't want to pay for anything."

Emboldened by the results of the 2015 election and concerned about
the ongoing teacher exodus, the Resistance unexpectedly gained new
allies on March 9, 2016, when students at Ponderosa High School held a
rally during school hours to protest teacher turnover. The organizer of the
student protest was a fifteen-year-old student named Grace Davis. Grace
was upset because many of her favorite teachers were leaving, including
fifteen in the previous year alone. Ponderosa High had a teacher turnover
rate of 21 percent, higher than the rest of the district or the state.

Five days before the planned protest, two school board members—the
president, Meghann Silverthorn, and vice president, Judith Reynolds—
called Grace Davis to meet with them. She said they asked to meet off-
campus, but she said she was fifteen, didn't have a driver's license, and
didn't want to ask her parents to leave work to take her to meet with
school board members. Grace thought that they wanted to speak with
her for a few minutes. The board members came to the school and sat
down with her for ninety minutes, without her parents' knowledge or
permission. She missed her Spanish class while they harangued her about
why she was protesting, why she thought that teachers were evaluated

unfairly, what ideas she had for evaluating teachers, why the protest was wrong, why she and her parents would have financial liability if anything went wrong at the protest, how dangerous it was to stage a protest because someone might get hurt, and why her understanding of the First Amendment was deficient. Unbeknownst to the adults, Davis taped the meeting. Davis knew it was legal to do so in Colorado because she had studied criminal justice a year earlier. After the meeting, she said that she was shaking the whole time. She claimed that the board members had bullied her, trying to get her to call off the protest. She released the tape to the media. The board president later said on a local radio show that she believed Davis was manipulated by the teachers' union, which the union denied.

About a hundred students joined Davis in a protest on the soccer field of Ponderosa High. They skipped classes and held signs that motorists could see, protesting the high number of teacher resignations. One sign said, "We (Heart) Teachers." Another said, "My Education is *not* your Business Opportunity." Others read, "Why Are Teachers Leaving?" and "Where Are Our Teachers?"

When the school board held its regular meeting on April 19, Grace Davis spoke up and called for the resignation of the two board members who had interviewed her, accusing them of trying to intimidate her. The minority of three members supported Grace; the majority of four promised an investigation. The board hired a lawyer to investigate the board members' actions. When the investigation was concluded two months later, the lawyer determined that no board policy had been violated because there was no board policy that forbade Silverthorn and Reynolds from meeting with a student without her parents' permission and making covert threats intended to block a planned protest. The investigation cost nearly $180,000.

Superintendent Elizabeth Fagen announced a month later that she was leaving DougCo to become superintendent in Humble, Texas, a district much smaller than DougCo, where her salary was increased to $298,000. Parents in Humble read about what had happened in DougCo, and more than 1,300 signed a petition opposing her selection. However, she was the Humble board's unanimous selection, and she moved there.

After Fagen left DougCo, she was soon followed by other top administrators, including Brian Cesare, the chief human resources officer who designed the market-based pay system.

Then came the 2017 school board race. Before the election, the board was split 4–3, with pro-voucher members in control. Four seats were up for grabs. Locals called it "the most important school board election in the country," held in the fifth wealthiest county in the nation and one of the highest-achieving districts in the state. The incumbents and those allied with them called themselves the "Elevate Slate." The opposition, backed by parent and community groups, called their anti-voucher slate the "Dream Team." An article in *The Colorado Independent* described the role of outside money in the campaign, with most of it given to the Elevate Slate by wealthy conservatives. It also identified a shadowy conservative group called the Leadership Program of the Rockies (LPR) that had trained three of the pro-voucher DougCo incumbents as well as the interim superintendent who succeeded Fagen. LPR "is valued among conservatives for teaching free market principles, but its greatest value may be in connecting its graduates to a statewide network of alumni and in at least several cases, wealthy board members." Run by former Republican congressman Bob Schaffer, LPR opened the door to campaign funds from voucher supporters such as Dick and Betsy DeVos of Michigan.

The election was held on November 7, 2017. The anti-voucher Dream Team swept all four seats, winning nearly 60 percent of the vote. That meant that the entire board, the four new members and the three incumbents, was opposed to vouchers. At its first meeting on December 4, 2017, the new board voted to abandon the district's appeal to the courts on behalf of vouchers. The victorious candidates said that the fight over vouchers was a "distraction" and that they wanted to restore calm to the district after eight years of constant turmoil and controversy.

In January 2018, the Colorado Supreme Court dismissed the case of *Taxpayers for Public Education v. The Douglas County School District* "as moot at the request of both parties." Cindy Barnard, president of Taxpayers for Public Education, said, "We are very pleased with the court's decision and that the misuse of public school funds to pay for private education in Douglas County is over. The dismissal of the appeal, together with the election of a new anti-voucher slate of school board members in the Douglas County School District, ensures that the district's focus will now turn to using public dollars to strengthen public schools."

In mid-2018, the board hired a new superintendent, Thomas Tucker, whose previous experience was in Ohio and Kansas. Tucker, the son of Arkansas sharecroppers, had a reputation as a conciliator and a bridge builder. His first order of business was to persuade taxpayers to approve a $250 million bond issue to upgrade buildings and security, as well as a $40 million tax levy to pay for higher teachers' salaries and more school counselors.

Tucker got his wish, as did the parent Resistance of Douglas County. In November 2018, voters passed the first tax increase for the schools in twelve years. The district said it would use $40 million to increase teacher pay and hire more counselors and dedicate the $250 million bond measure to pay for building repairs and transportation. Public confidence in the public schools of Douglas County was restored.

No one can predict what the future will hold for Douglas County and whether the scars and wounds of the Disruption era will heal or will lead to a renewal of hostilities. But the struggle in Douglas County demonstrates that divisiveness is a dead end. There should not be winners and losers. Schools should not be a battlefield for contesting ideologies. Comity matters. All parents, educators, and citizens should work together amicably for the good of the students.

CHAPTER II

The Resistance Goes National

M any millions of people have a stake in the public schools, as students, graduates, parents and grandparents, as educators and retired educators. When they learn about the efforts by billionaires to turn their public schools over to private management, they are not at all pleased. In public polls, parents say that they like their public schools and that they like their children's teachers. They don't want their local schools to be taken over by corporations with boards that may be located in other cities or states. When asked to vote, they overwhelmingly oppose sending public money to religious schools and they do not like the idea of outsourcing their community schools to corporations. That is why the privatizers prefer to operate by stealth, employing deceptive names for their organizations (such as "Families for Excellent Schools" or "StudentsFirst") or buying votes in the legislature or Congress, where their campaign contributions get them what they want.

As more people understand the nature of the privatization movement, as they learn that it is funded by billionaires and financiers, as they grasp its opposition to accountability and transparency, as they see that it draws money away from their local public schools, the Resistance grows larger and stronger.

It was a major victory for the Resistance when the nation's most venerable civil rights organization made clear that school choice is *not* "the civil rights issue of our time."

In July 2016, the national convention of the NAACP unanimously passed a resolution calling for a moratorium on charter school expansion until charters accepted accountability and transparency in their operations, until they stopped shedding students they didn't want, and until they stopped diverting funding from public schools. In October 2016, the national board of directors of the NAACP appointed a twelve-member Charter School Task Force—renamed the Task Force on Quality Education—to hold hearings across the country. Its charge was to make recommendations about the steps needed to improve the quality of education for children of color in inner city schools and "to ensure the sustainability of an effective public education system for all children." The Task Force held hearings in New Haven, Memphis, Orlando, Los Angeles, Detroit, New Orleans, and New York City.

The Task Force found that charter schools had been "created with more flexibility because they were expected to innovate and infuse new ideas and creativity into the traditional public school system." Unfortunately, they said, this promise had "never materialized." The Task Force recognized that "many traditional inner city public schools are failing the children who attend them, thus causing parents with limited resources to search for a funded, quality educational alternative for their children." The Task Force worried that as charter schools grew in number and became increasingly concentrated in low-income communities, issues emerged with the "quality, accessibility, and accountability" of charters, as well as "their broader effects on the funding and management of school districts that serve most students of color." Presenters in Detroit and New York City warned that having "too many charter schools in some communities, while neighborhood schools are shut down, contributes to a chaotic educational system for many families of color living in low-income neighborhoods."

What the Task Force wanted was high-quality schools for all children. The Task Force acknowledged that "while high-quality, accessible, and accountable charters can contribute to educational opportunity, by themselves, even the best charters are not a substitute for more stable, adequate and equitable investments in public education in the communities that serve our children. Multiple parents and community members described the need for the state or district to govern all schools—traditional and charter—so that there's one system of democratically-accountable, high-quality schools."

At the NAACP hearings, parents complained about charters that excluded their children or "cherry-picked" those they wanted. The testimony from parents was powerful. Irene Robinson, a parent in Memphis, made this impassioned statement:

> We are here to say that we have been impacted by school closings and the birth of charter schools and school privatization. . . . Our choices have been taken from us. And, as parents, we don't have any choices. The public officials and the board took it from us. In fact, doing that, who will be hurt the worst? Our children. Every child deserves a world-class education. As you closed fifty schools, you opened up fifty charter schools, meaning where is the money coming from? It's coming from our neighborhood schools. [Charters] have pushed children out, which has destroyed our community, destroyed the history of our schools. Our schools are the heart of our community and the root of our history.

Caroline Watkins, a parent in New York City, complained about the explosion of charters in her Harlem neighborhood. She said:

> We have thirteen elementary schools in less than a quarter mile radius from where I sit in my apartment. That is a tiny little section of Harlem, if you compare it to the Upper West Side, where there might be one or two schools, there are thirteen schools accepting kids in kindergarten. That is not choice. That's consumer vertigo. We do not have choice when parents don't have the opportunity, the resources, the time, and the support to analyze test scores and marketing materials and go on tours and talk to principals and talk to other parents. Parents who live in Harlem are faced with complete lack of opportunity to explore those choices.

After its hearings, the Task Force called for equitable and adequate funding for all schools, providing early childhood education, requiring charter schools to admit and retain all who apply, modifying the harsh disciplinary practices of "no-excuses" charter schools, and blocking the practice of not allowing new students to enroll after certain grades (such as barring new enrollments after grade four). "Charter schools," the Task Force held, "should be required to follow the same state regulations regarding discipline as public schools." Furthermore, charter schools should be required to hire certified teachers, and for-profit charter schools and for-profit management corporations should be completely eliminated.

The ACLU, the nation's leading civil liberties organization, was not fooled by the rhetoric of the privatization movement. It documented charter school abuses and filed multiple complaints about charter schools that excluded students with disabilities, promoted racial segregation, and punished children because of their dress or their hair.

In mid-2016, the ACLU of Southern California released a blistering report titled "Unequal Access: How Some California Charter Schools Illegally Restrict Enrollment." It accused some charter schools of excluding certain groups of students, even though state law required charters to admit all who apply, subject only to space limitations. The same law prohibited charters from discouraging the admission of students based on their income, national origin, language proficiency, academic performance, or other factors. The ACLU found that more than 20 percent of the state's charter schools openly discriminated against certain classes of students and acknowledged their illegal restrictions on their websites. Some refused admission to students unless they had strong grades and test scores, while others pushed out students who did not have strong grades and test scores. Some required essays or interviews with the intention of discouraging applicants. Some charters accepted students only if their parents agreed to volunteer their time or pay fees, which was illegal. The charters it identified, the report said, were only "the tip of the iceberg" because those were the ones that advertised their discriminatory practices on their websites. The ACLU warned that these exclusionary policies "threaten to turn public schooling into a two-tier system where the students who need the most resources receive the fewest."

In 2015, the Delaware ACLU filed a complaint with the U.S. Office of Education's Office for Civil Rights stating that charter school admission policies in that state were causing the resegregation of public schools, "erasing decades of progress." The state's first charter school, called the Charter School of Wilmington, was backed by the Wilmington business community. It was predominantly white and had "an exclusive entrance process," which enabled it to boast of its high test scores. The same cherry-picking approach was utilized by Sussex Academy, which was 81 percent white and 2.9 percent African American in a district that was 53 percent white and 14 percent African American. Kathleen MacRae, executive director of ACLU Delaware, said,

> When high-performing charter schools (or vo-tech and magnet schools) admit a disproportionate number of higher-income white students with no disabilities, the local community public schools are left with the difficult and costly task of educating the students most challenged by poverty or special education needs. This system just about ensures that schools in poor urban and poor rural areas will fail, and our children will suffer. The whole State of Delaware is worse off as a result. . . . Of course schools will succeed if they require high test scores, parent essays and completion of advanced gifted and talented programs at the elementary and middle school levels and enroll children whose families can pay for uniforms.

In 2017, the Arizona ACLU released a report titled "Schools Choosing Students" stating that many charter schools in that state had discriminatory and illegal admissions policies that excluded students with disabilities, English learners, and others that the charters did not want. By law, charters in Arizona are supposed to accept all who apply, subject only to space limitations. Of the 471 charter schools in the state that the ACLU was able to investigate, most of them actively violated state law and discriminated against certain groups of students. Some barred students with prior suspensions on their record; some limited the admission of students with disabilities; some required an interview or an essay. Some refused to provide their enrollment criteria to the ACLU. "'School choice' means that families should be choosing schools, not the other way around," said Alessandra Soler, executive director of the ACLU of Arizona. "But Arizona's charter schools, and the state agencies they're accountable to, have ignored deeply troubling and sometimes illegal enrollment policies that deny low-income students, English learners, students with disabilities, and other vulnerable student populations, opportunities to attend the schools of their choice."

Many charter schools make racial and ethnic segregation part of their identity and are run by people who believe that this is all right. In Minneapolis, for example, John Hechinger of Bloomberg News discovered charter schools intentionally organized for African American students, for Somali students, for Native American students, for Hmong students, and for white students. The white school is a "German immersion" school. The Dugsi Academy educates "East African children," all of whom are black, and in this school, girls wear "traditional Muslim headscarves and flowing ankle-length skirts" and study Somali and Arabic. Three quarters of the charter schools in the Twin Cities, Hechinger found, were "highly segregated," even though the state is 85 percent white. In Minneapolis, he wrote, it felt as though the U.S. Supreme Court's *Brown v. the Board of Education of Topeka* decision of 1954 had never happened.

The Civil Rights Project at UCLA found that the charter school sector "is even more segregated than the public schools" are. For many states, especially in the South, but not only in the South, charters found ways to skirt antidiscrimination laws and establish publicly funded schools that were almost all-white or all-black. A 2018 report by the Civil Rights Project asserted that charter schools were "drivers" of the resegregation of public schools in Charlotte, North Carolina; it found that "while national discourse presents charter schools as an alternative to underperforming schools of poverty, in the Charlotte region, the majority of charter schools are located in suburban areas and serve primarily academically proficient, middle-class students who are largely white or Asian." The departure of academically proficient white and Asian students to charter schools increased racial isolation of black students and segregation in the public schools. In 2019, a private school in Halifax County, North Carolina, which had been created in 1969 as a "white flight academy," won the approval of the State Board of Education to become a charter school, thus relieving its parents of the need to pay annual tuition of $5,000. The school, Hobgood Academy, is 87 percent white in a county where the local public schools are 4 percent white.

A California-based nonpartisan organization called In the Public

Interest (ITPI) monitors the privatization of public goods and services. It has tracked the growth of the charter school movement, which ITPI considers an insidious form of privatization that undermines the viability of public education. In 2018, ITPI published a report titled "Breaking Point: The Cost of Charter Schools for Public School Districts," written by Gordon Lafer of the University of Oregon.

In "Breaking Point," Lafer assessed the "stranded costs" of charter schools to three public school districts in California. In the 2016–17 year, charter schools cost the Oakland Unified School District $57.3 million, the San Diego Unified School District $65.9 million, and Santa Clara's East Side Union High School District $19.3 million. He wrote, "When a student leaves a neighborhood school for a charter school, all the funding for that student leaves with him or her, while all the costs do not. This intensifies fiscal pressure to cut core services like counseling, libraries, and special education, and increases class sizes at neighborhood schools." The schools have fixed costs that cannot be reduced when a portion of students leaves, such as the cost of maintenance, heating and cooling, repairs, and transportation. These are "stranded costs." The arrival of charter schools compels the neighborhood public school to lay off teachers; curtail classes in music and art; cut custodial, clerical, library, nursing, and IT staff; and make other economies that reduce the attractiveness of the public school to parents and students. Lafer writes,

> While charter schools are required by law [in some places] to accept any student who applies, in reality they exercise recruitment, admission, and expulsion policies that often screen out the students who would be the neediest and most expensive to serve—who then turn to district schools. As a result, traditional public schools end up with the highest-need students but without the resources to serve them.

The fiscal pressure on public schools can send them into a death spiral, creating more customers for charter schools.

California's charter law, Lafer wrote, is unusually permissive. A charter may open without the consent of the district where it is sited and with no consideration of the fiscal impact on the host district. Lafer concluded that the charter movement was helping to create a dual school system, at a price paid by the public schools whose doors are open to all. It makes no sense to provide "choice" for a small minority of students while harming the quality of education available to the vast majority.

Two of the nation's most respected civil rights organizations—the Education Law Center (ELC) and the Southern Poverty Law Center—became engaged in efforts to stop the privatization of public funds and to curb testing abuses. In 2012, the ELC called for regulation and oversight of charter schools, saying that they should welcome all students, rather than choosing the ones they wanted; that they should be free of conflict of interest and should not enrich any individuals, organizations, or businesses, and that they should be authorized and monitored by local school districts and elected school boards. ELC successfully blocked the use of PARCC tests as a graduation requirement in New Jersey. In 2016, it won a parent-initiated lawsuit in Nevada to block public funding for "education savings accounts," or vouchers.

In 2016, the Southern Poverty Law Center filed a lawsuit on behalf of parents and taxpayers against the state of Mississippi for passing legislation that diverted funding from taxes raised by local school districts and assigning them to charter schools. SPLC contended that the Mississippi Charter Schools Act violated the state constitution, which clearly states that schools must be under the supervision of the state and local boards of education to be eligible for public funding. Under the new legislation, charter schools are exempt from oversight by the state board of education, local school boards, and the Mississippi Department of Education. In a strained interpretation of the law, the Mississippi Supreme Court ruled against the plaintiffs. However, Presiding Justice Leslie D. King dissented, asserting that the funding mechanism for charter schools clearly violates the state constitution. He said, "This Court should not be a rubberstamp for Legislative policies it agrees with when those policies are unconstitutional. . . . The sole issue before this Court is whether the Legislature has the authority to require local school districts to fund charter schools using their ad valorem tax receipts." Do "charter schools belong to the district? No, he concluded, they do not. A school district clearly does not possess, control, or own charter schools. Charter schools are unaccountable to the district in which they are geographically located." By the definition of a charter school in the Charter Schools Act, they do not belong to the district in which they are located. Nevertheless, the majority upheld the right of privately managed charters to take tax monies from local school districts.

Despite the setback in Mississippi, the Southern Poverty Legal Center remains opposed to any efforts to advance privatization to the detriment and cost of public schools.

What matters is that in the battles to come, the NAACP, the ACLU, the ELC, and the SPLC—all highly respected national organizations— have joined the fight to preserve democratically controlled public education.

CHAPTER 12

Dark Money in Massachusetts
and Connecticut

Disrupters decided that Massachusetts was ripe for charter expansion. They already had strongholds in Republican-dominated states. They set their sights on the bluest of the blue states. Two other blue states were charter-friendly because of their governors: Andrew Cuomo in New York, who relied on hedge funders for his campaign treasury; and Jerry Brown in California, who had opened two charter schools when he was mayor of Oakland. Massachusetts would be a big prize for the Disruption Movement.

Beginning in 2012, the Disrupters began planning a three-part strategy: first, convince the legislature to lift the cap on charter schools; if that failed, put a referendum on the ballot, which they felt certain would pass because of their vast resources; and, at the same time, file a lawsuit in state courts claiming that the state's cap on charter schools was unconstitutional.

When the legislature failed to act, charter advocates immediately sought to place a referendum on the ballot to lift the state's cap (or limit) on charter schools. The state already had seventy-eight charter schools and openings for nearly thirty more. But the Disrupters wanted more; they wanted to remove the cap altogether. The charter lobby assumed that charter schools were so popular that the public would vote to increase the number of new charter schools. They pitched their campaign as a civil rights issue, a plea to open more charters that would "save" poor children of color from "failing public schools."

No other state had held a referendum on charter schools. Why Massachusetts? It was a strange choice for an epic battle over charter schools because Massachusetts is usually the highest-performing state school system in the nation, as measured by scores on the National Assessment of Educational Progress (NAEP). Every city and town except Boston has an elected school board, the symbol of grassroots democracy; Boston's public schools are governed by a board appointed by the mayor. There was no widespread demand to disrupt this successful state system. But the state had a Republican governor, Charlie Baker, who had appointed a choice-friendly state board of education, and charter advocates were eager to increase the percentage of students in charter schools, which was only 4 percent.

The referendum to expand the number of charters was called Question 2, and it was placed on the ballot for the election in November 2016, coinciding with the presidential election. The ballot measure proposed to increase the number of charters by twelve a year indefinitely, to be located in any district in the state.

Ultimately, Question 2 became a pitched battle between two narratives: opponents said that charter schools would harm public schools by draining away money and forcing budget cuts; proponents argued that charter schools would help disadvantaged children.

Governor Baker campaigned for Question 2. It was endorsed by the pro-charter Democrats for Education Reform (hedge fund managers based mainly in New York), the Massachusetts Taxpayers Foundation, the Massachusetts Charter School Association, and the Alliance for Business Leadership. U.S. secretary of education Arne Duncan supported Yes on 2. The campaign for Yes on 2 was coordinated by an organization called Great Schools Massachusetts. The major funding agency for Yes on 2 was the New York City–based Families for Excellent Schools-Advocacy (FESA), which bundled money from outside donors and tried to conceal the names of those donors. Yes on 2 was endorsed by *The Boston Globe*, the major newspaper in the state.

No on 2 was led by a group called Save Our Public Schools, a coalition composed of teachers' unions, labor unions, almost every elected school committee in the state, progressive groups, many city councils across the state, the Democratic Party state committee, Martin Walsh (mayor of Boston), author Jonathan Kozol, Maura Healey (the state attorney general), the state NAACP, Black Lives Matter, Senator Elizabeth Warren, and Senator Bernie Sanders of Vermont.

In the spring of 2016, polls commissioned by charter advocates showed overwhelming support for Yes on 2. It led in some polls by as much as 30 points, even 50 points. However, when the election was held on November 8, 2016, Question 2 was defeated by a vote of 62 percent to 38 percent.

The outcome was a devastating defeat for the charter lobby.

The amount of money spent on Question 2 was more than had ever been spent on any referendum in the state's history: $40 million. Supporters of Yes on 2 spent $25 million. Supporters of No on 2 spent $15 million.

A small number of wealthy individuals contributed most of the money for Yes on 2, most of it bundled by Families for Excellent Schools-Advocacy (FESA). "Families for Excellent Schools" had a name suggesting that it represented ordinary folks, perhaps poor families of color, but in fact it was comprised of billionaires, hedge fund managers, and tycoons. (In 2014, FESA had spent $9.4 million successfully lobbying against New York City mayor Bill de Blasio's efforts to limit the expansion of charter schools and encouraging Governor Andrew Cuomo to pass laws favoring charter schools.)

Among the biggest donors to the Yes on 2 campaign were Seth Klarman, a billionaire hedge fund manager in Boston ($3.3 million); Amos B. Hostetter Jr., a cable television magnate from Boston ($2 million); Jim Walton of the Arkansas Walmart family ($1.125 million); and his sister, Alice Walton, the richest woman in the world ($750,000); Paul Sagan, managing partner of a venture capital firm called General Catalyst and chair of the state Board of Elementary and Secondary Education ($496,000); Mark Nunnelly, a former Bain Capital executive and a member of Governor Baker's cabinet ($275,000), matched by his wife; the Fisher family of California ($500,000); Jonathan Sackler of Connecticut ($70,000); former mayor Michael Bloomberg of New York City ($490,000). Another ballot committee called Expanding Educational Opportunities raised nearly $600,000 from seven businesses in the state. Nearly $800,000 came from financial executives managing pension funds, including those of the public school teachers they were fighting.

The money for No on 2 came mostly from the dues of teachers who belonged to the Massachusetts Teachers Association, the American Federation of Teachers, and the National Education Association. The biggest single contributor to No on 2 was the Massachusetts Teachers Association, an organization of 110,000 teachers, whose annual convention voted to spend $9.2 million to fight the expansion of charter schools. There was no Dark Money in the No on 2 campaign. The financial reports filed by Save Our Public Schools showed a long list of small donations, mostly from individuals, many as small as $5 or $10 (there was even one for $1). The largest donations by out-of-state individuals were $50 (there were two of them, one from Pennsylvania and another from California).

After the campaign, the Massachusetts Office of Campaign and Political Finance (OCPF) punished FESA for failing to disclose the names of its donors before the election. The OCPF required FESA to pay a fine of $426,000 (emptying its bank account) and barred it from operating in Massachusetts for the next four years. This was the largest fine for a campaign finance violation in the state's history. But matters worsened for "Families for Excellent Schools" in early 2018. Jeremiah Kittredge, the chief executive officer of FES, was fired after an investigation "into allegations of 'inappropriate behavior toward a non-employee.'" The incident occurred at an annual "reformer" conference in Washington, D.C., hosted by Education Reform Now, the policy affiliate of Democrats for Education Reform. Within days, the organization closed its doors and was no more.

How did the No on 2 forces prevail?

First, their message was clear: charter schools take money away from public schools. That message resonated more credibly than did the billionaires' claim that the expansion of charters was a "social justice" issue. Most voters realized that the funding for new charter schools would be subtracted from their own public schools. They were not willing to see their local public schools lose teachers, electives, the arts, libraries, nurses, and other staff and programs so that a few more students could attend privately managed charter schools.

Second, the opponents of charter schools had a better ground game than the charter advocates did. While the charter groups spent millions on what seemed to be an unending deluge of television ads, public school supporters not only paid for television commercials but also enlisted thousands of volunteers, many of whom were teachers and parents, to knock on doors, operate phone banks, and organize house parties for their neighbors.

Third, the billionaire-funded campaign had a credibility problem in persuading voters of their sincere commitment to social justice. The No on 2 campaign benefited by reminding the public that Yes on 2 was funded by billionaires.

Fourth, endorsements by elected officials and civil rights and social justice groups undercut the huge resources of the Yes on 2 campaign. The Massachusetts State Democratic Committee overwhelmingly passed a resolution stating that "Massachusetts Democrats are committed to investing in public education" and that the $400 million in taxpayer money already diverted to charter schools had forced budget cuts to public schools while funding charter schools that enrolled fewer English language learners and fewer students with disabilities than public schools and used "hyper-disciplinary policies and suspensions for minor infractions to push out students."

The much admired author Jonathan Kozol wrote an article in *The Boston Globe* urging a no vote on Question 2, in which he said,

> Slice it any way you want. Argue, as we must, that every family ought to have the right to make whatever choice they like in the interests of their child, no matter what damage it may do to other people's children. As an individual decision, it's absolutely human; but setting up this kind of competition, in which parents with the greatest social capital are encouraged to abandon their most vulnerable neighbors, is rotten social policy. What this represents is a state-supported shriveling of civic virtue, a narrowing of moral obligation to the smallest possible parameters. It isn't good for Massachusetts, and it's not good for democracy.
>
> This commonwealth has been an exemplar of democratic public education ever since the incubation of the common school idea at the

midpoint of the 19th century. For all its imperfections and constant need of diligent repair, it remains a vision worth preserving. The privatizing forces from outside of this state have wisely recognized the symbolic victory they'd gain by turning Massachusetts against its own historic legacy. I urge my friends not to let this happen. Vote "no" on Question 2.

Boston mayor Martin Walsh, usually a supporter of charter schools, opposed Question 2 because "it would radically destabilize school governance in Massachusetts . . . by super-sizing an already broken funding system to a scale that would have a disastrous impact on students, their schools, and the cities and towns that fund them." The fiscal impact, he warned, would have a devastating impact on the city's budget. He wrote, "Our charter school assessment is 5 percent of the city's entire budget. Under the ballot proposal, it would grow to almost 20 percent in just over a decade. It's a looming death spiral for our district budget, aimed squarely at the most vulnerable children in our city. It's not just unsustainable. It's unconscionable."

Almost every local school committee in the state passed a resolution opposing the charter referendum. The few boards that voted yes were in affluent suburban districts that never expected to have a charter school in their town. In Boston, Worcester, Springfield, Cambridge, Newton, Quincy, Somerville, Lowell, Brockton, and Plymouth, the nays had it by large margins.

The biggest votes against Yes on 2 came from districts that already had charter schools. They had already absorbed budget cuts, due to the introduction of charters, and did not want to cut more.

Worcester was the first school committee in the state to vote against Question 2. The small city already had two charter schools, which were taking $24.5 million out of the public schools' budget. The district schools had already cut staff to make up for a budget deficit. Molly O. McCullough, a member of the Worcester School Committee, said that losing more money to additional charters "would be devastating."

The Yes on 2 cause was damaged when Moody's Investors Service released a warning on the eve of the election that if the referendum passed and the number of charter schools was expanded, this might have

Barbara Madeloni was president of the Massachusetts Teachers Association in 2016 at the time of a historic referendum on whether to lift the state cap on charter schools. Madeloni successfully organized teachers, parents, and school boards in opposition to the referendum.

a negative impact on the credit ratings of Boston, Lawrence, Fall River, and Springfield.

The leader of the fight against Question 2 was Barbara Madeloni, the president of the Massachusetts Teachers Association. Madeloni won the presidency of the union in 2014 in an unconventional manner. It was customary in the MTA for the vice president to succeed the president. There were contests for vice president, but never for president. Madeloni upended this tradition. She ran as an insurgent, beating the heir apparent, although she had never held any office in the union. She was, as an admirer wrote, "a pure rank and file candidate."

Madeloni earned a doctorate in psychology, practiced psychotherapy for fifteen years, then earned a master's degree in education at the University of Massachusetts in Amherst. She taught high school English in the Bay State, then became a professor of secondary education and director of the program to prepare high school teachers at the University of Massachusetts. After nine years leading the program, she set off a national controversy in 2012 when she refused to administer a new test designed by Pearson to evaluate and certify new teachers, called the edTPA (Teacher Performance Assessment). Michael Winerip of *The New York Times* wrote about her act of defiance. He said that it was customary for university professors and teachers to decide whether to grant a license to new teachers after six months of classroom teaching. The Pearson test "would decide licensure based on two 10-minute videos that student teachers submit, as well as their score on a 40-page take-home test." Madeloni and sixty-seven of her sixty-eight students boycotted the test. She told Winerip, "This is something complex, and we don't like seeing it taken out of human hands." She said, "We are putting a stick in the gears." For her defiance, the university fired her.

In 2014, two years later, Madeloni was elected president of the MTA, the state's largest union. She ran on a pledge to fight "the corporate assault on public education." After winning the MTA presidency, Madeloni immediately engaged in a series of confrontations with the Massachusetts Department of Elementary and Secondary Education. She killed a state plan to test and videotape kindergarten students. She blocked a proposal to tie teacher performance to standardized tests, one that would have stripped teachers with low ratings of their license to teach anywhere in the state. The state wanted to negotiate and offered three alternatives; the MTA's response was "none of the above." The state backed off. When the state informed the MTA that it planned to increase the number of charter schools, the MTA board directed Madeloni to negotiate with legislators and charter forces. She told legislators, "We are glad to talk, but we will not accept *any* deal that involves *any* new charter schools. Now, what do you want to talk about?"

The pro-charter forces were not afraid of Madeloni and the MTA. They were certain that charters were immensely popular because the relatively few charters in the state had higher test scores than did the nearby public schools. They thought that the union would make a deal rather than take their chances with a referendum. They felt sure that they would win a referendum, based on early polling, with the help of the governor and massive spending.

The Disrupters were wrong. Yes on 2 suffered a humiliating defeat. It was beaten by the Resistance by 62 percent to 38 percent.

The Walton Family Foundation commissioned a study to understand what went wrong. The study, prepared by an organization called Global Strategy Group, was supposed to be top secret, but it was leaked to the media. The funders for charters began planning an initiative to increase the cap in 2012, the report said. These funders expected the legislature to lift the cap in 2014 but were stymied in the state senate. They then asked Families for Excellent Schools, which had been successful in New York, "to develop a legislative strategy." The election of Governor Baker in 2014 raised their spirits, but when the legislature failed to increase the number of charters, they turned to the ballot. Then they made a crucial error. Previous proposals limited new charters to those districts with test scores in the bottom 25 percent of the state; the Yes on 2 ballot initiative called for up to twelve new charter schools a year that could open *anywhere* in the state for chapter expansions. Charter advocates thought that this language would scare legislators into compromising to protect their own districts. But, given the intransigence of the union, there was no compromise, and the charter advocates' gamble "handed the opposition their winning message" (that charters could open anywhere and take money from anyone's local public schools). Despite the early polling data that predicted an easy victory for charters, the only majority support on election day came from registered Republicans. The partisan divide was sharp. Only 27 percent of Democrats supported Question 2.

The Yes on 2 campaign assumed that Governor Baker would persuade voters, but he turned out to be irrelevant. The Waltons' secret analysis said that voters "turned to, and trusted, the opposition's primary messengers: teachers. . . . Teachers appeared all over the state to voice their opposition: in classrooms, in commercials, in newspapers, and in their communities." Their voices ultimately convinced voters that Question 2 "would have a detrimental impact on the traditional public school system."

The report blamed the "unprecedented" opposition by the union for the defeat of Question 2 and heaped criticism on Barbara Madeloni, calling her "ideological" and "uncompromising." The report "assailed Madeloni "as a rabble rousing, outsider, activist, leftist . . . She's Occupy Wall Street and into claiming that education reform is all about corporatization." Madeloni was responsible for "mobiliz[ing] a grassroots campaign of teachers by attacking charter schools as corporate interests." Furthermore, the unions "capitalized on the Yes campaign's out-of-state and corporate funding as a rallying cry for their active base of teachers. Funders, including the Waltons, were specifically called out for their donations on 2."

There was some irony in the fact that Madeloni's rallying cry was accurate. The funding for Yes on 2 was indeed reliant on out-of-state and corporate contributions.

The consultants were surprised by the "massive war chest" assembled by the teachers, which funded "the vast mobilization of classroom teachers, the early TV spending, the digital ads, the t-shirts and bumper stickers." It just wasn't fair that the No on 2 forces had raised so much money. The Yes on 2 advocates had spent $10 million more than the teachers and had expected to overpower the Resistance with their massive resources. But their large pocketbook was not enough to win the hearts and minds of the voters.

Another disadvantage for the Yes on 2 proposition was that it was seen as a Republican initiative. The Walton report singled out a tweet by Barbara Madeloni saying: "Real Democrats support public education and say #NoOn2." The consultants found this highly offensive. Unlike the Waltons and their allies, Madeloni just didn't play fair.

The consultants made several recommendations for future battles. They urged that charter teachers be fully mobilized for the next contest, so they could counter the union's ground game. (Strange to think that the teachers of 4 percent of the students in the state might effectively counter the teachers of the overwhelming majority of students.) They proposed that the charter groups "test owning the progressive mantle on education reform and charters: this is about social justice, civil rights, and giving kids a chance." They didn't understand why voters might not trust a social justice message framed by billionaires like the Waltons, who pay low wages to nonunion workers. In light of the beating that charter schools took in the election, the consultants urged rebuilding "the charter brand." They urged funders to "develop a base of support to rival the union's base of teachers." Perhaps parents might serve that purpose. Otherwise, the consultants advised, keep looking for "a trusted voice," though they were stumped about where to find that trusted voice to counter that of the teachers. Appeal to Democrats so that charter schools do not get identified with Trump and DeVos. Cultivate legislative leaders or elect new ones "sympathetic to our goals."

Inadvertently, the study by the Global Strategy Group provides an excellent road map to defeating referendums in other states. It demonstrates that people power, if well organized and amply funded, can defeat money power, especially when the money power has no connection to the lives of the people it seeks to control. It suggests that the most effective strategy to defeat privatization is to take the issue to the voters, even though the billionaires can deploy superior resources to peddle their alleged concern for equity and social justice. If they are called out and identified, they lose.

But who would call out and identify the privatizers and billionaires?

Maurice Cunningham, that's who. He was an unsung hero in this epic conflict. Cunningham, a professor of political science at the University of Massachusetts at Boston, blogged at the website of Boston Public Radio station WGBH. He was relentless in investigating the money behind the Yes on 2 campaign. He focused on one issue: Follow the money. The No on 2 alliance was easy. It came from teachers, their unions, and small individual contributions.

The Yes on 2 funding, however, was mysterious and opaque. Cunningham shone a bright light on that funding. He was fascinated with Dark Money, and he often reminded readers that "money never sleeps." He referred to the Corporate Disrupters as the Financial Privatization Cabal.

Maurice Cunningham is a political science professor at the University of Massachusetts at Boston whose influential blog about money and politics awakened the public to the role of Dark Money during the charter referendum of 2016.

Cunningham noted that the No on 2 campaign was kicked off at a public rally featuring Governor Baker surrounded by children and parents, all wearing matching bright blue T-shirts and carrying signs that said "YES ON 2: GREAT SCHOOLS NOW" and "#LiftTheCap." Missing from photos of the event, he pointed out, were the people who paid for it, associated with Great Schools Massachusetts. Of its 148 contributors, a mere 14 had "kicked in $475,000, or 96 percent."

Thirteen of the fourteen were individuals, and one was a group called Strong Economy for Growth, which Cunningham identified as a "money laundering operation." All the investors were from the hedge fund world (or married to hedge fund managers). Cunningham concluded that "the pro-charter operation is the tool of hedge fund and big finance players." The most important of these was Seth Klarman, who had been described by *The Boston Globe* as "New England's number one campaign contributor." Klarman had given $400,000 in 2014 to Republican Karl Rove's American Crossroads fund. He had contributed $850,000 to a libertarian political fund. He was a donor to campaigns in New York that supported charter schools and kept Republicans in control of the New York State Senate.

In August of 2016, as the campaign began to heat up, Cunningham explored the web of organizations that was funding Yes on 2 with Dark Money, hiding the names of donors. He zeroed in on a Massachusetts group called Strategic Grant Partners. The Massachusetts-based Strategic Grant Partners made large grants to Gates-funded, Oregon-based Stand for Children. "Once upon a time, Stand for Children was a grassroots organization of parents and educators, but by 2009 it had been taken over by corporate privatizing interests," Cunningham wrote. In the year from 2013 to 2014, Strategic Grant Partners gave $2.5 million to Educators for Excellence, a Gates-funded organization made up of young teachers who usually opposed teachers' unions and teachers' rights; $700,000 to Leadership for Educational Equity, an affiliate of Teach for America that encourages TFA alumnae to get involved in politics; $63,400 to Education Reform Now, an affiliate of Democrats for Educational Reform; $1,350,000 to Families for Excellent Schools of New York to help establish its organization in Massachusetts; and $600,000 to Teach for America, which supplies the teachers for charter schools. He identified six families that were funding the Great Schools Massachusetts ballot committee. "Tracing this money is no casual task and the interconnections are vast. The privatization effort is much more expensive and hidden than we realized and there is no grassroots."

In mid-August, the Yes on 2 campaign began to air misleading television ads during the Olympics saying "Yes on 2 for Stronger Public Schools." The ad listed five organizations as sponsors. Cunningham reviewed the financial reports and lobbying records that the five groups had filed with the state and concluded that all of the groups were conduits for Dark Money. The groups, he reported, were associated with Wall Street and hedge funds and were "active Republican dark money operations." He concluded: "This is our campaign finance farce-ocracy at work, and it's dark."

The sources of Dark Money for the Yes on 2 campaign remained hidden because final financial reports to the state were not filed until after the election. In the closing days of the campaign, a new Dark Money group appeared called Advancing Obama's Legacy on Charter Schools. President Obama had nothing to do with this group. It was led by Liam Kerr of Democrats for Education Reform Massachusetts and Frank Perullo, "a political consultant who channels Alice Walton's Walmart inheritance." On October 25, 2016, Kerr of DFER announced that the Advancing Obama's Legacy group would spend $500,000 "to shore up diving support among Democrats." DFER's affiliate, Education Reform Now Advocacy, "slid $155,000 to Advancing Obama's Legacy." However, most of the money for this group came from another pro-charter group called Campaign for Fair Access to Quality Public Schools. Charter advocates refer to charter schools as "high-quality" in contrast to regular public schools, which they imply are "low-quality." Who funded the Campaign for Fair Access to Quality Public Schools group? Cunningham wrote:

> If you're thinking low pay and lousy benefits then you're picking up the trail—Walmart heir Jim Walton gave the group $1.1 million in September. And Alice Walton gave $710,000 to the Yes on 2 ballot committee, which funneled $703,770.89 to Fair Access. It

shuffled the rest to entities controlled by the ubiquitous and well-compensated Mr. Perullo, who also consults for—you will never guess—Democrats for Education Reform. . . . Confused yet? That's by design. "Advancing Obama's Legacy" may sound like a Democratic group, but it was funded by Republicans.

Cunningham compared the attack of Dark Money on teachers' unions to the attack of the Great White Shark on innocent swimmers in *Jaws*. He urged the Massachusetts Office of Campaign and Political Finance to conduct an investigation of the Dark Money in the 2016 charter school campaign. Cunningham observed that "a good chunk of state education policy is being purchased by a handful of plutocrats."

The Massachusetts Office of Campaign and Political Finance did investigate the role that Families for Excellent Schools played in the 2016 campaign. It issued a report on September 8, 2017, announcing that the New York–based FESA had agreed to pay $426,466, all of its cash on hand, because it had

> violated the campaign finance law by receiving contributions from individuals and then contributing those funds to the Great Schools Massachusetts Ballot Question Committee in a manner intended to disguise the true source of the money . . . Between July 2016, when the ballot question qualified for the ballot, and the state election on November 8, the Great Schools Massachusetts Ballot Question Committee reported receiving more than $15 million from FESA— 70 percent of the $21.7 million in receipts reported by the committee.

The announcement of the agreement included a list of the donors and the amounts of the contributions that FESA had promised to keep secret. The OCPF did not investigate the Dark Money contributed by the other organizations that added millions more to the Yes on 2 campaign without identifying their donors. None of the funders in Massachusetts, New York, California, Arkansas, Texas, or elsewhere was ever held accountable for funding the referendum in Massachusetts without disclosing their identities.

The final blow against the charter advocates occurred eighteen months after the failed referendum, in the spring of 2018, when the Massachusetts Supreme Judicial Court threw out the complaint by charter advocates that the cap on charter schools violated students' rights. The opinion was unanimous. The justices ruled that even when a public school was getting poor results, it didn't mean that the state was failing in its constitutional duties, nor did it mean that opening more charter schools was a necessary remedy. The court ruled that "the education clause provides a right for all the Commonwealth's children to receive an adequate education, not a right to attend charter schools." The decision noted that more funding for charter schools means less funding for public schools. And it recognized a legitimate rationale for limiting charter schools because they are governed by private boards of trustees, a departure from local democratic control over public schools by local school committees.

Dark Money seems to be a common theme in the billionaires' campaign for more charter schools. In 2018, Common Cause in Connecticut issued a report about the role of Super PACs and Dark Money in local school board elections. Its report was called "Who Is Buying Our Education System?" It began:

A small group of corporate executives, wealthy individuals, and advocacy groups for the charter school industry [has] collaborated to reshape Connecticut's educational system by pumping more than a half million dollars into our elections in the last three years. The common thread among this group is their advocacy for charter schools—publicly funded schools that are run by private boards, independent of the local school district. Most of these donors have been involved in the management of charter schools or charter school advocacy groups as board or staff members.

Common Cause warned that large sums were being expended by charter organizations "to make more money for itself, shift control of public education to private hands, and drive wedges between parents in communities of color and teacher unions." It pointed out that the small number of wealthy donors has "management ties" to charter schools.

The charter school PACs were "funding an electoral megaphone that

Alice Walton, one of the heirs of the
Walmart fortune (her net worth of more
than $50 billion makes her the richest
woman in the world), is deeply devoted
to charter schools, as is the Walton
Family Foundation, which is both
pro-charter and anti-union.

drowns out the voices of Connecticut parents, citizens, and candidates
who are concerned about the future of our schools." Ordinary parents
and citizens could not compete with the large sums of money coming from the PACs. The PACs were corrupting the state's electoral system. "The shifting and vague names of these super PACs mask a thinly
veiled shell game played by a small group of advocacy groups, wealthy
donors, and charter school board members." Most of the money contributed to the six Super PACS came from out-of-state sources. Ten donors
accounted for 91 percent of the money contributed to the six Super
PACs. The biggest donor was Alice Walton, whose personal fortune was
said to be more than $50 billion; she does not live in Connecticut.

Common Cause said, "Few voters would have any idea that the Build
CT and Change Course CT PACs are funded by the wealthiest woman
in the world in her effort to rework the school system to shift control
of public education to private boards." In almost every state, it seemed,
Walton money was actively promoting privatization and charter schools.
Most of the PAC money went to Democratic candidates, even to candidates who had no opposition, especially in black and Puerto Rican

districts, to "curry favor" with a sure winner. In some cases, the PACs supported both candidates running against each other to be sure that the eventual winner would be influenced by their financial support.

The loser in this cynical deployment of money was democracy, as well as Connecticut's highly regarded public schools. The authors of the Common Cause report wondered: "What candidate would affirmatively want mountains of money spent on their behalf by Alice Walton, the nation's largest spender on efforts to destroy public education and whose fortunes are based on a business model that undermines small businesses and keeps people in poverty?"

Will the voters of Connecticut wake up to this stealth attack on their public schools? Will voters in other states pay attention when they learn that state and local candidates are funded by billionaires, many from out of state, whose goal is to privatize their public schools? Do candidates in school board elections have a fair chance when their opponents' campaign chests are overflowing with money from Super PACS? The same donors pop up again and again, in state after state, most of them contributing to races in states where they are not residents. Sunlight is surely essential to reveal this calculated attack on our public schools and our democracy. As teachers, parents, and school committees in Massachusetts showed, sunlight combined with political action is the best formula for success in the contest between citizens and predatory billionaires who are undermining our schools and our democracy.

CHAPTER 13

The Miracles That Weren't

New Orleans and Florida

The shining star of the charter industry is New Orleans. After Hurricane Katrina swept away much of the city and its public schools in 2005, the state's leaders replaced most of the city's public schools with charters. Eventually all were turned into charter schools. With one fell swoop, the white men who control the Louisiana state legislature decided that the local black majority could not be trusted to control its own school system. Without consulting the people of New Orleans, who had scattered because of the hurricane, the state closed the public schools and fired all the unionized teachers, most of whom were African Americans, many of whom were replaced by young white college graduates from out of state, trained for five weeks by Teach for America. To some locals, the transformation seemed like colonialism. In 2010, I visited Dillard University, a historically black institution in New Orleans; parents and educators turned out in large numbers to complain about the new charter system. One said, "First they stole our democracy, then they stole our schools." But to Disrupters, New Orleans was a stellar example of the triumph of the free market, a market that eliminated democratic control, banished the teachers' union, and replaced the public school system with privately managed charter schools.

By the metrics of Disruption, New Orleans was a success story, a district that was completely torn apart, an exemplar the privatizers desperately needed given the failure of their strategies everywhere else. A closer look, however, belies the use of the word "success." Test scores rose in the years after 2005, yet the test scores of the district remained well below state averages in one of the nation's lowest-performing states on the National Assessment of Educational Progress. The district went from being a poorly managed, underfunded public school system before the hurricane to being a better funded, highly stratified, privatized district after the hurricane, where, according to a Stanford University study, "the most advantaged students attend the best performing schools, while the neediest students attend [the] lowest performing schools." The same Stanford study characterized the New Orleans charter district as "a low-scoring district in a low-performing state," with the lowest graduation rate and almost the lowest average ACT score of any district in the state. In 2018, the all-charter New Orleans district was in the bottom third of the sixty-nine districts in the state. Only 26 percent of students in the Orleans Parish Recovery School District achieved mastery level or above on the state tests, compared to the state average of 34 percent. Forty percent of the charters in the New Orleans Recovery School District were rated D or F by the state, and students in the D and F charters were almost completely African American.

Nonetheless, in 2018, Douglas N. Harris and Matthew F. Larsen of the Education Research Alliance at Tulane University produced a report claiming significant gains for students in New Orleans and attributing these largely to the free market reforms that followed Hurricane Katrina. Test scores were up, graduation rates were up, college admissions were up, college persistence and graduation rates were up, they said. On the day after the report was released, the Trump administration's Department of Education awarded $10 million to the Education Research Alliance at Tulane and designated it as the National Center for Research on Education Access and Choice, with a mission to study how "different approaches to school choice, such as voucher programs and charter schools, can better serve disadvantaged students."

A New Orleans reporter questioned why the report "does not detail the recent flatline in public school progress—New Orleans schools have been outpaced by other districts in the past five years—the group said it would examine that phenomenon in a future review."

That "future review" appeared in 2019 in a report by the same Tulane research group. It lauded the Disruptive reforms for improving "average school quality," yet admitted that "quality peaked around 2013 and has either stagnated or started to decline during 2014–2016." And, "the average school improved from the first to the second year after it opened, but school performance remained mostly flat afterwards." This was hardly a ringing endorsement of Disruption!

In an analysis of the 2018 study commissioned by the Network for Public Education, Bruce Baker of Rutgers University challenged the Tulane authors' view that the free market reforms were the causal factors of any gains. He questioned whether it was necessary to fire all the experienced, unionized teachers and privatize the management of the public schools to get the same improvements.

Baker identified two significant changes that Harris and Larsen had minimized: first, there was a major increase in spending after the hurricane thanks to federal aid and the generosity of major philanthropies; second, the city experienced significant demographic changes due to the exodus of some of the city's poorest families, who never returned after their neighborhoods were devastated by the storm. The New Orleans schools enrolled 65,000 students before the storm but 48,000 a dozen years later.

Baker noted that spending increased significantly after Hurricane Katrina, by nearly $1,400 per student. A large share of the new resources was allocated to administration and transportation, while the cost of instructional staff was "artificially low due to the influx of a relatively inexperienced teacher workforce and changes to pensions and other benefits. It is likely that these expense reductions are not sustainable over time, meaning that total spending will either have to increase to maintain the system or that other expenses will need to be substantially reduced."

After the storm, Baker wrote, poverty was less concentrated than it had been. He cited a 2015 study from the Brookings Institution showing that New Orleans before the hurricane ranked second among American cities in concentrated poverty in 2000 but fell to fortieth by the period 2009–2013. This decline in concentrated poverty in New Orleans occurred at the same time that other big cities saw an increase in concentrated poverty due to the effects of the Great Recession of 2008–2009. Baker wrote that "population change cannot be ignored. . . . The effects of child poverty and more specifically spatially concentrated child poverty, intergenerational poverty, and the duration of poverty exposure, all matter greatly when it comes to short and longer-term outcomes. . . . Disrupting child poverty may be one of the most effective reform strategies possible."

Baker concluded that the new spending and the demographic changes might have accounted for almost all the gains seen after the hurricane.

Choice advocates and journalists who favored choice saw the Tulane study as an endorsement of free market reforms, which they believed could be applied to any city. Harris, however, cautioned that

> New Orleans was uniquely situated for these reforms to work. The district was extremely low-performing and pretty much everyone agreed that some type of major change was in order. It's easier to improve from such a low starting point. Also, the national interest in rebuilding the city and being part of the reform effort made it easier to attract educators, especially in the earlier years. Cities tend to have advantages over suburbs and rural areas as well. In short, I don't think we can extrapolate New Orleans to most of the country. It's more like a best-case scenario.

Thus, it would seem that the New Orleans formula of firing all the experienced teachers, eliminating the teachers' union, and privatizing all the public schools would not get the same results in other cities unless there was also a substantial boost in spending and a sharp reduction in poverty. Despite the sustained Disruption in New Orleans over fifteen years, the students in most of the city's charter schools scored well below the state average on state tests. There was no miracle.

Whatever the gains in New Orleans, there were substantial losses. Andrea Gabor of Baruch College in New York City assessed the human side of the story:

For all its youthful, twenty-first-century philanthro-capitalist trappings, the first decade of the New Orleans charter revolution hearkens back to an early age of oligopoly, union-busting, and top-down hierarchy. For most of the city's poor African American parents, school choice has boiled down to a thin-gruel menu of test-prep and strict-discipline, no-excuses schools. For teachers, it has been an unsustainable slog of long hours and low pay, which has created sky-high teacher-turnover rates. For charter operators, especially the smaller, less-well-connected ones, there are the perils of a low-margin business—too many operators hoping to outperform the market for test scores, chasing a limited supply of philanthropic dollars. For children, there is the Darwinian game of musical chairs—with the weakest kids left out when the music stops and failing schools close, or when they are counseled out of schools that can't, or won't, deal with their problems. And all this among a population of children and families displaced—often for years—and traumatized by the devastating storm in a state that offers poor children virtually no mental-health supports.

Behind this new regime are a handful of wealthy, unelected, mostly out-of-town organizations and benefactors, and their acolytes, who control the shots and help set the city's education agenda. Many, no doubt, have been motivated by a genuine desire to rebuild the inundated school system and to avoid the considerable mistakes— and corruption—of the past. But they are also driven by a deep and blinding animus [toward] unions, a distrust of grassroots organizing in poor communities, and an ideological belief in the power of markets and their ability to transform American education.

Another in a long line of miracle stories is Florida. Jeb Bush and Betsy DeVos point to Florida as a model of the success of school choice strategies. It might be more apt to point to Florida as a model of lawlessness and greed.

Florida's state constitution contains strong and explicit language protecting public schools.

Article 1, Section 3 of the state constitution makes clear that public money is to be spent only on public schools. It reads,

Religious freedom.—There shall be no law respecting the establishment of religion or prohibiting or penalizing the free exercise thereof. Religious freedom shall not justify practices inconsistent with public morals, peace or safety. No revenue of the state or any political subdivision or agency thereof shall ever be taken from the public treasury directly or indirectly in aid of any church, sect, or religious denomination or in aid of any sectarian institution.

Article IX of that constitution sets clear limits on what can be done with state education funds:

Section 1: Public education.—The education of children is a fundamental value of the people of the State of Florida. It is, therefore, a paramount duty of the state to make adequate provision for the education of all children residing within its borders. Adequate provision shall be made by law for a uniform, efficient, safe, secure, and high-quality system of free public schools that allows students to obtain a high quality education and for the establishment, maintenance, and operation of institutions of higher learning and other public education programs that the needs of the people may require. . . .

Section 6: State school fund.—The income derived from the state school fund shall, and the principal of the fund may, be appropriated, but only to the support and maintenance of free public schools.

The state constitution could not be more clear. It explicitly bans public funding of religious schools; furthermore, its requirement of a "uniform, efficient, safe, secure, and high-quality system of free public schools" directly contradicts the establishment of privately managed charter schools, including for-profit charter chains.

Because the state constitution is unambiguous, former governor Jeb Bush tried to change it by referendum in 2012. He and his allies proposed to repeal the ban on public funding of religious schools with an amendment they called the Florida Religious Freedom Amendment, hoping that voters would support "religious freedom" without noticing that the real purpose of the amendment was to allow public money to flow to religious schools via vouchers. The voucher forces knew that state refer-

Jeb Bush was governor of Florida from 1999 to 2007. His "Florida model" emphasizes testing, charter schools, vouchers, and online learning. Jeb Bush is a national leader of the Disruption movement; he is opposed to public schools. He is closely aligned with Betsy DeVos, who served on the board of his organization before she became secretary of education.

endums favoring vouchers for religious schools had always gone down to defeat, usually by huge margins, as such a referendum had in deeply conservative Utah in 2007, where it lost by 62 percent to 38 percent. However, the deceptive language was not enough to fool the majority of voters. Voters rejected the amendment by 55 percent to 45 percent. Had it been honestly represented as a vote to permit vouchers for religious schools, the margin of defeat would likely have been even larger.

Jeb Bush and his allies were unfazed by the defeat of their referendum. Instead, he and his fellow advocates of privatization set about circumventing the state constitution and ignoring their decisive defeat at the polls. The Republican-dominated Florida legislature enacted multiple voucher programs and encouraged the proliferation of charter schools, including for-profit charters. By 2018, Florida had the largest voucher program for private and religious schools in the nation, enrolling 140,000 students at a cost of $1 billion per year. Nearly 80 percent of voucher students attend religious schools.

Florida imposes strict standards, tests, and accountability on public schools and on charter schools, but not on voucher schools. Voucher-friendly legislators in Florida refuse to regulate voucher schools, even though they are funded with public money. Teachers in voucher schools are not required to be certified or even to have a college degree. Voucher schools do not have to meet any academic standards or report their graduation rates or make their budgets public. They are permitted to teach religious curricula. They are, in the words of an investigative series in the *Orlando Sentinel,* "Schools Without Rules," where children may learn that slavery was benign and that humans rode around on dinosaurs in prehistoric times. The financial and academic abuses within Florida's voucher schools are ignored by legislators, who want more vouchers. Richard Corcoran, then house speaker of the legislature, claimed that he wanted to "voucherize" the entire state. He said in a speech to a Republican club that "education needs to be more of a free market system, with more options for parents." As it happened, his wife operated a charter school. When Corcoran was term-limited out of office, the new governor of Florida, Ron DeSantis, named Corcoran the state's commissioner of education, despite his lack of any education credentials or experience.

As $1 billion flowed from the state's coffers to support vouchers for religious and private schools, another $2 billion was transferred to support privately managed charter schools. Unlike the voucher schools, the charter schools are required to administer the state tests and to hire certified teachers, although they are not required to comply with the state's building codes. In 2017–18, Florida had about 650 charter schools enrolling nearly 300,000 students (of a total state enrollment of three million students). Every year, new charter schools open, but almost as many close due to financial or academic failure. In 2016, twenty-six new charter schools opened, but twenty-five charter schools closed.

Many parent groups sprang up across Florida to fight privatization and to demand adequate funding of public schools. These groups included PTAs; the League of Women Voters; Fund Education Now; Support Dade Schools; Save Duval Schools; Teaching, Not Testing; and 50th No More. Several of these parent groups coalesced in 2012 and again in 2013 to block the enactment of a "parent trigger law," which would allow professional organizers to collect parent signatures to turn public schools over to charter operators. The bill was promoted by Jeb Bush and Michelle Rhee. Responding to grassroots pressure from constituents, six

Republican members of the state senate defected to kill the bill. Since then, new parent groups have sprung up, such as POPS (Protect Our Public Schools) in Sarasota and Manatee Counties. Citizens for Strong Schools filed a lawsuit to force the legislature to fund the public schools, but the State Supreme Court rejected their claims. In Alachua County, a group called Parents Against Corporate Takeovers made enough noise to block a for-profit charter chain that wanted to open in their county.

Among the most effective of the grassroots groups is the League of Women Voters. In 2014, the League published the results of a yearlong study of charters across the state. Although Florida prohibits for-profit charter schools, at least one-third of its charters in that year were operated by for-profit management companies like Charter Schools USA, Academica, and Imagine. The League reported that the state's charter schools had a high teacher turnover rate, low salaries, high levels of racial segregation, and a high rate of closures. In addition, 50 percent of the state's F-rated schools in 2011 were charters, and some charters were operated by religious groups. The report explained why the legislature ignored the plentiful evidence of charter failure and fiscal chicanery. Several key legislators had egregious conflicts of interest: the chair of the Senate Education Committee was the cofounder and business administrator of a charter school; a state senator on the Senate Education Committee was on the board of a charter school; the chair of the House Budget Committee was on the board of a charter school; the wife of then–House Speaker Richard Corcoran (who was also chair of the House Appropriations Committee) was in charge of a charter school; a state senator from Miami was president of a for-profit charter school; the chair of the House Education subcommittee on appropriations was married to the president of a for-profit charter chain and was the brother of the vice president of the same chain.

In 2016, Pat Hall and Sue Legg, state leaders of the League of Women Voters, examined the real estate practices of Charter Schools USA, a for-profit corporation then managing forty-nine charter schools in the state, as well as schools in several other states. Founded by noneducator Jonathan Hage, a veteran of Republican politics, Charter Schools USA is connected to a development company, a construction company, a foundation, a curriculum software company, and another three hundred limited liability corporations. The for-profit corporation charges fees for facilities financing, land acquisition, site clearing, construction, and bond financing, and collects many millions of dollars on leases to its schools. One company charges another for its services, and leases are flipped among related companies. In addition, the corporation charges management fees to its charter schools. Tracking the expenditure of taxpayers' money, they wrote, was "impossible due to for-profit business practices which are not transparent." The report estimated that about 40 percent of the public money received by the charter was not spent instructing children.

Florida demonstrates the danger that charter schools pose to public schools. In 2018, an independent government watchdog organization called Integrity Florida issued a blistering report about the risks of privatizing public education in the state and the need to regulate charter schools. Integrity Florida directly linked the underfunding of public schools, which enroll the vast majority of students, to the growth of charter schools. The authors asked how long the charter sector would grow and answered their own question: "Growth will continue unabated as long as private charter companies consider public schools a profit-making opportunity and they find receptive audiences in the legislature." They feared that the goal of charter advocates was to become the predominant system of schools, transferring a public responsibility to a private, for-profit industry. They noted that for-profit companies were operating nearly half the charter schools in the state (a substantial increase since the League of Women Voters' report only four years earlier). On average, charter schools were not more successful than public schools, nor were they more innovative than public schools. In the previous two decades, nearly four hundred charter schools had closed. Meanwhile, the proliferation of charters was straining the budgets of public school districts. The growth in charter schools was fueled by an aggressive for-profit industry that, since 1998, had given more than $13 million to political campaigns to influence state education policy. Integrity Florida noted that the legislature had enhanced the funding of new charters even though "some public officials who decide education policy and their families are profiting personally from ownership and employment in the charter school industry, creating the appearance of a conflict of interest." Thanks to the legislature's actions, "lax regulation of charter schools has created opportunities for financial mismanagement and criminal corruption."

Florida is an example for the nation of *what not to do.* Its leadership is intent on defunding public schools, expanding privately managed charter schools, increasing enrollment in religious schools at public expense, and enriching entrepreneurs. Students do not come first. They come last. Profits come first.

So long as the choice-crazed Republicans hold the governorship and a majority in both houses of the legislature, they will continue to reward the choice lobby. But the Resistance—the PTAs, the parent groups, the teachers' union, and the Florida League of Women Voters—is prepared to fight them at every turn from further eroding the state constitution's guarantee of a uniform system of high-quality public schools. The challenge for the Resistance in Florida is to elect officials who respect the state constitution and are determined to improve public schools.

CHAPTER 14

Common Core and a Gaggle
of Other Failed Reforms

About the year 2000, billionaire Bill Gates decided that he wanted to reform American public education. Neither he nor his children had ever attended public schools, and his knowledge of them was limited. But he had big ideas. His first plan was to break large schools into small schools. He said that "rigor, relevance, and relationships" would produce higher test scores. Creating small schools was not a bad idea, but when it didn't raise test scores, he abandoned that plan in 2008. The opportunity for another bold reform presented itself to him in that same year when he was visited by entrepreneur David Coleman and Gene Wilhoit of the Council of Chief State School Officers.

Coleman and Wilhoit went to Seattle to sell Bill and Melinda Gates on the biggest idea of all: an audacious, historic effort to create national standards that would drive testing, curricula, teacher training, and everything else. The federal government was prohibited by law from funding it. But Gates could. They recited woeful statistics about American education, and they claimed that national standards were the answer. They left with Gates's personal pledge to provide whatever funding was needed. As Lyndsey Layton of *The Washington Post* recounted their meeting, the pair asserted that "a fragmented education system stifled innovation because textbook publishers and software developers were catering to a large number of small markets instead of exploring breakthrough products. That seemed to resonate with the man who led the creation of the world's dominant computer operating system." Gates was convinced that creating a national marketplace would induce large corporations to develop new products. Gates appreciated the importance of standardization, which ensured that an electric appliance, plugged in anywhere in the United States, would get power. After the Common Core standards were developed, he touted their virtues to exemplary teachers who belonged to the National Board for Professional Teaching Standards (to which he had given $5 million in the previous five years). Gates told these teachers, "If you have fifty different plug types, appliances wouldn't be available and would be very expensive." Once an electrical outlet becomes standardized, he explained, many companies can design appliances and competition ensues, creating variety and better prices for consumers. Standardization would serve the needs of large corporations and consumers.

What Bill Gates never understood is that children and teachers are not toasters. You can't plug them in and expect them to produce the same results. They differ in their needs and interests and cannot be standardized.

The Common Core standards were supposed to revolutionize American education. The Bill & Melinda Gates Foundation spent hundreds of millions of dollars on their development and implementation, then invested many millions more to pay education groups to endorse and advocate for them. Supporters of the Common Core standards were sure that these standards would raise academic achievement across the nation, close achievement gaps between children from different races and income levels, and propel American students to the top of international assessments. So sure were their backers that they didn't think it necessary to conduct any field trials of the standards.

Gates sensed that he was finally at the center of the action in American education, and he was eager to get change quickly, "scaling up" as soon as possible. As one of the richest men in the world, he had practically unlimited resources with which to fund his ideas, and his newest passion was the Common Core State Standards.

Bill Gates gave many millions to education organizations, civil rights

Bill Gates, one of the richest people in the world, uses his wealth to promote public health in poor nations, but, less successfully, to transform public education in the United States in ways that have thus far failed. Gates believes in standardized testing, in measuring students and teachers by test scores, and in charter schools.

groups, both national teachers' unions, conservative and liberal think tanks, the National PTA, United Way, and the Chamber of Commerce to endorse the new Common Core standards. Every group that received his millions dutifully proclaimed the Common Core to be wonderful. Corporate America had long supported common national education standards. Its leaders preferred standardization to diversity; they knew that markets work best when products are standardized. Rex Tillerson, at that time the CEO of ExxonMobil and chairman of the Business Roundtable, starred in a television commercial in support of the Common Core. Joel Klein and Condoleezza Rice, former secretary of state in the George W. Bush administration, chaired a commission at the prestigious Council on Foreign Relations, whose report proclaimed that the Common Core was vital to America's national security. All this enthusiasm was generated before the Common Core had been implemented in classrooms and produced any results. Gates may have spent as much as $2 billion to develop, implement, and promote the Common Core. Forty-five states adopted the new standards, not because they were exceptionally good but because states were required to endorse common national standards (and the Common Core happened to be the only ones around) if they wanted to be eligible to compete for a share of the federal government's Race to the Top billions. Robert Scott, then the state superintendent in Texas, refused to endorse the Common Core standards because he would not accept them sight unseen. Most states were not so scrupulous and assumed that the standards could be merged with their own or ignored.

In 2010, I was invited to meet some of President Obama's key advisors—Melody Barnes, director of the Domestic Policy Council; Rahm Emanuel, the president's chief of staff; and Richard Rodriguez, the president's chief education advisor. They asked me what I thought of the Common Core standards. I said they should give grants to three to five states to conduct field trials, to find out how they worked in real classrooms with real teachers and students. If they did that, they could work out any kinks. They would find out whether the standards made a difference in student achievement, for good or bad. Their response was, "We can't wait. The standards must be in place before the 2012 election."

The Common Core was an unprecedented attempt to create a completely integrated system of standards, curricula, assessments, teacher education, textbooks, online resources, and teacher training, all calibrated to a single bullet list. Representatives of the major college admission testing corporations—the SAT and the ACT—served on the committee that wrote the Common Core standards and agreed that their tests would be redesigned to align with those standards.

Disrupters thought that if there were a fully aligned system, in which all the parts were systemically connected, then everyone would learn the same things in the same way at the same time, and everyone would end up educated well. They imagined that standardization would create equality of educational opportunity and leave no child behind and America would race to the top.

Despite the munificent funding provided by Bill Gates and the carefully stage-managed publicity campaign he underwrote, this audacious attempt to standardize the nation's schools was a massive flop.

Standardization was a great idea for the production of automobiles and mechanical devices, but it made no sense for children and schools. Even similar students in the same classroom with the same teacher, getting the same daily lessons, do not progress at the same rate and do not end up in the same place. Some excel, others do not. Variation is inevitable because individuals vary; some students work harder than others; some care about particular subjects more than others; and some are completely disengaged from their studies for reasons of their own. Some live in spacious homes where both parents are college graduates, and others live in small apartments with parents who are working two jobs or are unemployed. Actual teachers in actual classrooms need the flexibility to respond to the variations in students' needs, interests, and abilities.

When the Common Core was released in 2010, organizations representing English language learners, students with disabilities, and very young children warned that the standards were inappropriate for the students they represented. The more that teachers used the new standards, the less they liked them. The standards ran into a buzz saw of controversy and opposition. Gates must have been stunned when teachers and parents objected to his grand project and the Common Core became controversial, even radioactive.

Although the federal government was prohibited by law from attempting to control curricula or instruction, it could use its resources to support new tests. Arne Duncan funded two testing consortia at a cost of $360 million to create new tests aligned with the Common Core standards. One was called the Smarter Balanced Assessment Consortium (SBAC); it initially enrolled thirty-one states. The other was the Partnership for Assessment of Readiness for College and Careers (PARCC); it enrolled twenty-six states (the numbers fluctuated as states dropped in or out). A few states signed up for both. The two consortia decided to set very high cutoffs for passing their tests, ones that they considered appropriate to "college and career readiness."

The test designers in the two consortia knowingly chose cut scores (passing marks) that were certain to fail most students, a truly bizarre decision given that these tests were supposed to have high stakes: students would have to pass them in order to advance to the next grade level or— in some states—to receive their high school diplomas. In 2014, Catherine Gewertz of *Education Week* reported that one of the two federally funded testing consortia chose to align its passing marks with the "proficient" level on the National Assessment of Educational Progress. They knew when they made this decision that *most* American students had *never* scored "NAEP proficient." NAEP itself did not treat that ranking as a passing mark but as a mark of outstanding performance, surpassed only by "advanced," which very few students reached.

Gewertz wrote,

> In a move likely to cause political and academic stress in many states, a consortium that is designing assessments for the Common Core State Standards released data Monday projecting that more than half of students will fall short of the marks that connote grade-level skills on its tests of English/language arts and mathematics.
>
> The Smarter Balanced Assessment Consortium test has four achievement categories. Students must score at Level 3 or higher to be considered proficient in the skills and knowledge for their grades. According to cut scores approved Friday night by the 22-state consortium, 41 percent of 11th graders will show proficiency in English/language arts, and 33 percent will do so in math. In elementary and middle school, 38 percent to 44 percent will meet the proficiency mark in English/language arts, and 32 percent to 39 percent will do so in math.

PARCC, the other federally funded testing consortium, set even tougher passing marks, guaranteeing that most students would fail again and again. Both testing consortia knew when they chose the passing marks that most students would fail to reach "proficient."

As the dismal results of Common Core tests were released, and as state after state reported that most students were "failing" to reach "proficiency," parents were understandably furious. Disrupters like Michelle Rhee and Campbell Brown gleefully pointed to the high failure rates as evidence that the public schools were failing. The "failure" rate was highest among the poorest students, the students who did not know English, and students with disabilities. Knowing that most students would never graduate high school if they stuck with these tests, state after state dropped out of the two testing consortia. By 2018, only a small number of states continued to use either PARCC or SBAC.

The media did not tell the public that the passing marks were not based on objective criteria. Those in charge of standard setting can make the test easier or harder, depending on where they set the bar.

Tom Loveless, a scholar at the Brookings Institution, patiently explained that NAEP proficient does not mean "grade level." NAEP's achievement levels, he pointed out, are of dubious validity and have been challenged repeatedly by independent scholars, by the National Academy of Education, and by the National Academy of Sciences. He noted that most students in private schools fail to score "NAEP proficient," as would students in most nations in the world.

When judged by the Disrupters' own metric—test scores—the Common Core was a failure. Adopted by forty-five states and the District of Columbia, it produced little or no gains in test scores on the National Assessment of Educational Progress. Some of the few states that did not adopt the Common Core got higher scores on NAEP than those that did adopt it. It did not reduce achievement gaps between different racial and economic groups. States spent billions of dollars in changing their standards, teacher training, textbooks, online materials, and tests, and billions more to install computers on which students would take the Common Core tests, but none of this made any difference. Common Core was hated by many parents as a form of federal overreach; many teachers and parents saw it as an attempt to standardize curriculum and instruction and to repress creative teaching and pedagogical innovation. The only beneficiaries were a few large corporations that expected to sell standardized products to a national marketplace.

The architect of the Common Core standards was entrepreneur David Coleman, who had worked at McKinsey, the global management consulting firm, before launching his own testing business. He sold his testing company to McGraw-Hill for millions of dollars, then opened a company called Student Achievement Partners, which led the development of the Common Core standards.

David Coleman believed that American schools were spending too much time on literature and personal essays. The standards included a chart showing what percentage of students' time should be devoted to reading nonfiction or fiction at different grade levels. In elementary school, it decreed, the division between fiction and "informational text" should be 50-50. In grade eight, it should be 45 percent literary and

55 percent informational text. By high school, the division should be 30-70, favoring informational text. There was no scientific basis for this dictate; it simply copied the instructions that the governing board of the federal National Assessment of Educational Progress gives to developers of the reading assessments. The ratios were intended for those who were designing tests, not as directions for teachers in classrooms across the nation.

Coleman confidently assumed that the Common Core standards would raise test scores. He told a reporter, "One of the striking things in American education is that reading scores at the fourth-grade level have been frozen for 40 years." Coleman continued, "We've hit a wall in reader literacy that these standards respond to." He anticipated a sharp rise in fourth grade reading scores. But this did not happen. Fourth grade reading scores remained flat. The fourth grade NAEP reading scores for the lowest-performing students actually declined in 2017.

Coleman emphasized "close reading" of text, believing that students should be able to read and understand passages without any background or context (a bizarre idea given that texts only make sense in context). Students were supposed to decipher the meaning that resided "within the four corners of the text." A student might, for example, read Dr. Martin Luther King Jr.'s "Letter from Birmingham City Jail" without the teacher providing background information about the history of racial segregation or the civil rights movement. Coleman disparaged student essays about their personal views or their lives. Teachers who had once encouraged students to write about their own experiences of the world or their reactions to what they read were informed that this was wrong. Coleman spoke out against personal essays in a professional development session in Albany, New York:

> Do you know the two most popular forms of writing in the American high school today? . . . It is either the exposition of a personal opinion or the presentation of a personal matter. The only problem, forgive me for saying this so bluntly, the only problem with these two forms of writing is as you grow up in this world you realize people don't really give a shit about what you feel or think. . . . It is rare in a working environment that someone says, "Johnson, I need a market

analysis by Friday, but before that I need a compelling account of your childhood."

Coleman had never been a teacher. He did not realize that students should be encouraged to use vivid, concrete detail and evidence when they write. Kids, because they are kids, don't yet know much of the world. But they do know a lot about their own lives, so personal writing is a useful way for them to learn to write, as it is for many professional writers. Teachers know this. Coleman, the standards architect, did not.

After adoption of the Common Core, critics bemoaned the decline in teaching "whole books" and the loss of classic novels and other literature. As early as 2015, Tom Loveless reported a significant decline in teaching fiction, accompanied by a significant increase in teaching nonfiction. Jamie Gass of the conservative Pioneer Institute in Massachusetts complained that the Common Core had destroyed the Bay State's excellent literature standards and driven out classics such as *Frankenstein* and *The Count of Monte Cristo*. In 2018, the conservative Thomas B. Fordham Institute, which had received millions of dollars from the Gates Foundation both to evaluate and to advocate for the Common Core, lamented that 70 percent of teachers were emphasizing informational text, as the Common Core recommended, while devoting less time to teaching "classic works of literature" because "there is no longer room for them in the curriculum." The folks at Fordham, who had dutifully testified in state legislative hearings on behalf of the Common Core, found it "concerning" that classic works of literature were being sacrificed in response to the Common Core, not acknowledging their own role in creating the problem.

The Disrupters were impatient. They wanted more change faster: more charter schools, more testing, more turmoil. The pace of change was too slow. So, they came up with a cornucopia of strategies to hasten the process of disruption.

All of these strategies failed.

One of the most unpopular and ineffective Disruption proposals was the mandate to evaluate teachers by the test scores of their students. This idea was a key feature of Obama's 2009 Race to the Top competition. States that wanted to be eligible for a slice of the $4.35 billion prize offered by the U.S. Department of Education had to change their laws to evaluate teachers by the test scores of their students. Almost every state complied with this requirement. Such evaluation is known as "value-added measurement," or VAM, meaning that teachers would be judged by the value they added as measured by their students' test scores. If scores went up, the teacher was effective; if not, she or he was ineffective.

The concept of VAM was originally developed by William Sanders, an agricultural statistician experienced in measuring the growth of cattle and corn. Why not do the same for teachers? Sanders applied VAM to education and insisted that his measurements would reliably identify the best and the worst teachers. If states and districts used his secret and patented value-added methods, he claimed, they could evaluate teachers objectively by the rise or fall of their students' test scores.

But VAM, too, was a mighty flop. This flop was entirely predictable because social scientists had long known that the biggest influence on students' academic success is not their teachers but their families' income, education, English language ability, and consistent support for education. Teachers are important; teachers make a big difference in the lives of their students; but it is a rare teacher who can have a greater impact on students' academic success than is made by circumstances outside the school, like hunger, homelessness, exposure to violence, and poor health; or, on the other hand, educated parents who make sure their children have regular medical checkups, read to them as toddlers, meet with their teachers, take them to the library and museums, talk about their schoolwork, and provide other advantages.

Secretary of Education Arne Duncan was an enthusiastic supporter of VAM. He often claimed that critics of VAM were trying to cover up for failed teachers. When the *Los Angeles Times* created its own VAM ratings and published online the names of teachers with their ratings, teachers objected that the ratings were inaccurate and unfairly damaged their reputations, but Duncan applauded the paper's release of these ratings as courageous.

In Colorado, a politically ambitious young state senator, Michael Johnston, wrote a bill (SB 191) to base 50 percent of teachers' and principals' job ratings on test scores, creating the most test-focused teacher evaluation system in the nation. A former member of Teach for America who had briefly served as a school principal, Johnston insisted that his plan would produce great teachers, great principals, and great schools. His bill passed in 2010 over the strenuous objections of the Colorado Education Association. By 2017, Van Schoales, one of the state's leading "reformers," admitted that Johnston's SB 191 had failed. Most districts, he wrote, had no ineffective teachers, not a single one! He noted with puzzlement that Aurora Central High School, one of the lowest-performing schools in the state, had 100 percent effective or highly effective teachers in 2014–15, "not much different than in 2009 when the school was struggling just as much as today." Fewer than 1 percent of teachers in Colorado were rated ineffective. Schoales said that the only results of the turmoil were alienated teachers and the creation of "a massive bureaucracy" to oversee the evaluation system. Johnston, however, refused to disown his bill, and the legislature did not repeal it.

VAM failed, first of all, because it was a nonsensical idea. Teachers are not solely responsible for raising or lowering their students' test scores. Students are not randomly assigned. Social scientists have reported many times that the influence of teachers on test scores matters less than the students' home life—family income, family education, family support for education. Lovers of VAM ignored decades of research and assumed that the teachers just didn't want to be evaluated.

In addition, VAM was impractical because 70 percent of teachers do not teach the subjects that are tested every year (reading and mathematics in grades 3–8). Teachers in the early grades and in high schools do not produce VAM scores, nor do teachers of the arts, physical education, science, vocational studies, or other subjects. How to evaluate the 70 percent? Some states assigned VAM ratings to teachers based on subjects they did not teach, generated by students they never taught. Florida teachers sued in federal court to stop the practice of evaluating them by the scores of students they never taught. However, the teachers lost in federal court; the judge ruled in 2014 that the state's program was "unfair" but not unconstitutional.

In practice, VAM proved notoriously unreliable and ineffective. In many states and districts, almost every teacher was rated "effective" or "highly effective." In Miami-Dade County, fewer than 1 percent of teachers were rated "unsatisfactory," and in New York State, only 3 percent of teachers were declared "ineffective." Despite these ratings, which refuted the claim that schools were overrun by "bad teachers," the test-based evaluation system caused massive demoralization, and many teachers cited it as the reason they were leaving the profession. VAM contributed to widespread teacher shortages, as teachers retired early and the number entering the teaching profession dropped precipitously. Some teachers were reluctant to teach the neediest students for fear of getting a low VAM score and being fired.

Teachers knew that it was unfair to judge them by the performance of their students, because test score gains and losses depend to a large extent on which students are in their classes. Teachers of students with disabilities and those who teach the most challenging classes are not likely to see the same gains as those who teach children from educated, affluent families.

Late in 2011, a new study by prominent economists gave powerful ammunition to believers in test-based accountability and value-added measurement. The study was reported on the front page of *The New York Times,* discussed on the *PBS NewsHour,* and mentioned by President Obama in his State of the Union Address in 2012. The following year, its lead author, Raj Chetty, won a MacArthur Foundation "genius" award, largely because of this study. The economists—Raj Chetty of Harvard University, John N. Friedman of Harvard University, and Jonah E. Rockoff of Columbia University—concluded that teachers who raise test scores in the elementary and middle school years have a lasting impact on the lives of students, including adult earnings, college-going rates, and even teenage pregnancy rates. The authors told *The New York Times* that "a student with one excellent teacher for one year between fourth and eighth grade would gain $4,600 in lifetime income, compared to a student of similar demographic who has an average teacher. . . . Replacing a poor teacher with an average one would raise a single classroom's lifetime earnings by about $266,000." Friedman told *The New York Times* that "the message is to fire people sooner rather than later." Chetty added, "Of course there are going to be mistakes—teachers who get fired who do not deserve to get fired." But he thought that using value-added scores would lead to fewer mistakes in the firing process. Disrupters immediately hailed the study as a wondrous breakthrough.

With the imprimatur of the Chetty study, school districts were supposed to start firing teachers who didn't raise test scores and close achievement gaps. These findings came at a time when many thousands of teachers had already been laid off because of the budget cuts that followed the recession of 2008–2009, and teacher shortages were widespread.

The Chetty study was widely hailed by VAM-lovers, but almost no attention was paid to a sharp refutation of its findings by Columbia University economist Moshe Adler. Adler noted that the Chetty findings about increased income applied to workers at age twenty-eight, but that an earlier version of the paper concluded that teacher value-added had "no effect on income at age thirty." The Chetty group, he charged, failed to report their own finding that the effects of teacher value-added faded out after age twenty-eight. Even at age twenty-eight, the income gain in the original version of the paper was only $182 a year per person, about enough to buy a cup of coffee once a week, hardly a cause for popping the champagne cork or for presidential salutations in the State of the Union Address.

Chetty's paper arrived at the very time that the Disrupters had shaped a seamless narrative about American education. The Disrupters' narrative, honed by Michelle Rhee and repeated endlessly by Bill Gates, Arne Duncan, and their allies, went like this: American education is failing. It must be rebuilt from scratch. The blame for this abject failure lies with bad teachers. Blame teachers' unions, which protect bad teachers. Blame tenure and seniority, which give teachers a lifetime job without accountability. Blame locally elected school boards, which lack the courage to fire bad teachers. That is the critics' narrative, and it is false.

This narrative was echoed by major media, especially *Time* and *Newsweek* magazines, which put Michelle Rhee on their covers, portraying her as the transformational leader who would fearlessly fire those incompetent teachers and principals who were causing low-income and minority children to get low test scores.

In 2014, *Time* had a cover story about "bad teachers" called "Rotten Apples: It's Nearly Impossible to Fire a Bad Teacher: Some Tech Millionaires May Have Found a Way to Change That." The cover was illustrated with four apples, one of which was rotten, visually implying that one of every four teachers was a "rotten apple." The story inside the magazine was titled "The War on Teacher Tenure." It described the Vergara lawsuit in California, funded by a wealthy Silicon Valley entrepreneur who hoped to strip teachers in that state of their job protections. The plaintiffs won in the lowest state court, but ultimately the state's highest court threw out the case and said that the legislature, not the courts, should make decisions about teachers' job rights. The case was silly on its face, since students in high-scoring districts were even more likely to have tenured teachers than were those in low-scoring districts.

Encouraged by the Chetty study, Disrupters like Arne Duncan and Bill Gates determined to bear down even harder on teacher evaluation by test scores. This monomaniacal focus on using test scores to evaluate teachers and fire "bad teachers" coincided with the after-effects of the Great Recession of 2008–2009. Most states cut education spending. About half of them never restored those cuts. Health care costs for teachers and other school personnel were rising. In many states, teachers were barely earning a living wage. States didn't need reasons to fire teachers. They had trouble holding on to those they had.

The Learning Policy Institute at Stanford, headed by scholar Linda Darling-Hammond, warned that the supply of teachers was diminishing. Following the 2008 recession, school districts laid off teachers to save money. At the depths of the recession, states enacted austerity policies. But when the economy improved, and many districts wanted to hire teachers, the supply was not there. In a report published in 2016, the Learning Policy Institute wrote that the revival of hiring came "at a time when teacher attrition is high, and as teacher preparation program enrollments have fallen 35 percent nationwide in the last five years, a decrease of 240,000 teachers in total." These shortages were occurring across the nation, especially for teachers of mathematics and science, bilingual education, and special education. Some teachers retired, but many quit because of poor working conditions, lack of respect, and punitive accountability programs like those required by No Child Left Behind and Race to the Top. The schools hurt most by teacher shortages were those in the poorest communities. Districts responded to the teacher shortage by increasing class sizes or by hiring teachers who were not certified in the subjects they were teaching. The neediest schools were likeliest to have the highest teacher turnover and to employ the most inexperienced teachers. The Learning Policy Institute pointed out that high teacher turnover, which Chetty and company treated as a positive goal,

> negatively affects student achievement, and the detrimental effects extend to all of the students in a school, not just to those students in a new teacher's classroom . . . The resulting churn undermines student achievement as a function of teacher inexperience, under-preparation, and overall instability. Schools suffer from diminished collegial relationships, a lack of institutional knowledge, and the expense of training new teachers who, oftentimes, will not stay.

Teachers were not invited to participate in this national discussion about their effectiveness; the stage was monopolized by economists, policymakers, think tank denizens, celebrities, and other outside-the-classroom "experts." But teachers understood that the Disrupters were labeling them as the enemies of children. They knew that they had become punching bags for the national media. They knew intuitively that they were responsible neither for the academic struggles of students with difficult home circumstances nor for the impressive test scores of the most advantaged students. As teachers, they took pride in influencing the lives of their students, but they did not measure their influence by their students' standardized test scores but by their students' ambition, inspiration, motivation, self-discipline, love of learning, classwork, in-class assessments, and other qualities that tests do not measure.

The legitimacy of VAM suffered a devastating blow when the American Statistical Association released a statement in 2014 criticizing the use of test scores to evaluate individual teachers. It cautioned that VAM measures correlation, not causation. It warned that teachers account for about 1 percent to 14 percent of the variability in test scores and that most of the opportunities for quality improvement are found in system-level conditions.

The courts began to step in, this time on the side of teachers whose rights were violated. In 2015, a state judge in New Mexico enjoined the state from using the value-added model to punish or reward teachers because of doubts about the reliability and validity of the model, which would count for 50 percent of a teacher's evaluation. In 2017, a federal judge in Houston threw out the school district's test-based evaluation system, ruling that the teachers were judged by a "secret algorithm" and that they had "no meaningful way" to ensure that their scores were correctly calculated, which violated their due process rights. The Houston judge ruled, "The [teacher's] score might be erroneously calculated for any number of reasons, ranging from data-entry mistakes to glitches in the computer code itself. Algorithms are human creations, and subject to error like any other human endeavor."

VAM suffered the biggest blow to its validity when an evaluation of the Gates Foundation's VAM program was released in 2018. The program cost $575 million, of which the foundation supplied $212 million; the balance was paid by taxpayers. The grants were awarded to three school districts—Hillsborough County in Florida, Memphis, and Pittsburgh—and to four charter chains—Alliance College-Ready Public Schools, Aspire Public Schools, Green Dot Public Schools, and Partnerships to Uplift Communities Schools. The grant recipients agreed to evaluate teachers by test scores and by "peer evaluators." The goal of the program was to improve staffing decisions and to get more highly effective teachers working with the neediest students.

The Gates Foundation engaged the RAND Corporation and the American Institutes for Research, two well-respected research organizations, to evaluate the program over a six-year period. The RAND-AIR report concluded that the $575 million did not improve student achievement, did not affect graduation rates or dropout rates, and did not change the quality of teachers.

Carol Burris reviewed the RAND-AIR evaluation of the Gates program and concluded that the program may have done more harm than good. It wasted district resources that would have been better spent reducing class sizes or improving teachers' salaries, she said. The program carried an astronomical cost to taxpayers. After adding the indirect costs of the time of administrators and teachers, she said, the actual cost of the Gates program across the seven sites might have been as high as $1 billion. Florida's Hillsborough County Public Schools paid a hefty price: "Its program alone cost $262.2 million. Federal, state and local taxpayers paid $178.8 million, far more than the Gates Foundation's contribution of $81 million. Gates used his money as a lever to open the public treasury to fund his foundation's idea. The taxpayers picked up the lion's share of costs."

Across the seven sites hosting the Gates Foundation program, the results were negative. Some experienced increased teacher turnover. The neediest students did not get the most effective teachers because teachers feared that their VAM scores might fall if they taught high-needs students. Although Disrupters expected that the rate of teacher firings might rise as high as 20 percent, the actual dismissal rate was only 1 percent, as we saw in Colorado and Miami, the same as it had been before the program was launched. Burris, a retired principal, concluded that the hugely expensive program had no effect on teacher quality or student test scores because it defied common sense: "The project failed because evaluating teachers by test scores is a dumb idea that carries all kinds of negative consequences for achieving the goal we all want—improved teaching and learning. Every good principal knows that improvement in teaching requires coaching built on a relationship of trust and mutual respect—not boxes and metrics intended to determine whom to punish and whom to reward."

The foundation decisively proved that the methods it believed in, the methods embedded in Race to the Top's requirements, didn't work. Gates has never publicly admitted that his multimillion-dollar investment in VAM was a bust. Perhaps being a billionaire makes it difficult to admit error or to acknowledge that his core belief that "bad teachers" cause low test scores was wrong.

VAM was a sham. But despite the RAND-AIR evaluation of the Gates program, despite legal victories in Houston and New Mexico, where judges enjoined the district and the state from using VAM for high-stakes purposes; despite its demonstrated ineffectiveness in states and districts across the country, most states continued to use value-added measurement to evaluate teachers. Why? In the absence of a judicial ruling or different elected officials or massive political pressure, legislatures are slow to repeal bad laws. In 2019, Michelle Lujan Grisham, the new governor of New Mexico, issued an executive order in one of her first official acts eliminating that state's test-based teacher evaluation system and withdrawing from the Common Core–aligned PARCC test.

The privatizers rolled out another initiative in 2010, along with Common Core and VAM, to advance their goal of disrupting public schools. They persuaded the California legislature to endorse a parent trigger law. The idea behind the parent trigger was that parents were so unhappy with their public schools that they should be allowed to petition to take control of their school and turn it over to a charter operator or fire the teachers or the principal. The parent trigger was tailor-made for a new Disrupter organization called Parent Revolution, created in 2009 and funded with millions of dollars by the Walton Family Foundation, with additional millions from the Bill & Melinda Gates Foundation, the Eli and Edythe Broad Foundation, the Laura and John Arnold Foundation, and other pro-charter philanthropies. Right-wing groups liked the parent trigger idea so much that ALEC, the American Legislative Exchange Council, drafted model legislation for all states to consider. The parent trigger idea, in my view, is akin to a law allowing passengers in a public bus, if they are dissatisfied with the service, to commandeer the bus and give it to a private bus company. It is just plain ridiculous.

Parent Revolution sent organizers into poor communities to gather parent signatures on petitions enabling the parents to seize control of their public schools and hand them over to charter operators. Wherever the Parent Revolution organizers went, they fomented controversy and divided communities.

The first target of Parent Revolution was McKinley Elementary School in Compton, California. Parent Revolution collected enough signatures to make possible a parent takeover, but the school district challenged the validity of the signatures. Some parents revoked their signatures, and Parent Revolution sued. Eventually, the effort to privatize the public school collapsed, and the new charter school opened a few blocks away. Very few McKinley families signed up.

The second attempt to pull the parent trigger was at Desert Trails Elementary School in Adelanto, California, a poor desert town where the school enrolled mainly Latino and African American students. Adelanto's population was 32,000. Its per capita yearly income was $12,000. Nearly two thirds of the people in the city were Latino, many of them undocumented, and another 20 percent were African American. Parent Revolution rented a house for its organizers and began collecting signatures. Amid allegations of fraud and harassment, the battle over the future of the school ended up in court when some of the parents who signed the petition tried to withdraw their names, claiming they had been misled; they thought they were signing a petition to improve their school, not to change its management. The judge ruled against the parents, and ultimately only 53 of the 466 original signers of the parent trigger petition voted to turn Desert Trails over to a private charter operator.

Millions of dollars from foundations were expended to convert one public school into a charter school.

Inspired by California's example, Mississippi, Texas, Indiana, Louisiana, and other states passed parent trigger laws. None of them, however, has ever had a public school converted by parents to a charter school.

The Disrupters were busy on many fronts in their campaign to destabilize public schools. In Tennessee, Michigan, Ohio, and other states, they embraced the concept of state takeovers as their solution to the problems of schools with low test scores.

Tennessee was one of the first states to win a grant from Obama's Race to the Top competition. It won $500 million to adopt the Common Core, measure teacher "effectiveness," increase the number of charter schools, and transform its lowest-scoring schools into high-performing schools. Part of the Tennessee plan was to establish an Achievement School District (ASD) to "turn around" the schools that were in the lowest 5 percent in the state; most of those schools were in Memphis, with a few in Nashville and Chattanooga. The state education department, headed by Disrupter Kevin Huffman, selected a charter school star, Chris Barbic, to manage the new ASD. Barbic had previously led the YES Prep charter chain in Houston. Barbic boldly pledged that the low-performing schools in the ASD would reach the top 25 percent in the state rankings within five years.

The ASD opened in 2012 with six schools, and the countdown clock began ticking. The annual cost was estimated at $22 million a year for five years. In year four, Barbic had a heart attack and resigned from his leadership role to join the staff of the Laura and John Arnold Foundation. By the end of year five, none of the initial six schools in the ASD had reached the top 25 percent. All but one were still mired in the bottom 5 percent, and that one had reached the 6th percentile. By 2018, studies by Vanderbilt researchers concluded that the schools in the ASD showed no significant academic improvement.

The ASD experiment failed. Yet in true Corporate Disrupter style, where bad ideas are quickly turned into templates without regard to evidence, the ASD concept spread to other states, including Nevada and North Carolina, all eager to copy the latest new thing without waiting to learn if it actually made a difference and helped students.

Michigan launched a state takeover to improve low-performing Detroit public schools, and it too was a disaster. In 2009, Democratic governor Jennifer Granholm appointed Robert Bobb as emergency manager of the Detroit public schools. He was a recent graduate of the unaccredited Broad Academy, which encourages closing public schools and replacing them with privately managed charter schools. Bobb's salary of $280,000 was enhanced by another $145,000 from the Broad Foundation. At the time, the city's schools had a deficit of nearly $300 million; under Bobb's control, the deficit grew even larger. Bobb successfully disrupted the district. He closed dozens of public schools, fired principals, laid off teachers, and opened charter schools. As more charter schools opened, enrollment in the Detroit public schools dwindled, revenues fell, and the deficit increased.

In 2011, Republican governor Rick Snyder created the Education Achievement Authority, whose mission was to take over the state's lowest-performing schools—those in the bottom 5 percent—and dramatically improve them. The first fifteen schools were located in Detroit and enrolled ten thousand students: twelve were public schools, and three were charter schools. The first leader of the new authority was John Covington, also a graduate of the unaccredited Broad Academy; he was superintendent in Kansas City when he received a call from billionaire Eli Broad telling him that he was needed in Detroit. Covington abandoned Kansas City and took the Detroit job.

The Education Achievement Authority was mired in controversy from the beginning. Covington fired all the staff of the fifteen schools and required them to reapply for their jobs; only 20 percent were rehired, and many were replaced by inexperienced Teach for America recruits. The EAA boasted about "personalized learning," "student-centered learning," and dramatic test score gains, but students spent hours as guinea pigs using computer programs that were not fully developed. Contrary to the EAA's claims, student test scores stagnated and declined, students left EAA schools to return to the Detroit public schools, and an air of failure enveloped the project. In early 2016, the Eastern Michigan University Board of Regents announced that it was withdrawing its sponsorship of the EAA, and Republican legislative leaders declared that it was finished. In June 2017, the EAA closed its doors, and its fifteen schools were reabsorbed into the Detroit public school system. The short and unhappy life of the EAA was marked by low student performance, declining enrollment, and frequent charges of mismanagement and corruption. Michigan State University professor David Arsen described the EAA as "a train wreck of educational policy." It was certainly not a model for any other state.

Policymakers are supposed to seek evidence before they impose a new governance structure on a community institution like public schools. But Republican legislators did not seem to care that state takeovers in Tennessee and Michigan had failed to achieve any of their goals. Undeterred, legislators in Ohio, Arkansas, North Carolina, and other states continued to take control of school districts with low scores, even though the state education department had no new ideas about what to do once they had grabbed the reins of power.

Despite failure after failure, the Disrupters kept driving forward, uninterested in analyzing their failures. There was so much money undergirding their multiple and overlapping organizations that the failure of their experiments did not matter. There was no grassroots support for their efforts to quash democratic control of public schools. Their continued forward momentum was guaranteed by the many millions of dollars available to keep trying. There would always be people eager and willing to promote Disruption, regardless of its track record, because that's where the money was.

CHAPTER 15

The Teachers Revolt

After the passage of No Child Left Behind, the lives of teachers in American schools changed dramatically. Their careers and their reputations were increasingly tied to standardized test scores. Government at all levels—district, state, and federal—expected test scores to rise every year, and teachers were expected to raise them. No one asked whether it was reasonable to expect that children in third or fourth or fifth or sixth or seventh or eighth grades this year would get higher scores than their predecessors last year, and that scores would go up year after year for every cohort. Yet teachers were given this assignment by politicians who didn't give much thought to whether their demands were reasonable. They left it to teachers to figure out how to meet politically determined goals.

We now know what teachers and the public did not know during the heyday of high-stakes evaluation and the "fire teachers sooner rather than later" craze. In response to the deep economic recession that began in 2008, most states cut funding for education. The federal government enacted the American Recovery and Reinvestment Act to shield schools from the worst effects of the recession, but the federal money soon ran out. In the decade after the recession ended, more than half of all states were still spending less for education than they did before the recession. At the same time, many of these states cut income taxes and corporate taxes, further reducing the revenues needed to fund education. According to the Center on Budget and Policy Priorities, "Twenty-nine states provided less overall state funding per student in the 2015 school year than in the 2008 school year, before the recession took hold." The states that cut state funding the most, by percentage change, adjusted for inflation, from 2008 to 2015 were Arizona (36.6 percent), Florida (22.0 percent), Alabama (21.6 percent), Idaho (18.0 percent), Georgia (16.6 percent), Texas (15.9 percent), Oklahoma (15.6 percent), and Utah (14.6 percent).

When a state has less money to spend on education, that means that there will be teacher layoffs, larger classes, fewer electives, as well as less money for teacher salaries, for social services that poor students need, and for libraries, the arts, and repairs. Between 2008 and 2015, capital spending for new buildings and renovations dropped by $23 billion, or 31 percent. In the era of austerity, teachers' salaries declined, in real dollars, in thirty-nine states. The number of people employed in schools fell, while student enrollments grew.

If they really wanted to help students, the foundations and billionaires might have spent their money calling attention to the sharp decline in education budgets and advocating for higher taxes to increase funding for the public schools. But they did not.

At the very time that states cut funding for essential services, the privatizers demanded the diversion of funding from public schools to charter schools, vouchers, untested methods of teacher evaluation, and the Common Core. As the schools struggled to pay teachers, Disrupters demanded that they fire teachers based on their students' test scores. Teachers coped with larger classes, stagnant wages, and media that portrayed them as villains. Many districts were forced to shorten the school year or reduce the school week from five to four days. Many schools eliminated arts programs, nurses, and libraries. Necessary repairs were ignored. In Georgia, 70 percent of schools shortened the school year, and 42 percent eliminated art and music classes. Twenty percent of the school districts in Oklahoma shortened the school week to four days. The American Federation of Teachers called the era from 2008 to 2018 the "decade of neglect."

In these circumstances, the decision to teach was an act of courage, dedication, and self-sacrifice. But even the most selfless of individuals can reach a breaking point, because teachers, like everyone else, have to pay for food, shelter, transportation, health insurance, and the other necessities of life.

This is the economic and cultural context in which to understand what happened in the spring of 2018, the Education Spring, the spring in which thousands of teachers walked out of their schools to demand better conditions for teaching and learning and reasonable pay.

It started in West Virginia, one of the poorest states in the nation. Teachers decided that enough was enough. After months of planning, every teacher in the state walked out. Teachers united with other school employees to demand change, for themselves and their students. The West Virginia teachers were fearless, and they were strategic.

They walked out for higher pay and for relief from soaring health care costs. The average teachers' salary was about $45,000, the forty-seventh in the nation, with only Oklahoma, Mississippi, and South Dakota paying less. The state's governor, billionaire Jim Justice, had offered them a 1 percent a year raise for each of five years, but that raise was sure to be outpaced by inflation. To add insult to injury, Governor Justice referred to the state's teachers as "dumb bunnies." The state hiked health care insurance costs for public sector workers by $300 per month (and more for retirees) and required them to use a "wellness app" to track their steps and threatened to fine them if they failed to do so. Teachers considered this mandate an invasion of their privacy.

The state had hundreds of unfilled teacher jobs, and some classes were taught by people uncertified in the subjects that they were teaching. Teachers were leaving the state to work in nearby states with higher salaries. The legislature proposed to fill the vacancies by lowering standards for new teachers.

On February 22, 2018, teachers across West Virginia walked out. The statewide action was carefully thought through and well planned. Every public school closed in all fifty-five counties. West Virginia is a right-to-work state where collective bargaining is forbidden, where no one is required to join a union, and where striking by public sector workers is illegal. But every school in the state closed down, and most of the state's twenty thousand teachers descended on the state capitol in Charleston to present their demands, in alliance with about fourteen thousand other public sector workers.

West Virginia has a long history of strikes by coal miners, including the famous Battle of Blair Mountain in 1921, when thousands of coal miners fought a pitched battle with thousands of lawmen and strike-breakers hired by the mine operators. Eventually, the U.S. Army was dispatched to end the conflict. Some of the teachers were grandchildren of the miners, and they knew about the state's history of labor activism. Nor was this the first teachers' strike in the state. In 1990, teachers in forty-seven of the state's fifty-five counties had gone on an eight-day strike that concluded with a pay raise.

This time was different. In 2018, every teacher in every county went on strike. Planning for the strike began in the southern part of the state, which had once been the center of coal mining. The superintendents agreed with the teachers and closed the schools, so the teachers were technically not striking and not breaking the law. Every employee of the schools across the state, including bus drivers and cafeteria workers, joined the teachers. The strike was preceded by much discussion and planning in every county. Some of the organizing and communications was facilitated through a Facebook group called West Virginia Public Employees United, which had 24,000 members. Rank-and-file teachers were aided by state affiliates of the American Federation of Teachers and the National Education Association (which teachers join as a matter of choice). Teacher groups made arrangements with churches and other community organizations to provide meals and safe spaces for children. The teachers' outreach to parents ensured public support for their strike. Many teachers were living "from paycheck to paycheck," and many worked second jobs, wherever they could pick up extra work to make ends meet. They taught in the midst of a devastating opioid crisis, which damaged the families of their students. But the legislature was obsessed with tax cuts for corporations.

In the early morning of February 22, teachers packed the hallways of the state capitol, wearing red bandanas and T-shirts. Teachers were everywhere.

In mid-strike, the walkout leaders announced a deal with Governor

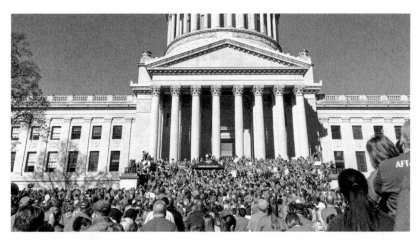

The teachers of West Virginia (*above*) engaged in a mass, statewide walkout at the State Capitol Building, Charleston, West Virginia, in February 2018 to protest the state's financial neglect of public schools and to oppose charter schools. Their walkout inspired a rolling wave of teachers' strikes across the nation.

The Chicago Teachers Union went on strike for eleven days in October 2019 and won commitments to limit class sizes and to provide a nurse, a librarian, a student counselor, and other essential services in every school, as well as a limit on new charter schools, and a pledge to restore an elected school board.

Justice offering a 5 percent pay raise for teachers and a 3 percent raise for other public workers; the strikers refused to accept any settlement unless it included a 5 percent raise for all public sector workers and until it was passed by the legislature. The strikers did not trust the governor or the legislature to keep their promises. Nothing was real until it was enacted. The strikers chanted, "Back to the table!" and "We are the union bosses."

The strikers kept every public school in the state closed for nine days, until the legislature passed a pay raise of 5 percent for every public employee. Republican leaders warned that the state would pay for the raises by cutting Medicaid, but the governor promised that he would not let that happen. Teachers wanted their raises to be paid for by raising taxes on the energy industries that had been showered with tax cuts. The governor promised to create a task force to review health care insurance costs.

The biggest victory for the teachers was the fact that they had united as #55Strong, had stood together with other public employees, and had won respect. Governor Justice also agreed to block charter schools and to veto anti-union legislation. One of the strike leaders, middle school teacher Jay O'Neal, said that the lesson of the strike was that "if we can do it, anybody can do it. It's not like we're a special group of activist teachers who have been studying for twenty years about how to mobilize the working class. We're not." A year later, the legislature attempted to pass legislation authorizing both charter schools and vouchers, and the teachers went on strike again to block the proposed legislation, knowing that privatization would strip funding from their schools. But in 2019, as the teachers feared, the governor and the legislature double-crossed the teachers and passed a charter bill, with every Democrat voting against the bill. There was a ray of hope, however. The charter lobby in Washington, D.C., complained that the West Virginia bill allowed only local districts to authorize new charters, which would severely restrict the number of new charters.

One important lesson from the West Virginia strike was that persistent efforts by the right wing to eliminate labor unions were fruitless. Even as the strike in West Virginia was in full swing, the United States Supreme Court was considering the anti-union *Janus* decision, which was handed down in June 2018. In that decision, the high court ruled that public sector unions could no longer collect mandatory fees from workers who did not wish to join the union even though they would continue to enjoy the benefits that unions negotiated for them. *Janus* was intended to cripple unions by depriving them of members and revenue. The West Virginia strike demonstrated that workers could organize themselves with or without unions and that wildcat strikes like the one in West Virginia were even more difficult to control in the absence of collective bargaining agreements.

Teachers in Oklahoma were inspired by the militancy of their colleagues in West Virginia. There, the situation for teachers and public schools was even worse than in West Virginia (incredibly, West Virginia spends 40 percent more per pupil than Oklahoma does). The state's 42,000 teachers made an average salary of $45,000, near the lowest in the nation. There had been no salary increase for teachers or any other state workers in a decade. Teachers were leaving Oklahoma for neighboring states to earn more money. Oklahoma's 2016 teacher of the year and his wife, also a teacher, left for better pay in Texas (the move across the state line increased their family pay by $40,000). According to the Center on Budget and Policy Priorities, Oklahoma legislators had cut the education budget by a billion dollars, or 28 percent, between 2008 and 2018.

Efforts to increase funding for public schools and teachers' salaries had failed repeatedly in the Oklahoma legislature and at the ballot box. The legislature had cut income taxes, corporate taxes, taxes on oil and energy companies and had exempted capital gains income from taxation. But it required a vote of 75 percent of the legislature to raise taxes. While the legislature was penurious toward its public schools, which enrolled the vast majority of students, it generously funded two voucher programs with tax credits for individuals and corporations and with direct subsidies to privately managed charter schools and virtual charter schools.

Alberto Morejon, an eighth grade history teacher, organized a Facebook group called Oklahoma Teacher Walkout—The Time Is Now! Overnight, the group enrolled 21,000 members and soon had 72,000.

The legislature and governor in Oklahoma favored the oil and gas industry, not schools and teachers. Thanks to tax breaks and incentives, the richest man in the state was multibillionaire Harold Hamm, whose profitable fracking had helped to make Oklahoma "the earthquake capital of the world." As Eric Levitz reported in *New York* magazine, "Before the fracking boom kicked off in 2008, Oklahoma experienced an average of one to two earthquakes of 3.0 magnitude or higher per year. In 2014, the state was rattled by 585." Rivka Galchen of *The New Yorker* wrote that earthquakes had become such a common phenomenon in Oklahoma that they were included in daily weather reports by local weathermen. This was the devil's bargain that the state's policymakers had made: cut the budgets of the public schools to protect the vast wealth of Harold Hamm and the fossil fuel industry, and to hell with the state's environment and its children.

Oklahoma teachers decided that the only way anything would change was if they took direct action. They walked out on April 2, 2018, and they made three demands: higher salaries, greater funding for their schools, and increased taxes on the energy industry to pay for the package. Their protest lasted for two weeks. "During the walkout," *The New Yorker* reported, "the demonstration at the capitol was attended by as many as eighty thousand people," a huge number in a state with a population of less than four million. "The scene had the high spirits of a music festival and the nerdiness of people who really love school. 'Can we please put the smart people in charge now?' one sign read. Many signs referred to Oklahoma's infamously high incarceration rate and its private prison system, and to the fact that the state spends twice as much per prisoner as per student: 'If we dress our kids in stripes, will you fund education?,'" said another placard.

In response to the strike, the legislature agreed to give teachers a wage increase of about $6,000 per year but refused to increase funding for the schools or to raise taxes on the wealthy. As legislators tabled motions to increase taxes to pay for education, billionaire Harold Hamm sat in the galleries watching the action and reminding the legislators who was in charge in Oklahoma. The teachers ended their strike and vowed to take their fight for more funding to the voters. Teachers and their supporters ran in the Republican primaries and walloped those who had opposed taxes for education. Of the nineteen Republicans who voted against the tax increase for education, only four survived the Republican primaries. Voters ousted the most outspoken critics of education funding, replacing them with moderate Republicans. In the general election, sixteen educators were elected to the state legislature, expanding the education caucus to twenty-five, including sixteen Republicans and seven Democrats. In addition, teachers helped to elect Kendra Horn to Congress, the first Democrat elected from her district in forty-four years and the first female member of Congress from the state.

In the remarkable spring of 2018, teachers in other states followed the examples of militancy displayed by their colleagues in West Virginia and Oklahoma. Teachers in Colorado walked out in late April to demand better salaries, higher funding for the schools, and better management of their pension funds. Unlike the walkout in West Virginia, the Colorado walkout was not statewide, and many schools did not close. The teachers' grievances were similar to those in other states, but the demands in Colorado were blunted by the state's Taxpayer Bill of Rights (TABOR), which prohibits raising taxes without voter approval. In 2013, voters rejected a $1 billion bill to increase funding for education. As a result, half the districts in the state were open only four days a week. There were thousands of vacancies in the state's public schools. The legislature found some new funding without raising taxes, and the teachers' action ended with a 2 percent pay raise and a small increase in overall education funding.

In Kentucky, thousands of teachers rallied at the state capitol against the governor's effort to eliminate dedicated pensions for future teachers. Pension funds in Kentucky had been depleted by mismanagement and raided by politicians of both parties to pay for other state projects. Teachers in Kentucky count on their defined-benefit pensions as compensation for low wages; they do not receive Social Security. Despite the teachers' opposition, the governor and legislature abandoned traditional, defined-benefit pensions and replaced them with a hybrid plan for future teachers that relies on 401(k) accounts. At the urging of teachers, the legislature increased taxes to fund the schools, by raising the cigarette tax by 50 cents and the sales tax on some services like home and auto repairs. Matt Bevin, the Republican governor, vetoed the tax increases to fund education, but the Republican legislature overrode the governor's veto, which was an important victory for the teachers.

Only weeks after the teachers were rebuffed by Kentucky's governor, they got a measure of vengeance when middle school math teacher Travis Brenda of Rockcastle County High School entered the Republican primary in May and defeated Jonathan Shell, the House majority leader, who was considered a rising conservative star in the national party. Brenda was elected in the general election. He was one of fifty-one educators who ran for seats in the legislature; most were running as underfunded, little-known Democrats in heavily Republican districts. Fourteen won their races. In Louisville, special education teacher Tina Bojanowski defeated Republican incumbent Phil Moffett, a frequent critic of the public schools.

As the teacher walkouts moved west, the last big battleground of the Education Spring was Arizona, where teacher pay and per-pupil spending were among the lowest in the nation. The state government, controlled by libertarian conservatives, was dedicated to low taxes, low spending, and school choice. The state had cut personal income tax rates by 10 percent in 2006, cut corporate tax rates by 30 percent in 2011, reduced taxes on capital gains, and reduced other taxes wherever possible, starving the state of revenues to fund education and other public services. The Center for Budget and Policy Priorities stated that Arizona's school system "is the second-least adequately funded" in the nation. It was spending 14 percent less on education in 2018 than it had before the 2008 recession. Due to low pay, "over 60 percent of teacher positions are either vacant or filled by people who don't meet standard teaching requirements." Arizona is a right-to-work state, but teachers organized on their own to press their demands for higher salaries and a commitment by the state to spend more on schools. Two groups led the teachers: the Arizona Education Association (which claimed 20,000 of the state's 57,000 teachers as members) and a grassroots Facebook group called Arizona Educators United, created by a young teacher named Noah Karvelis.

The protests in Arizona started in March, after Karvelis, a twenty-three-year-old teacher in Phoenix, put up a post on Facebook creating Arizona Educators United and asking teachers to wear red on March 7 to demand more funding for the public schools. Days later, over six thousand teachers had signed on, and the number kept growing. Karvelis and other activists declared that every Wednesday would be Red for Ed day. Veteran education writer Dale Russakoff wrote about the Arizona teachers' revolt and reported: "Across the state, teachers were taking in roommates, working second and third jobs and leaving the profession in such waves that substitutes without standard certifications were leading more than 3,400 classrooms statewide. Two thousand more couldn't be staffed at all." In addition to low pay, Arizona teachers had nearly the highest average class size in the nation. Arizona's average per pupil spending of $8,141 was well below the national average. "Arizona school counselors had an average caseload of more than 920 students each, the highest in the country."

Teachers voted for a statewide walkout on April 26; Governor Doug Ducey tried to head off the walkout by offering teachers a 20 percent pay increase by 2020. He pledged a raise of 10 percent in 2018, and 5 percent in each of the next two years. Teachers were dubious about Ducey's offer because he was committed to tax cuts and did not propose a new revenue source to fund his offer.

The teachers walked out on April 26. Phoenix turned into a sea of red as tens of thousands of teachers and their supporters wearing red T-shirts marched to the state capitol chanting "Red for Ed." The crowd

In 2018, teachers in Arizona walked out to protest low pay and the state's under-investment in public education. Tens of thousands of teachers gathered wearing #RedForEd T-shirts and handmade placards. #RedforEd became the watchword of teachers across the nation.

encircling the capitol was estimated to be fifty thousand. They sought funding increases of $1 billion to restore the budget to where it was before the recession and a 20 percent raise in teachers' salaries. Some of the signs during the #RedforEd march said, "This Republican family supports #RedforEd"; "History is Watching"; "I Support My Students—I Should Be Able to Support My Family"; "Arizona's Top Exports: Citrus, Copper, Teachers." The strike lasted for six days, until May 3, when Governor Ducey signed a bill raising teacher pay by 20 percent by 2020 (at a cost of $644 million) and agreed to restore $371 million to the education budget that had previously been cut.

The teachers didn't get any sympathy from House Majority Leader John Allen from Scottsdale. A year earlier, he had said that teachers, like legislators and everyone else, chose to take a second job so that they could enjoy the "finer things in life." "They're making it out as if anybody who has a second job is struggling. That's not why many people take a second job," Allen said. "They want to increase their lifestyles. They want to improve themselves. They want to pay for a boat. They want a bigger house. They work hard to provide themselves with a better lifestyle. Not everyone who takes a second job does it because they're borderline poverty." Allen made these comments after passing a bill to lower standards for entry into the teaching profession. According to state data, more than 40 percent of teachers quit after two years in the classroom. Democrats wanted to raise teachers' salaries, but Republicans insisted that the answer to getting more teachers was to reduce "regulations" (that is, standards) by allowing people to teach without any formal teacher education.

One Republican senator, Sylvia Allen of Snowflake, Arizona, said that her grandmother had taught in a one-room schoolhouse even though she never went to high school, which was her evidence that regulations and standards were "not the answer" to the teacher shortage. The legislature passed the bill to waive teacher qualifications and lower standards for new teachers.

In the wake of the 2008 recession, Russakoff reported, Arizona "cut funds that districts relied on to pay teachers, maintain buildings, update curriculum and technology and much more. Salaries were frozen, funding for all-day kindergarten was eliminated and class sizes climbed year by year as teachers left for higher-paying jobs and principals were forced to combine orphaned classes." The legislature and the Republican governor at that time, Jan Brewer, kept cutting taxes in hopes of stimulating the economy. Voters approved a temporary 1 cent sales tax in a 2010 referendum, mostly for education, but then voted it down in 2012. Doug Ducey, then the state treasurer, led the opposition to extending the sales tax. He was a "no new taxes" guy. In 2014, when he ran successfully for governor, he pledged to cut taxes and "drive income taxes in Arizona 'as close to zero as possible.'" Governor Ducey was funded in large part by the Koch brothers and their network of Dark Money groups.

At the same time that Arizona's #RedforEd movement was capturing the attention of the state and the nation, teachers and parents in Arizona were fighting on another front to block vouchers for private and religious schools. Governor Ducey and the Republican-dominated legislature were pushing to expand the state's voucher program by sixfold, from five thousand to thirty thousand students. The Republicans' goal was to expand vouchers incrementally until every one of the 1.1 million students in the state was eligible for one. The state's voucher program started in 2011, with an offer of "scholarships" for students with disabilities (which was ironic, since students with disabilities abandon their federally protected rights when they leave public schools). Year after year, the legislature had added other protected groups—students living on reservations, foster children, military children, students enrolled in D- or F-rated schools—to the list of those eligible to receive what they called Empowerment Scholarship Accounts. Families who received a "scholarship" received a debit card worth 90 percent of the money that would have gone to their local school district and were expected to use it to pay for religious or private schools or homeschooling. Ducey's new voucher proposal was limited to thirty thousand students, but critics expected that the cap would be eliminated in the near future, posing a mortal threat to the state's underfunded public schools. A study by *The Arizona Republic* found that nearly 70 percent of the students using vouchers were leaving A- or B-rated districts to attend private schools, while only 7 percent of the money was used by students from low-performing districts.

Opponents of the voucher bill were led by Save Our Schools Arizona (SOS Arizona). The group started with six women who met while attending legislative hearings in hopes of persuading legislators not to enact vouchers. They were in the legislative chambers when the bill passed in April 2017. They left the building and wondered what they should do next. They exchanged phone numbers, and the Arizona Resistance was born. Their story was written up by Laurie Roberts in *The Arizona Republic.* The group's founders were "Sharon Kirsch, a college professor of literature; Melinda Iyer, who trained camp counselors; Beth Lewis, a fifth-grade teacher; Alison Porter, a retired software engineer; Dawn Penich-Thacker, a college English professor and former Army public information officer; and Cathy Sigmon, a retired account officer. They researched the law and found that citizens of this state have a constitutional right to a referendum—to gather signatures and put the work of our leaders on hold, giving voters the final say in whether it will go into effect."

They learned that they had ninety days after the legislature adjourned to gather 75,321 signatures to freeze the law and put it on the ballot in November 2018. The voucher advocates scoffed at these volunteers and predicted they could never succeed. Yet in the heat of the summer of 2017, thousands of volunteers canvassed the state and collected 111,540 signatures on petitions requesting a referendum on the voucher bill. No one expected them to get so far, and lawyers funded by the Goldwater Institute, the Alliance for Children, and Americans for Prosperity (the Koch brothers' organization) tried to invalidate the signatures. When they failed to accomplish that, they asked the courts to throw the referendum off the ballot. That failed too. Then there was talk that the legislature would repeal the bill and pass it under another name, so that the volunteers would have to start all over again, exhausting their energy and their funds. But the referendum won court battle after court battle, and the volunteers persisted.

SOS Arizona was up against formidable opponents. The network of donors led by the billionaire Koch brothers had declared that K–12 education would be its target for the year and that it was "low-hanging fruit"; Arizona was ground zero for its efforts to privatize public education. The Koch brothers' network consisted of seven hundred donors who had each given a minimum of $100,000. The Kochs were Governor Doug Ducey's principal donors. They had contributed $5.2 million to his 2014 campaign. Ducey went to the Kochs' 2018 seminar to boast about his new voucher law and said, "I didn't run for governor to play small ball. I think it is an important idea." Betsy DeVos's American Federation for Children had spent $257,000 in 2016 to elect a legislature in Arizona that would pass a voucher law. Both the Koch brothers and members of the DeVos family contributed to Governor Ducey's reelection campaign in 2018.

As journalist Laurie Roberts noted, the Kochs and their allies were outraged by the prospect of a referendum; they "came unglued at the prospect of a public vote." Public referendums are not friendly territory for privatization, especially vouchers for religious schools.

Despite the well-funded attempts by the Koch brothers to stop them, the volunteers of SOS Arizona got their referendum, Prop 305, on the ballot. When the votes were counted on November 6, 2018, Governor Ducey's voucher plan was overwhelmingly defeated, by a vote of 65 percent to 35 percent.

Educators tried to place two other issues on the ballot, but the Arizona Supreme Court blocked them. One was a referendum called "Invest in Ed," which sought to create a dedicated revenue stream of about $700 million annually for the schools by taxing the highest incomes in the state. Another was a referendum called "Outlaw Dirty Money," which would have required the disclosure of the names of those who contributed at least $10,000 to a campaign. Both proposals were taken off the ballot by the court.

After their dismal failure on Prop 305, the Goldwater Institute and DeVos's American Federation for Children were quick to issue statements asserting that the battle for vouchers was not over. They promised that they would be back, despite the voters' decisive rejection of public funding for private and religious schools. Dawn Penich-Thacker, the spokesperson for SOS Arizona, promised that SOS Arizona would rise up again to counter their efforts.

In the election of 2018, not only did Prop 305 go down in flames, but voters elected Kathy Hoffman, an educator and a Democrat, in a hotly contested race for state superintendent of instruction. Ducey was reelected, and Republicans continued to control both houses of the legislature, but by smaller margins. A few teachers were elected to the legislature. #RedforEd posted a message for Governor Ducey on Facebook:

Dear Governor Ducey,

In the November 6 election, Arizona's citizens spoke loudly and clearly that we do not want to pursue ESA accounts and vouchers.

Now that the election is over, we ask you to please prioritize a plan to invest in building a public education system we can all be proud of in our state.

It was never only about teacher pay. We want fair wages for support staff. We want funding for repairing and updating our buildings. We would like to vastly improve the counselor to student ratio. We want our children to have updated textbooks and technology. We are asking for funding for transportation and safe buses. We want art and music and science supplies; to see no teacher ever need to pay out of pocket to teach; to have resources to meet every student's needs. And yes, to have fair salaries for educators so we can attract bright passionate graduates to the teaching profession. We care about Arizona's students, and we are asking you to care with us.

That's all it's ever been about.
Written on behalf of Arizona #RedforEd

The teachers' movement—from West Virginia to Arizona and beyond—had a dramatic effect on the portrayal of American teachers in the mass media. Where once they had been demonized as "bad teachers" and "rotten apples," the media changed their tune in response to the walkouts, protests, and strikes. *Time* magazine, which had published stories that were deeply hostile to teachers, had a conversion experience. In contrast to earlier cover stories that praised people who were intent on firing "bad teachers," *Time* reported on the strikes with three covers published simultaneously, each one featuring a teacher who was underpaid, overworked, and unappreciated. The cover story was called "I'm a Teacher in America." One cover showed a teacher in her classroom who said, "I have a master's degree, 16 years of experience, and donate blood plasma to pay the bills. I'm a teacher in America." Another cover, for the same issue, showed a teacher in a hallway in front of student lockers, who said, "I have 20 years of experience, but I can't afford to fix my car, see a doctor for headaches or save for my child's future. I'm a teacher in America." The third version showed a teacher in her classroom, who said, "My child and I share a bed in a small apartment, I spend $1,000 on supplies, and I've been laid off three times due to budget cuts. I'm a teacher in America." The story accompanying the covers focused on the lives and sacrifices of teachers as they dealt with "low pay, crumbling facilities, and outdated textbooks."

Almost overnight, America's teachers went from being portrayed as rotten apples to being celebrated as self-sacrificing heroes struggling to make ends meet under circumstances that would be unthinkable in other professions. The national discourse changed from the Disrupters' narrative about "failing" schools and "bad" teachers to the deplorable plight of teachers who work two or three additional jobs to pay their bills, who teach overcrowded classes, and who dig into their own pockets to pay for classroom supplies. The Disrupters had been saying for years that money didn't matter, that what was needed was charters, vouchers, and inexperienced teachers willing to work unlimited numbers of hours a week. But the teachers' revolt changed the subject and—for a time—silenced the Disrupters. When the mass media began telling stories of real-life teachers who chose teaching as a career and had to work at fast-food restaurants or sell their blood to pay their rent or their mortgage or their student loans, the Disrupters' attacks on teachers appeared as not only irrelevant but mean-spirited. For the first time in many years, teachers came to life in the nation's major media as recognizable people who were working hard and not getting the pay and respect they deserved.

The Teacher Revolt of 2018 inspired teachers across the nation. When the next major teachers' strike occurred, in Los Angeles in 2019, the public overwhelmingly supported the teachers. By striking, teachers realized that they had the power to demand a living wage, smaller class sizes, decent working conditions, and a halt to privatization.

The teachers taught the nation a lesson.

But more than that, they taught themselves a lesson. They united, they demanded to be heard, and they got respect. That was something that the Disrupters had denied them for almost twenty years. Teachers learned that in unity there is strength. Some ran for office. Some were elected; some were not. But united by their profession, they learned that they could achieve their goals if they stood together. No one, not even the most conservative, penny-pinching politician, wants to see the children of an entire state out of school, not for a day, not for a week. The politicians thought that they could silence teachers by breaking their unions. They were wrong. Teachers learned that together they had power. And they won't forget that lesson.

CHAPTER 16

Goliath Stumbles

Goliath was mighty and well armed. David was a young man, slight of stature, armed only with a slingshot. David felled Goliath with a single stone aimed at his head. The story of David and Goliath has given hope to every resistance movement. Today, among educators in the United States, it is a metaphor for the Resistance against the billionaire-funded movement to disrupt, monetize, and privatize public education, which gallingly dares to call itself a "Reform" movement. When the masks are stripped away, it is nothing more than a privatization movement, which relies on strategies of deception and propaganda.

Today's privatizers say they want world-class education, but they don't want to pay for it. They don't want to pay higher taxes to fund the schools that all children need and deserve. They don't want to pay the cost of higher salaries for professional teachers and wraparound services for students (like counselors, social workers, librarians, psychologists, and a nurse in every school). Disrupters insist that it does no good to spend more money on education because that's just "throwing money at the problem," although they don't mind throwing money at the schools their children attend. They oppose reducing class sizes, because it costs too much; they insist that a "great teacher" can teach successfully no matter how many students are in her class (research and common sense do not support this view). They offer choice as a low-cost substitute for funding.

The tide is turning against disruption and privatization masquerading as reform, which they are not. The mask is falling away. The NAACP's call for a charter moratorium in 2016 sent a loud signal that school choice is not the "civil rights issue of our time." The decisive defeat in 2016 of the Massachusetts referendum on charter expansion sent a clear message that the public does not want its public schools to lose funding to charter schools. In the same year, voters in Georgia rejected a change in the state constitution that would have created an "opportunity school district," controlled by the governor, to take over public schools with low test scores and give them to charter operators; it was modeled on Tennessee's failed Achievement School District. The measure failed by a decisive margin of 60 percent to 40 percent, even though there was no strong union, as there was in Massachusetts, to lead the opposition. Voters in Georgia did not want to abandon democratic control of their public schools.

Disrupters have used standardized testing to identify and take over or close schools with low scores, but they disregard standardized testing when it reveals the failure of charters and vouchers. Disrupters no longer claim that charter schools and inexperienced recruits from Teach for America will miraculously raise test scores. After three decades of trying, they have not been successful.

Nothing that the Disrupters have championed has succeeded unless one counts as "success" closing hundreds, perhaps thousands, of community public schools in low-income neighborhoods. The Disrupters have succeeded in demoralizing teachers and reducing the number of people entering the teaching profession. They have enriched entrepreneurs who have opened charter schools or developed shoddy new products and services to sell to schools. They have enhanced the bottom line of large testing corporations. Their fling with the Common Core cost states billions of dollars to implement but had no effect on national or international test scores and outraged many parents, child advocates, lovers of literature, and teachers. The Disrupters tried to encourage the collection of personally identifiable student data and monetize it, but this was stymied—at least temporarily—by well-informed parents who blocked the intrusion of Big Brother into their children's lives.

Since Disrupters must always have a new idea, especially when what they are selling is not working, they have latched on to "personalized learning," which is intended to replace teachers with computers for a significant part of the school day. The computer algorithms adapt to the skill level of the student so that each student gets a lesson or activity that matches his or her level. Parents and educators know that this bizarre concept of "personalized learning" is a hoax because its stony heart is defined by an interaction between a student and a machine, not between humans. Students in Kansas, Pennsylvania, New York, and Connecticut walked out of their schools to protest the adoption of Chan Zuckerberg's Summit Learning platform, which is meant to replace teachers with screen time. A parent in McPherson, Kansas, visited his son's fourth grade classroom and said, "We're allowing the computers to teach and the kids all looked like zombies," then removed his child from the school. Parents want their children to have a human teacher who sees them, listens to them, knows them, and cares about them. The students will remember the teachers who inspired them for the rest of their lives; they will not remember their Chromebooks and iPads.

The good news is that at least a few Disrupters realize that test scores are a poor measure of children's potential.

A prominent member of the Disruption establishment, Paymon Rouhanifard, denounced standardized testing when he stepped down as superintendent of the Camden, New Jersey, public schools after five years on the job. Rouhanifard had served as a high-level official on Joel Klein's team in New York City, where test scores were the all-consuming goal of education. Upon his arrival as superintendent of the impoverished Camden district at age thirty-two, he developed school report cards to rank every school mainly by test scores. But before he left, he abolished the school report cards. He changed his mind, he said, after hearing complaints from teachers, students, and parents about the time spent on testing and the time that was not available for the arts or global studies or foreign languages.

He acknowledged that the current accountability regime had raised test scores but questioned whether the test score gains were worth the weeks and months of instruction that were lost. Speaking to a conference of his allies, he concluded that the unnatural focus on tests in two skill subjects was corrupting education.

> I'll go out on a limb—most everyone in this room wouldn't tolerate what I described for their own children's school. Mostly affluent, mostly white schools shy away from heavy testing, and as a result, they are literally receiving an extra month of instruction—and usually with less overall time allotted to the school day. . . . The basic rule, what we would want for our own children, should apply to all kids.

That was what John Dewey had in mind when he wrote, "What the best and wisest parent wants for his own child, that must the community want for all of its children. Any other ideal for our schools is narrow and unlovely; acted upon, it destroys our democracy."

The Disrupters, as we know, include a long list of fabulously wealthy individuals who are accustomed to getting their way and who are unaccustomed to doubt. They ignore critics. But will they ignore one of their own? In 2019, Nick Hanauer, a venture capitalist and longtime funder of charters, publicly renounced his affiliation with the public-schools-are-failing camp. He published an article in *The Atlantic* in which he admitted he was wrong. He had been "captivated" by the simplistic idea that "failing schools" caused poverty and inequality. But after decades of contributing millions of dollars to the "reform movement," he concluded that "our education system can't compensate for the ways our economic system is failing Americans." He acknowledged that family income is "the single biggest driver of student achievement," and that the reform movement—by refusing to recognize that basic fact—was part of the problem. He pointed out that the nation's "philanthropic elite," forty of the fifty largest family foundations, agrees that schools are the basic problem, not wage stagnation and poverty. It was easier for his friends to blame the schools than to confront and address the issues associated with deeply entrenched economic inequality.

Will the Disrupters listen to Hanauer? If they stopped funding failed ideas, it would make room for thoughtful and sensible discussion about how to increase economic and educational opportunity.

Disrupters boast that three million students are enrolled in charter schools, 6 percent of all students, although many of those charter schools will close, to be followed by others that will open and then close. The outcome of disruption is disruption, not better education. The charter industry has not been able to create a stable sector of schools that consistently outperforms public schools. They have not created a model for American public education. High-performing charter schools are the exception, not the rule. Those charter schools that do not cull their students do not get better test scores than public schools do, and many get far worse scores. The best schools are not the ones with the highest test scores or the ones where students take the most Advanced Placement examinations but those that succeed in nurturing the talents and interests of every youngster who enters their doors. These are goals that standardized tests cannot measure.

Charter schools have fallen under a cloud. The backlash against privatization grows stronger with every new scandal. The scandals in the charter sector have become too frequent to ignore, and these scandals are the direct consequence of lax state laws that exempt charter operators from accountability and oversight. Nor can the public ignore the fact that funding charter schools means less money for public schools, which enroll most students. The Los Angeles teachers' strike in January 2019 directly criticized the "billionaire privatizers," meaning Eli Broad, Reed Hastings, and the many other billionaires who support charter schools. Many of the Democratic candidates for president rushed to express their support for the strike.

The backlash against charter schools affected elections. In California, the billionaires backed a pro-charter candidate for governor in 2018 who didn't make it into the runoff. They backed Marshall Tuck, a charter school champion, for the office of State Superintendent of Public Instruction, who lost in the general election to legislator and social worker Tony Thurmond, an outspoken proponent of public schools. In Los Angeles, the billionaires lost control of the city's school board when Jackie Goldberg, a pro-public-school candidate, won an overwhelming victory in a special election. In Milwaukee, where school choice had become the norm, a pro-public-education slate endorsed by the teachers' union and the Working Families Party won control of the school board in 2019. That same spring, Chicago elected Lori Lightfoot, a pro-public-education candidate, to succeed Rahm Emanuel, bringing an end to twenty-five years of control by Corporate Reformers. In New York, Democrats who support public schools won control of the state senate in 2018, thus ending Republican domination of that body and blocking future charter school favoritism and expansion. In the presidential primaries leading up to the 2020 election, not a single candidate stepped forward to endorse charter schools, which was a sharp rebuke to the Bush-Obama agenda of privatization. The embrace of charter schools by the Trump administration and the billionaire secretary of education Betsy DeVos was an embarrassment for Democrats who supported charter schools, and they fell silent.

Charter school growth began to decline in 2012–2013, for the first time since charter schools were established in the early 1990s. The National Association of Charter School Authorizers admitted that the number of new charter schools had slowed "dramatically," reflecting the lowest growth rate in the short history of charters. It said, "The relatively small number of openings in 2015–16 combined with a steady number of school closures made for the lowest net charter growth in history." In the 2012–13 year, 640 new charter schools opened; by 2015–16, only 329 new charters opened. The number of applications to open new charter schools had fallen by 48 percent in a few short years.

Robin Lake of the charter-friendly Center for Reinventing Public Education asked in 2017, "Is Charter School Growth Flat-Lining?" She answered her own question: yes. The rate of growth "pretty consistently held at 6 to 8 percent until the 2014–15 school year, when the rate slowed to around 4 percent. In 2015–2016, it slowed further to just barely over 2 percent, and then down to the current 1.8 percent." She opined that it was getting more difficult for charters to attract "great teachers and school leaders," in large part due to the "slowed growth of TFA." Teach for America was the primary source of low-wage, temporary teachers willing to work long hours, and as TFA's growth slowed, so did that of charter schools. Increased efforts by unions to unionize charters was also having a negative effect on their growth, she wrote. She admitted that even in "high-choice" cities, "high-performing charter schools were having a hard time attracting parents away from their default neighborhood schools." Somewhat gloomily, she concluded that "the days of easy, unfettered charter growth may be gone, at least for the near future."

In fact, the number of charter schools that closed each year was growing close to the number of new charter schools that opened each year. Every charter organization gives different numbers for the charters that close, making this statistic difficult to track. According to the National Association of Charter School Authorizers, about 7 percent of charters close every year. The National Alliance for Public Charter Schools (which insists that charter school growth is boundless, despite what others say) claims that "only" two hundred charter schools close every year. According to the U.S. Department of Education, the most authoritative source, 308 charter schools closed during the 2014–15 school year.

In some states, more charter schools closed than opened. In the 2016–17 school year, Delaware opened no new charters and closed 2; Georgia added 8 new charters and closed 17, for a net loss of 9; Illinois opened 3 charters and closed 5; Maryland opened 1 and closed 4; Michigan opened 7 and closed 8; New Jersey opened 4 and closed 5; Wisconsin opened 7 and closed 12. The states with the biggest charter sectors, in terms of numbers of schools, were California, Florida, Texas, Arizona, and Ohio. In California, which had 1,253 charters, 56 new charters opened, and 30 closed. In Florida, which had 656 charters, 26 new charters opened, and 25 charters closed. In Texas, which had 761 charters, 64 charters opened, and 30 closed. In Ohio, which had 362 charters, 8 new charters opened and 22 closed, for a net loss of 14 charters.

After three decades of explosive growth, after billions of dollars spent by billionaires and by the federal government to start new charters and expand corporate charter chains, what is striking is not how many charter schools there are, but how few. It is true that the charter industry is concentrated in big cities, where the largely black and brown population is relatively politically powerless (as compared to state legislatures, where decisions about charter expansion are made) and unable to protect their public schools. Many cities have significant numbers of students in privately managed charter schools, but the gains—if any—have been small or nonexistent.

Consider, after all the billions spent, that in Illinois, which has 2 million students, only 65,000 are in charter schools. That's 3 percent of students.

Consider that in Ohio, the number of charter schools is declining, as well as charter enrollments, despite the best efforts of former governor John Kasich and the legislature to promote charter schools. At the peak of the privatization craze in 2014, there were 395 charter schools in the Buckeye State, but four years later that number had fallen to 340. Charter enrollment in 2014 was 121,000 but declined by 17,000 over the next four years to 104,000, only 7 percent of the state's students. Two thirds of the state's charters received grades of D or F.

In Michigan, which has made a full-fledged commitment to charter schools and school choice for three decades, the majority of children still attend their neighborhood public schools. As of 2017, 69 percent of the state's 1.3 million students attended their neighborhood public schools; another 12 percent attended public schools in other districts. Ten percent attended private schools. Only 9 percent attended charter schools. About 146,000 of Michigan's students were enrolled in charter schools, out of a total enrollment of 1.48 million. In 2018–19, charter school enrollment actually declined for the first time in twenty-one years. In 2017–18, more charter schools in Michigan closed than opened. In a state that was a national leader in the school choice movement, the home of the DeVos family, a total enrollment of 9 percent in charter schools (and no vouchers) is nothing to brag about.

In most states, the proportion of students in charter schools is in the single digits. The states with the most students in charter schools are Arizona (17 percent), California (10 percent), Colorado (13 percent), Louisiana (11 percent), and Florida (10 percent), but charters in some of these states close almost as quickly as others open. In New York State, a hotbed of charter school advocacy due to the power of Wall Street money, only 5 percent of students are enrolled in charter schools. In Massachusetts, only 4 percent attend charter schools. Under the governorships of Mitch Daniels and Mike Pence in Indiana, charter schools are celebrated and praised, and there are no caps on the number that could open, yet only 4 percent of students in the state have chosen to enroll in a charter school as of 2018. The year before, nine charter schools closed in Indiana, and only five new ones opened.

Florida spends $1 billion each year to subsidize vouchers, and another $2 billion each year for charter schools, money that is subtracted from its ill-funded public schools, which enroll nearly 80 percent of the state's students. The high point for charter school applications was 2011, when some 350 applications were submitted to local school districts and the state, 35 percent of which were approved. By 2016, the number of applications to open new charter schools had fallen to only 75, of which about 40 percent were approved. The decline in applications was surprising because the state offers a generous, federally funded competitive grant of $550,000 to anyone who seeks to open a charter, no education experience necessary. If the charter never opens or closes its doors within a year, the money is lost. By 2018, charters enrolled about 300,000 students in the state, or 10 percent of all students. Enrollment growth was slowing, however, having increased by only 12,000 over the previous year. Several major counties, such as Palm Beach County, Broward County, Leon County, Lee County, and Monroe County, experienced declining charter enrollments.

In the quarter century since 1994, the federal government has doled out $4 billion to start new charter schools, but one third of those that were funded either never opened their doors or closed soon after they collected the money. About $1 billion in federal funds has been wasted on these "start-ups" that never got off the ground. Secretary of Education Betsy DeVos has used the federal Charter Schools Program—started during the Clinton administration in 1994 to launch start-up charter schools—to enrich established corporate charter chains like KIPP, IDEA, and Success Academy. In 2019, she gave $86 million to KIPP to open fifty-two new "no-excuses" schools and $116 million to the IDEA chain, based mostly in Texas, to grow its brand (she had previously given $67 million to IDEA). New York City's Success Academy, which is richly endowed by a bevy of billionaires, won nearly $10 million in federal funding.

How many more billions will be required to lift charter school enrollment to 10 percent? And why is it worth the investment, given that charter schools, unless they cherry-pick their students, are no more successful than public schools are and often far worse? Why should the federal government spend nearly half a billion dollars each year on charter schools that may never open when there are so many desperately underfunded public schools?

Vouchers have also been a major failure. Rigorous studies, even those funded by choice proponents, have consistently found that students lose ground when they use vouchers. Most voucher schools are low-cost religious schools that do not hire certified teachers, have low academic standards, and rely on textbooks that teach religious beliefs as facts. Worse, many religious schools teach and practice bigotry and treat the Bible like a science textbook. The Bible is a repository of ancient wisdom, and it remains an important source of inspiration and guidance to millions in the Judeo-Christian tradition, but using it to teach science is not education for the twenty-first century. It's indoctrination at public expense.

Despite the zealous advocacy of political figures like Betsy DeVos, Jeb Bush, the Koch brothers, and Mike Pence, very few students take advantage of vouchers, even fewer than those who enroll in charters. The two states that have been most enthusiastic in funding vouchers are Indiana and Florida, even though the state constitutions in both states explicitly ban the use of public money in religious schools. State leaders simply decided to ignore the state constitution.

The most important lesson to be learned from this account of the past few decades is that Reform doesn't mean reform. It means demoralization, chaos, and turmoil. Disruption does not produce better education.

There is no "Reform movement." The Disrupters never tried to reform public schools. They wanted to disrupt and privatize the public schools that Americans have relied on for generations. They wanted to put public school funding in private hands. They wanted to short-circuit democracy. They wanted to cripple, not improve, the public schools. They wanted to replace a public service with a free market.

The Disrupters don't care about growing racial segregation in the schools. They don't care that charters are usually more segregated than public schools are. They remain willfully ignorant of research that demonstrates the value of integrated schools.

The Disrupters insist that they are fighting for children, especially for "poor children trapped in failing schools," but they do nothing to alleviate poverty. They think that they can diminish poverty in some imaginary future by creating nonunion charter schools where strict discipline is sternly administered by inexperienced young college graduates, most of whom will leave teaching in two or three years. They cling fiercely to their belief that fixing schools will fix poverty. There is not a single district that Disrupters can point to where charter schools and vouchers have "fixed poverty." Poverty is not cured by schools but by macroeconomic changes that create jobs with good wages and decent housing.

Privatization fails for many reasons:

First, the schools that are publicly funded but privately managed are subject to extraordinary levels of waste, fraud, abuse, and corruption. Not every charter school is corrupt, but the absence of public oversight assures that many are. Public money should be accompanied by public oversight. In the absence of oversight and regulation, charter operators may engage in complex real estate deals that produce millions of dollars in profit for themselves and their family members. This is a corrupt use of taxpayers' money.

Second, privatization and school choice promote segregation of every kind—by race, income, social class, and religion. Public schools should diminish segregation to the greatest extent possible. Public schools should teach young people to live with others who are unlike them.

Third, privatization harms the public schools by taking away funding that rightly belongs to the public schools, not to their privately managed competitors. When charter schools open, they draw upon the same funding as the public schools, which means the public schools must fire teachers, enlarge class sizes, cut programs, and eliminate necessary services. Public schools in most states are already underfunded. Adding charter schools and vouchers makes the situation worse for the public schools that enroll most students. In effect, 85 to 90 percent of students get a worse education so that 10 to 15 percent can "choose" charter schools or religious schools that are usually no better than the public school. This makes no sense at all.

Fourth, privatization by charter school is a direct assault on democracy. A few big cities have school boards appointed by their mayors, but more than 95 percent of school districts are governed by elected boards. Although the privatizers object to democratically elected school boards, they finance campaigns to win seats on elected boards, as they have done in Nashville, Denver, St. Louis, Los Angeles, Atlanta, and other cities. Their lavish spending makes it difficult for ordinary citizens to compete for school board seats in their communities. Charter school boards operate outside of democratic norms; they are not elected and often their members do not live in the same communities where their charter schools are located. Charter board members are likely to be financiers. If charter parents are unhappy with a school decision, they are unlikely ever to meet a board member. If they bring a complaint to the charter principal, he or she is likely to tell them to find another school.

In many states, charters can be opened and operated by people with no experience in education. These may be businessmen or lawyers or politicians or entertainers or athletes or speculators. This makes no sense. Schools should be run by educators.

Why are charter schools allowed to take public money without public accountability? Why is this even legal?

Charter schools should be authorized only by their host districts. They should be operated by educators, not entrepreneurs. They should meet the needs that those districts cannot fill. They should hire only certified professionals. They should be subject to the same laws, regulations, and ethical standards as public schools are. If charters do not meet their goals, the students and facilities should be returned to the host districts as public school students and public school buildings. Anything purchased with public funds by a charter operator should be returned to the district if the charter closes, rather than becoming the personal property of the charter owner or corporation. For-profit charter schools and for-profit charter management organizations should be banned. Online courses should be offered by school districts, not by for-profit corporations.

The billionaire supporters of privatization insist on pouring good money after bad by continuing to fund disruption. How long will they continue to fund a hobby injurious to the common good? Do they really want to help the nation's poorest children? If they did, what might they do instead of privatizing public schools and undermining the teaching profession?

I have a few suggestions.

After the publication of my book *Reign of Error* in 2013, my first public appearance was in Pittsburgh. It was a festive event, with other speakers, a guitarist, steel drummers, and the Westinghouse High School "high-stepping" marching band. When it was time for the marching band to make its appearance, about twenty-five youngsters proudly marched down the aisle of the packed auditorium, with neither instruments nor uniforms. One of the students came to the podium to explain that the school could not afford to pay for musical instruments or uniforms. When I later suggested to a founder of DFER, Democrats for Education Reform, that he might buy uniforms and instruments so that these students had a proper marching band, he laughed.

So here are a few ideas for the billionaires, based on genuine needs and research: They could pay their share of taxes to support well-resourced public schools. They could open health clinics to serve needy communities and make sure that all families and children have regular medical checkups. They could underwrite programs to ensure that all pregnant women have medical care and that all children have nutritious meals each day. They could subsidize after-school programs where children get exercise, play, dramatics, and tutoring. They could rebuild the dramatics programs and performance spaces in every school. They could provide art supplies and the resources needed for teachers, marching bands, jazz bands, orchestras, and choral groups in schools. They could lobby their state legislatures to fund schools fairly, to reduce class sizes, and to enable every school to have the teachers, teaching assistants, social services, librarians, nurses, counselors, books, and supplies it needs. They could create mental health clinics and treatment centers for those addicted to drugs. They could underwrite programs based on "the Kalamazoo Promise," in which an anonymous donor guaranteed to underwrite the college tuition of every public high school graduate in that city in Michigan, a promise that has produced excellent results and an enthusiastic response from students, parents, and teachers. They could emulate the innovative public school that basketball star LeBron James subsidized in Akron, which admits only the lowest-performing students and gives them nurturing guidance, small classes, whatever services they need, and helps their parents earn a high school diploma. Those are just a few thoughts. It would be easy to fill another book with realistic proposals that could be funded by philanthropists who wanted to do good.

Philanthropies should respect the sound principle of giving to meet needs instead of giving to impose their ideas and take control of others.

Our current education policy is madness. It is madness to destroy public education in pursuit of zany libertarian goals. It is madness to use public funds to put young children into religious schools where they will learn religious doctrine instead of science. It is madness to hand public money over to unaccountable entrepreneurs who want to open a school but refuse to adhere to high ethical standards or to be held accountable for its finances and its performance. It is madness to ignore nepotism, self-dealing, and conflicts of interest. We sacrifice our future as a nation if we continue on this path of de-professionalizing our schools and turning them over to businessmen, corporate chains, grifters, and well-meaning amateurs. We sacrifice our children and our grandchildren if we continue to allow them to be guinea pigs in experiments whose negative results are clear.

The question that more and more Americans—parents, teachers, administrators, grandparents, and concerned citizens—are asking is whether we as a nation can continue on the path of blowing up our public education system without doing serious damage to the future of our nation and our democracy.

Across the country, in state after state, the answer is "no."

No genuine social movement is created and sustained by elites. The civil rights movement was supported by millions of people and did not rely on America's most powerful titans to survive. The abolitionist movement was a rebellion against the powerful, not its tool. The women's rights movement was broad-based, not a plaything for the wealthy. Any movement controlled by billionaires is guaranteed, as writer Anand Giridharadas wrote in his book *Winners Take All: The Elite Charade of Changing the World,* to preserve the status quo while offering nothing more than the illusion of change.

Michael Edwards, in his book *Small Change: Why Business Can't Save the World,* asks why billionaires should have more say over our lives than our democratic institutions, where we have a voice.

> If my government doesn't do what it is supposed to do, then I can hold it accountable by voting in a new one. If Bill Gates does something I don't like, there's nothing I can do because he's a private citizen in charge of his own foundation. However, Gates is as big an influence on global health and educational policy as any government, and the decisions he makes will affect the lives of millions. It's great that he and other philanthrocapitalists want to improve public schools in America, but why should his ideas about how to accomplish that task win out over others just because he's rich?
>
> Why should his private board of three family members decide how to change our public schools? What if he is wrong, as he has been thus far on every one of his education initiatives? Does it ever occur to him that the imposition of his ideas into education policy undermines the institutions of civil society?

The people are catching on. Teachers are fighting back. Parents are fighting back. Students are speaking out. They are sick of the pointless weeks of standardized testing. They are fed up with large class sizes. They are angry that their neighborhood schools are closed to make way for charters that choose their students and exclude the ones with the greatest need. They reject the replacement of teachers by computers. They object to the data mining of children. They are offended by the intrusion of hedge fund managers, politicians, entrepreneurs, corporations, and profiteers into their school board elections and into the daily work of their schools. They want teachers, experienced teachers, teachers who intend to join the profession rather than pad their résumés. They want schools where the healthy development of children and young people is treasured, not their scores on dubious standardized tests. They want schools that are child-centered, not centers of profit.

The great lesson of this story is that billionaires should not be allowed to buy democracy, although they are certainly trying to do so. The power of their money can be defeated by the power of voters. When privatization of public schools is on the ballot and its funders' names are revealed, it loses. When the issues are presented clearly to the voters, they choose the common good over private gain. When the public understands who is paying for the attack on their public schools, the billionaires lose.

This is the Resistance. The citizens who comprise it are not going away. No one pays them. They are motivated by a passion for children, a passion for education, a commitment to their community, a dedication to democracy, and a belief in the value of public schools. They can't be bought off. They are not for hire or for sale. They are the Davids who will never give up and can never be defeated. And that is why they are winning and why they will prevail.

Acknowledgments

No author can publish a book without the help of many friends and the sacrifice of those who are nearest and dearest. The dedication reflects my debt to my wife, Mary Butz, who sacrificed weekends, evenings, and vacation time and kept the wheels of daily life turning so I could concentrate on writing. And I kept on writing.

Most of the heroes of the Resistance featured in this book shared their stories with me, and I thank them. They continue to fight on, and they won't give up until they win the public schools that all children deserve. Their ranks will be continually replenished by students, parents, educators, civil rights leaders, grandparents, and others who care about our common future and our shared destiny.

I owe a huge debt of gratitude to Robert Shepherd, author, editor, and teacher, who offered to edit the book as it neared completion. He knew me from my blog, and I knew him as a brilliant commenter and blogger. He and I shared an intense exchange by email over several weeks and became friends, despite the fact that we have never met.

Many others helped by reading and commenting on parts of the book before it was finished, including Samuel Abrams, Carol Burris, Mary Butz, Anthony Cody, Cece Cunningham, and Leonie Haimson.

I thank Victoria Wilson, my friend and editor at Knopf, who believed in the book at every step along the way, read it with care, and offered many valuable suggestions, including its title (which I love). Thanks also to her able assistant Marc Jaffee and to Ryan Ouimet, who gathered the photographs for the book. I am grateful to my longtime literary agents, Lynn Chu and Glenn Hartley of Writers Representatives.

I also wish to acknowledge the powerful inspiration of the teachers who led the #RedforEd Movement, whose example of courage persuaded me that the tide is turning against the ideology of Disruption described in this book and that the true spirit of education may yet be recovered and reconstructed for the benefit of all children in our schools and for the future of our society.

Notes

I. DISRUPTION IS NOT REFORM!

11 But perhaps worst among the Disrupters' sins: Heather Koball, and Yang Jiang, *Basic Facts About Low-Income Children: Children Under 18 Years,* National Center for Children in Poverty, 2016. See also, "A New Majority Research Bulletin: Low Income Students Now a Majority in the Nation's Public Schools," Southern Education Foundation (2015).

2. THE ODIOUS STATUS QUO

13 They don't like grassroots democracy: Anand Giridharadas, *Winners Take All: The Elite Charade of Changing the World* (Alfred A. Knopf, 2018).

16 If an unfriendly foreign power: The National Commission on Excellence in Education, *A Nation at Risk: The Imperative for Educational Reform* (U.S. Government Printing Office, 1983), p. 1.

16 They candidly admitted: Anya Kamenetz, "What 'A Nation at Risk' Got Wrong, and Right, About U.S. Schools," "NPREd," April 29, 2018, https://www.npr .org/sections/ed/2018/04/29/604986823/what-a-nation-at-risk-got-wrong-and -right-about-u-s-schools, accessed January 5, 2019.

17 President George H. W. Bush convened: Diane Ravitch, *National Standards in American Education: A Citizen's Guide* (Brookings Institution, 1995), pp. 187–92.

17 They concluded that achievement: C. C. Carson et al., "Perspectives on Education in America: An Annotated Briefing," *The Journal of Educational Research* 86, no. 5 April 1992 (May—June, 1993), pp. 259–310, https://thewarreportonpublic education.files.wordpress.com/2015/04/perspectives-on-ed-in-america.pdf, accessed January 5, 2019.

18 The "crisis in education" was a politically: David C. Berliner and Bruce J. Biddle, *The Manufactured Crisis: Myths, Fraud, and the Attack on America's Public Schools* (Basic Books, 1995).

21 The state itself might take over: For a useful review of the No Child Left Behind law, see Frederick M. Hess and Michael J. Petrilli, *No Child Left Behind Primer* (Peter Lang, 2006).

23 They also had to collect data on: For further reading about Race to the Top, see Diane Ravitch, *Reign of Error: The Hoax of the Privatization Movement and the Danger to America's Public Schools* (Alfred A. Knopf, 2013).

24 "The development of common standards": Joanne Weiss, "The Innovation 'Mismatch': Smart Capital and Education Innovation," *Harvard Business Review,* March 31, 2011, https://hbr.org/2011/03/the-innovation-mismatch-smart.html, accessed January 5, 2019.

3. WHAT DO THE DISRUPTERS WANT?

29 Billionaire Reed Hastings, the founder of Netflix: Valerie Strauss, "Netflix's Reed Hastings Has a Big Idea: Kill Elected School Boards," *Washington Post,* March 14, 2014.

38 DFER, as it is deceptively called: Steven Brill, *Class Warfare: Inside the Fight to Fix America's Schools* (Simon & Schuster, 2011), p. 131.

40 The list includes such major corporations as: Gordon Lafer, *The One Percent Solution: How Corporations Are Remaking America One State at a Time* (Cornell University Press, 2017), p. 14; the list is reproduced as an appendix in the back of this book. To see a list of major corporations that resigned from ALEC, go to Sourcewatch.org, https://www.sourcewatch.org/index.php/Corporations_that_Have_Cut_Ties_to_ALEC.

40 Founded in 1992, SPN describes itself as: "State Policy Network," Sourcewatch .org, https://www.sourcewatch.org/index.php/State_Policy_Network.

45 Teach for America is a favorite: Annie Waldman, "How Teach for America Evolved into an Arm of the Charter School Movement," *ProPublica,* June 18, 2019. The article includes a link to TFA's 2018 tax filings.

46 *Time* and *Newsweek* devoted cover stories: Evan Thomas, "Can Michelle Rhee Save D.C.'s Schools?," *Newsweek,* August 22, 2008; Amanda Ripley, "How to Fix America's Schools," *Time,* December 8, 2008; Evan Thomas, "The Key to Saving American Education: Why We Must Fire Bad Teachers," *Newsweek,* March 5, 2010; Michelle Rhee, "I'm Not Done Fighting," *Newsweek,* December 13, 2010; Haley Sweetland Edwards, " 'Rotten Apples': It's Nearly Impossible to Fire a Bad Teacher: Some Tech Millionaires May Have Found a Way to Change That," *Time,* November 3, 2014.

48 In his final episode on PBS: Bill Turque, "No Evidence That Probe of Possible Cheating Was Pursued at Some D.C. Schools," *Washington Post,* September 7, 2009; Jack Gillum and Marisol Bello, "When Standardized Test Scores Soared in D.C., Were the Gains Real?," *USA Today,* March 30, 2011; Valerie Strauss, "Subpoena Everyone in D.C. Cheating Scandal—Including Rhee," *Washington Post,* March 30, 2011; John Merrow, "The Education of Michelle Rhee," PBS

Frontline, January 8, 2013, https://www.pbs.org/wgbh/frontline/film/education -of-michelle-rhee/; Jay Mathews, "Principal Slammed for Cheating Report," *Washington Post,* January 9, 2013.

49 This was her ugly, homophobic, sexist: Bryan Toporek, "Michelle Rhee's Olympic-Themed StudentsFirst Ad Rankles Educators," *Education Week,* July 24, 2012; the StudentsFirst video of 2012 can be found at: https://youtube.com /qeCz_ivXT9o.

50 As Michael Edwards, a former Ford Foundation executive: Michael Edwards, *Small Change: Why Business Won't Save the World* (Berrett-Koehler Publishers, 2008, 2010), pp. xii–xiii.

50 "Would philanthrocapitalists have helped": Ibid., p. 14.

4. MEET THE RESISTANCE

53 In 1999, the for-profit Edison Project took over: Samuel Abrams, *Education and the Commercial Mindset* (Harvard University Press, 2016), p. 97; Tali Woodward, "Edison's Failing Grade," "CorpWatch," https://corpwatch.org/article/edisons -failing-grade, June 20, 2002; Brent Staples, "Fighting the Culture of Poverty in a Worst-Case School," *New York Times,* March 4, 2002; Catherine Gewertz, "State-Run Pennsylvania District Battles Host of Woes," *Education Week,* March 1, 2005; "Edison Poised to Leave Chester, Pa., Schools Early," *Education Week,* April 12, 2005.

54 Michael Edwards, whom I quoted: Michael Edwards, *Small Change,* p. 78.

55 In the 1960s: Jonathan Kozol, *Death at an Early Age: The Destruction of the Hearts and Minds of Negro Children in the Boston Public Schools* (Houghton Mifflin, 1967).

55 Susan Ohanian, a teacher in Vermont: Susan Ohanian, *One Size Fits Few: The Folly of Educational Standards* (Heinemann, 1999); Susan Ohanian and Kathy Emery, *Why Is Corporate America Bashing Our Public Schools?* (Heinemann, 2004); Susan Ohanian, "Standardized Schools," *The Nation,* September 30, 1999.

55 In his books: Alfie Kohn, *Punished by Rewards: The Trouble with Gold Stars, Incentive Plans, A's, Praise and Other Bribes* (Houghton Mifflin, 1993).

55 She opened schools of choice: Deborah Meier, *The Power of Their Ideas: Lessons for America from a Small School in Harlem* (Beacon Press, 1995).

56 The National Education Policy Center: David C. Berliner and Bruce J. Biddle, *The Manufactured Crisis: Myths, Frauds, and the Attack on America's Public Schools* (Basic Books, 1995); David C. Berliner and Gene V. Glass, *50 Myths and Lies That Threaten America's Public Schools: The Real Crisis in Education* (Teachers College Press, 2014); Richard Rothstein, *The Way We Were? The Myths and Realities of America's Student Achievement* (Twentieth Century Fund, 1998); Richard Rothstein, *Class and Schools: Using Social, Economic, and Educational Reform to Close the Black-White Achievement Gap* (Teachers College Press, 2004); Helen F. Ladd,

"Education and Poverty: Confronting the Evidence," *Journal of Policy Analysis and Management,* March 28, 2012; "No Child Left Behind: A Deeply Flawed Federal Policy," *Journal of Policy Analysis and Management,* January 30, 2017; Bruce D. Baker, *Educational Inequality and School Finance: Why Money Matters for America's Students* (Harvard University Press, 2018); Eva L. Baker, Paul E. Barton, Linda Darling-Hammond, Edward Haertel, Helen F. Ladd, Robert L. Linn, Diane Ravitch, Richard Rothstein, Richard J. Shavelson, and Lorrie A. Shepard, "Problems with the Use of Student Test Scores to Evaluate Teachers," Economic Policy Institute, August 27, 2010; Edward H. Haertel, "Reliability and Validity of Inferences About Teachers Based on Student Test Scores," William H. Angoff Memorial Lecture Series, Educational Testing Service, 2013, p. 5; Christopher A. Lubienski and Sarah Theule Lubienski, *The Public School Advantage: Why Public Schools Outperform Private Schools* (University of Chicago Press, 2014); Daniel Koretz, *The Testing Charade: Pretending to Make Schools Better* (Harvard University Press, 2017); Audrey A. Amrein-Beardsley, *Rethinking Value-Added Models in Education: Critical Perspectives on Tests and Assessment-Based Accountability* (Routledge, 2014); American Statistical Association, "ASA Statement on Using Value-Added Models for Educational Assessment," April 8, 2014.

56   Noliwe Rooks coined the term "segrenomics": Pasi Sahlberg, *Finnish Lessons: What Can the World Learn from Educational Change in Finland?* (Teachers College Press, 2011); Yong Zhao, *Catching Up or Leading the Way: American Education in the Age of Globalization* (Association for Supervision and Curriculum Development, 2009); *World Class Learners: Educating Creative and Entrepreneurial Students* (Corwin, 2012); *Who's Afraid of the Big, Bad Dragon? Why China Has the Best (and the Worst) Education System in the World* (Jossey-Bass, 2014); Linda Darling-Hammond, *The Flat World and Education: How America's Commitment to Equity Will Determine Our Future* (Teachers College Press, 2010); Noliwe Rooks, *Cutting School: Privatization, Segregation, and the End of Public Education* (New Press, 2017).

57   Joanne Barkan wrote: Joanne Barkan, "Got Dough? How Billionaires Rule Our Schools," *Dissent,* Winter 2011; Katherine Stewart, *The Good News Club: The Christian Right's Stealth Assault on America's Children* (PublicAffairs, 2012); Jeff Bryant, "Charter Schools Are Pushing Public Education to the Breaking Point," *Salon,* February 8, 2019; "New Report Spurs Congress to Question Up to $1 Billion Wasted on Charter Schools," *The Progressive,* April 2, 2019; "Why Charter School Proponents Have Lost Many of the Democrats Who Once Supported Them," *Salon,* May 14, 2019.

59   The only new idea: National Research Council, 2009. *Letter Report to the U.S. Department of Education on the Race to the Top Fund* (The National Academies Press). https://doi.org/10.17226/12780.

60   Teachers are ready to be partners in reform: Anthony Cody, "Open Letter to President Obama," "Living in Dialogue," *Education Week,* November 2, 2009, http://blogs.edweek.org/teachers/living-in-dialogue/2009/11/open_letter_to

_president_obama.html; National Academies, "Education Innovations Funded by 'Race to the Top' Should Be Rigorously Evaluated; Value-Added Methods to Assess Teachers Not Ready for Use in High Stakes Decisions," press release, October 7, 2009, http://www8.nationalacademies.org/onpinews/newsitem.aspx?RecordID=12780.

60 After the call ended, Cody concluded: Anthony Cody, "Talking into a Tin Can on a String 3,000 Miles Long: Our Talk with Duncan," "Living in Dialogue," *Education Week,* May 24, 2010.

63 Peggy Robertson, parent and teacher: Peggy Robertson, "Occupy This," *An Activist Handbook for the Education Revolution: United Opt Out's Test of Courage* (Information Age Publishing, 2015), p. 66.

65 In addition to blogging, she published: Mercedes K. Schneider, *A Chronicle of Echoes: Who's Who in the Implosion of American Public Education* (Information Age Publishing, 2014); Mercedes K. Schneider, *Common Core Dilemma: Who Owns Our Schools?* (Teachers College Press, 2015); Mercedes K. Schneider, *School Choice: The End of Public Education?* (Teachers College Press, 2016).

65 In every such case, Rubinstein showed that: Gary Rubinstein, "The Case of the Missing Scholar," "Gary Rubinstein's Blog," June 17, 2018, https://garyrubinstein.wordpress.com/2018/06/07/the-case-of-the-missing-scholar/.

66 Anthony Cody persuaded: Anthony Cody, *The Educator and the Oligarch: A Teacher Challenges the Gates Foundation* (Garn Press, 2014).

66 She shattered one myth after another: Jennifer Berkshire, "These Charter Schools Are #1," "Edushyster blog," October 6, 2012, http://haveyouheardblog.com/these-charter-schools-are-1/; "Is TFA Undermining the Chicago Public Schools," "Edushyster blog," September 9, 2013, http://haveyouheardblog.com/is-tfa-undermining-the-chicago-public-schools/.

71 In 2019, Carol Burris and Jeff Bryant: Network for Public Education Action, "Hijacked by Billionaires: How the Super Rich Buy Elections to Undermine Public Schools" (2018); Carol Burris, "Charters and Consequences" (Network for Public Education, 2017); Carol Burris and Jeff Bryant, "Asleep at the Wheel: How the Federal Charter Schools Program Recklessly Takes Taxpayers and Students for a Ride," Network for Public Education, 2019; Valerie Strauss, "Report: U.S. Government Wasted Up to $1 Billion on Charter Schools and Still Fails to Adequately Monitor Grants," *Washington Post,* March 25, 2019; Matt Barnum, "Charter Networks KIPP and IDEA Win Big Federal Grants to Fund Ambitious Growth Plans," *Chalkbeat,* April 21, 2019.

71 When Kilfoyle retired as national director: Marla Kilfoyle and Melissa Tomlinson, "Badass Teachers: Fighting for Education in the Age of Corporate Reform," in *Resisting Reform* (Information Age Publishing, 2015), pp. 253–69.

71 The BATs strongly: Ibid., p. 259.

72 Many other teachers shared their stories: Ibid., p. 263.

72 The BATs have been effective: Badass Teachers Association webpage, http://badassteachers.blogspot.com/p/about.html.

5. THE BEGINNING OF THE END OF DISRUPTION

77 He suggested that the "reformers" should: Nicholas Kristof, "Beyond Education Wars," *New York Times,* April 23, 2015.

78 Martin West of Harvard described: Michael J. Petrilli, "NAEP 2017: America's 'Lost Decade' of Educational Progress," Thomas B. Fordham Institute, Flypaper, April 11, 2018, https://edexcellence.net/articles/naep-2017-americas-lost-decade -of-educational-progress; Martin R. West, "A Disappointing National Report Card," *Education Next,* May 2, 2018.

78 Arne Duncan praised the district as: Peter Jamison and Fenit Nirappil, "Once a National Model, Now D.C. Public Schools Target of FBI Investigation," *Washington Post,* February 2, 2018.

79 The graduation rate scandal: Kate McGee, "What Really Happened at Ballou, the D.C. High School Where Every Senior Got into College," WAMU.org, November 28, 2017, https://wamu.org/story/17/11/28/really-happened-ballou -d-c-high-school-every-senior-got-college/; Perry Stein, "D.C. Public Schools Graduation Rate on Track to Decline This Year," *Washington Post,* March 1, 2018.

79 The NAACP resolution pointed out: "Statement Regarding the NAACP's Resolution on a Moratorium on Charter Schools," NAACP, October 15, 2016, https:// www.naacp.org/latest/statement-regarding-naacps-resolution-moratorium -charter-schools/.

79 Nor did it weed out ineffective teachers: Carol Burris, "How the Gates Foundation Could Have Saved Itself and Taxpayers More Than Half a Billion Dollars," "Answer Sheet," *Washington Post,* July 17, 2018.

80 Greene, a champion of school choice: Jay P. Greene, "Does Regulation Improve the Political Prospects for Choice?," *Education Next,* October 8, 2015; Jay P. Greene, "Evidence for the Disconnect Between Test Scores and Changing Later Life Outcomes," *Education Next,* November 7, 2016; Jay P. Greene, "If You Care Mostly About Test Scores, Private School Choice Is Not for You," *Education Next,* April 28, 2017.

81 Milwaukee is both a model: Emma Brown and Mandy McLaren, "Nation's Only Federally Funded Voucher Program Has Negative Effect on Student Achievement, Study Finds," *Washington Post,* April 27, 2017.

81 The researchers concluded that: Michael Q. McShane, Patrick J. Wolf, and Colin Hitt, "Do Test Scores Even Matter? Lessons from Long-Run Outcomes in School Choice Research," American Enterprise Institute, March 19, 2018, http://www.aei.org.

82 In other words, the long-term effects: Will Dobbie and Roland G. Fryer Jr., "Charter Schools and Labor Market Outcomes," January 9, 2018, https://scholar .harvard.edu/fryer/publications/charter-schools-and-labor-market-outcomes.

83 The ship he launched: Arne Duncan, "People Are Saying Education Reform Hasn't Worked. Don't Believe Them," *Washington Post,* April 1, 2018; Emma Brown, "Obama Administration Spent Billions to Fix Failing Schools, and It Didn't Work," *Washington Post,* January 19, 2017; Thomas Dee, "School Turn-

arounds: Evidence from the 2009 Stimulus," NBER Working Papers: Working Paper 17990, April 2012, http://www.nber.org/papers/w17990.pdf.

84 His column read like an obituary: Frederick Hess, "5 Thoughts on the Teacher Strikes," *Education Next,* April 11, 2018.

84 "Over the last two decades, federal and state": Jay P. Greene and Michael Q. McShane, "Learning from Failure," *Phi Delta Kappan,* April 30, 2018, http://journals.sagepub.com/doi/full/10.1177/0031721718775678.

86 So, in this same sad spring: Arne Duncan and Margaret Spellings, "What Ails Education? An Absence of Vision, a Failure of Will and Politics," *Washington Post,* May 9, 2018.

87 Merrow wondered who the "we" was: John Merrow, "How Strong Is Education Reporting?," *The Merrow Report,* May 11, 2018, https://themerrowreport.com/2018/05/11/how-strong-is-education-reporting/.

87 "It's far easier to identify": Ibid.

6. THE RESISTANCE TO HIGH-STAKES STANDARDIZED TESTING

90 The results of standardized testing: Michael Young, *The Rise of the Meritocracy* (Thames & Hudson, 1958; revised 1994, Transaction), p. xvi.

94 He asks, why discard the informed: Todd Farley, *Making the Grades: My Misadventures in the Standardized Testing Industry* (Polipoint Press, 2009), p. 242.

94 But it can't tell the difference: Michael Winerip, "Facing a Robo-Grader? Just Keep Obfuscating Mellifluously," *New York Times,* April 22, 2012.

94 Perelman "tells students not to waste": Ibid.

95 " 'Privateness has not been' ": Steve Kolowich, "Writing Instructor, Skeptical of Automated Grading, Pits Machine Versus Machine," *The Chronicle of Higher Education,* April 28, 2014. You too can generate a meaningless but impressive-sounding essay on the Babel Generator by visiting this site: https://babel-generator.herokuapp.com/.

95 Despite this impressive record: Gail Robinson, "NYC Schools That Skip Standardized Tests Have Higher Graduation Rates," *The Hechinger Report,* October 30, 2015; "Educating for the 21st Century: Data Report on the New York Performance Standards Consortium: A Practitioner-Developed and Student-Focused Performance Assessment System," 2017, http://www.performanceassessment.org/research/.

97 State officials convened training sessions: Here is the video that was shown to inspire educators, but more likely frightened them: www.youtube.com/watch?v=L2zq TYgcpfg.

97 They anticipated a narrowing: New York Principals, APPR Paper, http://www.newyorkprincipals.org/email-updates/28-nov-2011; Michael Winerip, "Principals Protest Role of Test Scores in Evaluations," *New York Times,* November 27, 2011.

99 "I do not need a test to determine": Chris Cerrone, "Standardized Tests Are a Poor Assessment Tool," *Buffalo News*, April 3, 2012.

100 Parents and students demonstrated outside: Leonie Haimson, "The Pineapple and the Hare: Pearson's Absurd, Nonsensical ELA Exam, Recycled Endlessly Throughout Country," "NYC Public School Parents Blog," April 12, 2012, https:// nycpublicschoolparents.blogspot.com/2012/04/pineapple-and-hare-pearsons -absurd.html; Leonie Haimson, "The Lessons of Pineapplegate," "WNYC School- Book," June 6, 2012, www.wnyc.org/story/301545-the-lessons-of-pineapplegate/.

100 *The New York Times* editorialized, echoing: "New York's Common Core Test Scores," *New York Times*, August 7, 2013.

102 He was disappointed when: Susanne Craig and Jesse McKinley, "Cuomo Recasts Social Agenda for a New Term," *New York Times*, January 21, 2015.

102 He appointed a commission to review: Monica Disare, "In Big Shift, Regents Vote to Exclude State Tests from Teacher Evals Until 2019," *Chalkbeat*, December 19, 2015.

103 At the press conference, history teacher: Jesse Hagopian, "Our Destination Is Not on the Map," in *More Than a Score: The New Uprising Against High-Stakes Testing*, ed. Jesse Hagopian (Haymarket Books, 2014), p. 33.

103 Furthermore, the test narrows the curriculum: Sue Peters, "15 Reasons Why the Seattle School District Should Shelve the MAP Test," March 15, 2011, https:// seattleducation.com/2011/03/15/15-reasons-why-the-seattle-school-district -should-shelve-the-map®-test—asap/.

105 Hagopian wrote that "our determination": Ibid., p. 38.

106 "You are new to this district": Ibid., p. 41.

107 "Other students marched off": Ibid., p. 42.

107 The students erupted: Ibid., p. 45.

108 "We believe that we should graduate": Diane Ravitch, "Breaking News: Stu- dents in Providence Oppose High-Stakes Testing," "Diane Ravitch's Blog," January 30, 2013, https://dianeravitch.net/2013/01/30/breaking-news-students -in-providence-oppose-high-stakes-testing/.

109 High school student Claudierre McKay: Emily Boney, "Students Oppose Test in 'Zombie' Rally," *Brown Daily Herald*, February 14, 2013.

110 "Of course, it is true that many of these": Diane Ravitch, "Breaking News: Adults' Test Scores Released in Providence," "Diane Ravitch's Blog," March 19, 2013, https://dianeravitch.net/2013/03/19/adults-test-scores-released-in-provi dence/. Here is a video of adults taking the test: https://vimeo.com/62718799.

110 Gist called the event: Linda Borg, "Gist Irked by Mock NECAP," *Providence Journal*, March 19, 2013.

110 "The fundamental problem, though": "Flunking the Test," *Boston Globe*, April 11, 2013.

111 "We're told to sit and listen": Diane Ravitch, "Don't You Love the Providence Student Union?," "Diane Ravitch's Blog," April 30, 2013, https://dianeravitch .net/2013/04/30/dont-you-love-the-providence-student-union/.

112 He refuses, tosses the pencil: Emily Boney, "City Students Say State Testing

Inhibits Learning," *Brown Daily Herald,* October 17, 2013. Video of part of the event is at https://vimeo.com/76769828.

112 Jose Serrano, a sophomore: Whiting Tennis, "Operation Guinea Pig: Providence Students Protest NECAP," *Brown Daily Herald,* January 30, 2014.

113 Rhode Island was one of twenty-six states: Molly Schulson, "R.I. Public Schools Test NECAP Replacement," *Brown Daily Herald,* April 3, 2014; "U.S. Secretary of Education Arne Duncan Announces Winners of Competition to Improve Student Assessments," U.S. Department of Education, September 2, 2010, www .ed.gov/news/press-releases/us-secretary-education-duncan-announces-winners -competition-improve-student-asse.

113 If passing PARCC had been: Mark Schieldrop, "RI PARCC Results Out, and They're Not Pretty," *The Patch,* November 17, 2017, https://patch.com/rhode -island/narragansett/ri-parcc-results-out-theyre-not-pretty; Linda Borg, "Mixed Reaction to Dropping PARCC Requirement," *Providence Journal,* April 27, 2016; Linda Borg, "PARCC Results: R.I. Sees Improvement, but Achievement Gap Grows, *Providence Journal,* August 25, 2016.

114 Duncan believed that the dismal results: Valerie Strauss, "Arne Duncan: 'White Suburban Moms' Upset that Common Core Shows Their Kids Aren't 'Brilliant,'" "Answer Sheet," *Washington Post,* November 16, 2013.

114 As state after state learned: Catherine Gewertz, "Which States Are Using PARCC or Smarter Balanced?" *Education Week,* April 9, 2019.

7. REWARDS AND PUNISHMENTS ARE NOT GOOD MOTIVATORS

117 "Innovation and disruption are ideas": Jill Lepore, "The Disruption Machine: What the Gospel of Innovation Gets Wrong," *The New Yorker,* June 23, 2014.

118 Far from being innovative: As someone who spent years at Columbia University earning a doctorate in the history of American education, I recoil when I hear that word "scholar"—a mark of accomplishment—attached to children. Might as well hand out plastic stethoscopes to children and call them "doctors."

119 The Taylor System "involved the establishment": Raymond E. Callahan, *Education and the Cult of Efficiency* (University of Chicago Press, 1964), p. 33.

120 " 'Well, if you are a high-priced man' ": Ibid., p. 37.

123 At the start of his career: Edward L. Deci, *Why We Do What We Do: Understanding Self-Motivation* (Penguin, 1996), pp. 18–19, 22.

123 Throughout his career, he explored: Ibid., p. 22.

123 Deci himself became entranced: Ibid., p. 23.

124 Introducing rewards made the subjects: Ibid., p. 25.

124 "It seems that bigots were eager": Ibid., p. 26.

125 Not only do controls undermine: Ibid., p. 51.

125 The biggest controlled experiment with merit pay: Matthew G. Springer et al., *Teacher Pay for Performance: Experimental Evidence from the Project on Incentives*

in Teaching, National Center on Performance Incentives, Vanderbilt University, September 21, 2010, p. xi, https://my.vanderbilt.edu/performanceincentives/files/2012/09/Full-Report-Teacher-Pay-for-Performance-Experimental-Evidence-from-the-Project-on-Incentives-in-Teaching-20104.pdf.

126 "Cash will take you only so far": Ibid., p. 93.

127 The panel was sharply critical of: *Incentives and Test-Based Accountability in Education* (National Research Council, National Academies Press, 2011), p. 4, https://www.nap.edu/catalog/12521/incentives-and-test-based-accountability-in-education.

127 "The more any quantitative social indicator": Donald T. Campbell, "Assessing the Impact of Planned Social Change," in *Social Research and Public Policies: The Dartmouth/OECD Conference,* ed. G. Lyons (Dartmouth College Public Affairs Center, 1975).

127 The committee noted, "When goals": *Incentives and Test-Based Accountability in Education,* p. 29.

128 "In the process of creating": Joy Resnovits, "National Testing Push Yielded Few Learning Advances," *Huffington Post,* December 8, 2011.

128 This was surprising because it was produced: Sarah D. Sparks, "Panel Finds Few Learning Gains from Testing Movement, *Education Week,* May 26, 2011.

128 One of his biographers, Andrea Gabor: Andrea Gabor, *The Man Who Discovered Quality: How W. Edwards Deming Brought the Quality Revolution to America—the Stories of Ford, Xerox, and GM* (Penguin, 1990), pp. 250–53; Andrea Gabor, *After the Education Wars: How Smart Schools Upend the Business of Reform* (New Press, 2018).

8. BAIT AND SWITCH.
HOW LIBERALS WERE DUPED INTO
EMBRACING SCHOOL CHOICE

131 Shanker said he did not want to be: I describe his proposal in *The Death and Life of the Great American School System: How Testing and Choice Are Undermining Education* (Basic Books, 2010), pp. 122–23.

132 "That opened charter doors not only": Paul E. Peterson, "No, Al Shanker Did Not Invent the Charter School," *Education Next,* July 21, 2010, http://educationnext.org/no-al-shanker-did-not-invent-the-charter-school/.

132 Minnesota passed the first charter law: Albert Shanker, "Noah Webster Academy," *New York Times* (paid advertisement), July 3, 1994; "Risky Business," *New York Times* (paid advertisement), February 18, 1996.

133 They boldly claimed that "reformers": John E. Chubb and Terry M. Moe, *Politics, Markets, and America's Schools* (Brookings Institution Press, 1990), pp. 2, 12, 217.

135 Kansas charter law allows only: Center for Education Reform, "National Charter School Law Rankings and Scorecard, 2018: The Essential Guide for

Policymakers and Advocates" (2018), https://www.edreform.com/wp-content /uploads/2018/03/CER_National-Charter-School-Law-Rankings-and-Score card-2018_screen_3-21-18.pdf; Center for Education Reform, "Parent Power! Index," http://educationopportunityindex.edreform.com.

135 ALEC, the American Legislative Exchange Council: American Legislative Exchange Council, Next Generation Charter Schools Act, September 12, 2016, https://www.alec.org/model-policy/amendments-and-addendum-the-next-gen eration-charter-schools-act/.

136 But in time, charters demanded: Gary Miron and Jessica L. Urschel, *Equal or Fair? A Study of Revenues and Expenditures in American Charter Schools* (National Education Policy Center, 2010); Caitlin McCabe, "Report: Charter Adminis- tration Costs Double Those of Other Public Schools," *Philadelphia Inquirer,* August 19, 2016, http://www.philly.com/philly/education/20160819_Report __Charter_administration_costs_double_that_of_other_public_schools.html.

136 Of the seventy-two students who started: Alan Singer, "Why Didn't Chalk- beat Cover Student Unrest at Success Academy Charter High School?," *Daily Kos,* June 18, 2018, https://www.dailykos.com/stories/2018/6/18/1772810/-Why -Didn-t-Chalkbeat-Cover-Student-Unrest-at-Success-Academy-Charter-High -School?; Ben Chapman, "EXCLUSIVE: Success Academy Boss Eva Mos- kowitz Charters Radio City Music Hall for Annual 'Slam the Exam' Pep Rally," New York *Daily News,* March 3, 2017, http://www.nydailynews.com /new-york/manhattan/success-academy-eva-moskowitz-charters-radio-city -pep-rally-article-1.2987626?cid=bitly; Eliza Shapiro, "Internal Documents Lay Out Threats to Success Academy Model," *Politico,* May 11, 2016, www .politico.com/states/new-york/city-hall/story/2016/05/internal-documents -lay-out-threats-to-the-success-academy-model-101592.

137 In 2015, after completing a national survey: "Charter School Graduation Rates Way Behind Ohio's Urban Districts," *Columbus Dispatch,* December 26, 2017. These numbers do not include dropout recovery charter schools. Ohio Depart- ment of Education, "Annual Report on Ohio Community Schools," July 1, 2017–June 30, 2018, p. 17, http://education.ohio.gov/getattachment/Topics /Community-Schools/Annual-Reports-on-Ohio-Community-Schools /2017-2018-Community-Schools-Annual-Report.pdf.aspx?lang=en-US; Patrick O'Donnell, "Ohio's Charter Schools Ridiculed at National Conference, Even by National Charter Supporters," *The Plain Dealer,* March 4, 2015.

137 As private entities, charter schools are: Center for Education Reform, "Charter Schools Closure Rate Tops 15 Percent," December 21, 2011, https://www.edre form.com/2011/12/charter-schools-closure-rate-tops-15-percent/; National Edu- cation Association, "The Findings of the NEA Charter Taskforce in Support of the Proposed Charter Policy Statement," April 14, 2017, p. 4, http://www .eiaonline.com/NEACharterTaskForceReport2017.pdf.

138 The billionaires' referendum passed: "Hijacked by Billionaires: How the Super Rich Buy Elections to Undermine Public Schools," Network for Public Educa-

tion Action (2018), pp. 20–31; Carol Burris, "It's National School Choice Week. What Is That? (Possibly Not What You Think)," "Answer Sheet," *Washington Post,* January 21, 2018; Joanne Barkan, "A Case Study of How the Ultra-Wealthy Spend Millions to Get What They Want in School Reform," "Answer Sheet," *Washington Post,* May 2, 2016.

138 "The Gates Foundation spent more than": Barkan, "A Case Study of How the Ultra-Wealthy Spend Millions to Get What They Want in School Reform."

139 As such, they do not meet the state's definition: *League of Women Voters of Washington v. State of Washington* (2015), https://www.courts.wa.gov/opinions /pdf/897140.pdf.

140 Judge Madsen, Judge Mary Yu: Jim Camden, "Big Money Fuels Contentious Washington Supreme Court Races," *Spokane Times,* October 26, 2016; Jim Brunner, "Bill Gates, Others Donate Nearly $1 Million to Defeat Supreme Court Justice Wiggins," *Seattle Times,* October 26, 2016.

140 This created a revenue stream for the 3,500 students: Joseph O'Sulllivan, "Washington Supreme Court Ends Long-Running McCleary Education Case Against the State," *Seattle Times,* June 7, 2018; Dahlia Bazzaz, "What's Next for Washington State Charter Schools and Their Opponents Following Supreme Court Ruling," *Seattle Times,* October 27, 2018.

140 The bottom line was: Center for Research on Education Outcomes, "Charter School Performance in the State of Washington 2019," Stanford University (2019), p. 43.

140 Even more embarrassing for Bill Gates: Neal Morton, "More Charter Schools to Close in Western Washington, Citing Dwindling Enrollment," *Seattle Times,* June 8, 2019.

142 One man served as CEO of six: California Department of Education, "Fingertip Facts on Education in California, 2017–2018," https://www.cde.ca.gov/ds/sd/cb /ceffingertipfacts.asp; Carol Burris, "Charters and Consequences: An Investigative Series," The Network for Public Education, November 2017, pp. 4, 8.

142 Van Zandt, known as the "charter school king": Burris, "Charters and Consequences: An Investigative Series," p. 9; Maureen Magee, "SD Charter School Broker Sentenced to Home Confinement," *San Diego Union-Tribune,* April 6, 2016.

143 The most controversial of the charter chains: Burris, "Charters and Consequences," op. cit., p. 23; Paul Singer and Paulina Firozi, "Turkish Faith Movement Secretly Funded 200 Trips for Lawmakers and Staff," *USA Today,* October 29, 2015; Paul Singer, "U.S. Lawmakers Got Suspect Turkish Campaign Cash," *USA Today,* November 19, 2015; Liz Essley Whyte, "Turkish Opposition Subsidizes Scores of State Lawmakers' Trips," *USA Today,* February 9, 2017.

9. SCHOOL CHOICE, DEREGULATION, AND CORRUPTION

145 Starting in 2014: "Charter School Vulnerabilities to Waste, Fraud, and Abuse," The Center for Popular Democracy and Integrity in Education, May 2014; "The Tip of the Iceberg: Charter School Vulnerabilities to Waste, Fraud, and Abuse" The Center for Popular Democracy and The Alliance to Reclaim Our Schools, April 2015; "Charter School Black Hole: CMD Special Investigation Reveals Huge Gap on Charter Spending," The Center for Media and Democracy, October 2015; "Charter School Vulnerabilities to Waste, Fraud, and Abuse: Federal Charter School Spending, Insufficient Authorizer Oversight, and Poor State & Local Oversight Leads to Growing Fraud Problem in Charter Schools," The Center for Popular Democracy, May 2016; "Charter School Vulnerabilities to Waste, Fraud, and Abuse," The Center for Popular Democracy, May 2017; Carol Burris and Jeff Bryant, "Asleep at the Wheel: How the Federal Charter Schools Program Recklessly Takes Taxpayers and Students for a Ride," Network for Public Education, March 2019.

146 "Unlike truly public schools that have to": "Charter School Black Hole: CMD Special Investigation Reveals Huge Info Gap on Charter Spending," The Center for Media and Democracy, October 2015, p. 1.

146 He reported that 42 percent of the charters: Curt Cardine and David Wells, "Following the Money: Twenty Years of Charter School Finances in Arizona," September 17, 2017, http://grandcanyoninstitute.org/following-the-money-twenty-years-of-charter-school-finances-in-arizona/.

147 Seven months after the charter: Curtis J. Cardine, *Carpetbagging America's Public Schools: The Radical Reconstruction of Public Education* (Rowman & Littlefield, 2018).

147 As a result of the debt load: Ibid., p. 3.

147 Eddie Farnsworth opened: Craig Harris, "Charter School Vote Allows Eddie Farnsworth, School Operator and Lawmaker, to Make Millions," *Arizona Republic,* September 10, 2018; Laurie Roberts, "Arizona Rep. Eddie Farnsworth Is a Charter School Millionaire—and You Helped Pay for It," *Arizona Republic,* September 11, 2018.

147 Another charter operator, Glenn Way: Laurie Roberts, "Arizona Rep. Eddie Farnsworth Is a Charter Millionaire"; Craig Harris, "Primavera Charter CEO Gets $8.8 Million Despite Having Arizona's Third-Highest Dropout Rate," *Arizona Republic,* September 1, 2018; Craig Harris, "Arizona Charter School Founder Makes Millions Building His Own Schools," *Arizona Republic,* July 14, 2018.

149 When Yarbrough bought a car: Kevin Carey, "DeVos and Tax Credit Vouchers: Arizona Shows What Can Go Wrong," *New York Times,* March 2, 2017.

149 White and Asian students: Carol Burris, "What the Public Isn't Told About High-Performing Charter Schools in Arizona," *Washington Post,* March 30, 2017; Laurie Roberts, "BASIS Scores, and So Does Doug Ducey," *Arizona Republic,* May 1, 2017; E. J. Montini, "Did You Buy BASIS Charter School Founders an $8.4 Million NYC Condo?," *Arizona Republic,* May 7, 2018.

150 In 2009, Whitman became: David Whitman, *Sweating the Small Stuff: Inner City Schools and the New Paternalism* (Thomas B. Fordham Institute, 2008), pp. 70–71; Mitchell Landsberg, "Spitting in the Eye of Mainstream Education," *Los Angeles Times,* May 31, 2009.

150 Chavis said that iron discipline: Landsberg, "Spitting in the Eye of Mainstream Education"; Mark Hemingway, "Straight Outta Oakland," *National Review,* September 14, 2009. See the schools' Wikipedia page, which includes bigoted comments about students and teachers: https://en.wikipedia.org/wiki/American_Indian_Public_Charter_School.

150 His charters got spectacular scores: Diane Ravitch, "Rise and Fall of California's Most Celebrated Charter School," "Diane Ravitch's Blog," January 28, 2013, https://dianeravitch.net/2013/01/28/rise-and-fall-of-californias-most-celebrated-charter-school/.

150 AIMS's reputation was severely damaged: Joyce Tsai, "Ex-Oakland Charter Schools Director Charged with Grant Application Fraud, Money Laundering," *East Bay Times,* March 30, 2017; Nate Gartrell, "Oakland: Ex-American Indian Public Charter School Director Gets Probation in Grant Fraud Case," *Mercury News,* June 24, 2019.

150–51 After he pleaded guilty, he was: Vanessa McCray, "Latin Academy Charter School Founder, Thief Gets 20 Years," *Atlanta Journal-Constitution,* January 23, 2018.

151 In 2019, McFarlane was sentenced: Anna M. Phillips, Howard Blume, and Matt Hamilton, "Federal Agents Raid Charter School Network," *Los Angeles Times,* January 25, 2017; Anna M. Phillips and Adam Elmahrek, "Inside Celerity Charter School Network, Questionable Spending and Potential Conflicts of Interest Abound," *Los Angeles Times,* March 6, 2017; Anna M. Phillips, "L.A. Charter Schools Under Federal Investigation Part Ways with Their Parent Organization," *Los Angeles Times,* September 12, 2017; Anna M. Phillips, "Celerity Charter School Founder to Plead Guilty to Conspiracy Charge, Prosecutors Say," *Los Angeles Times,* December 21, 2018; Colleen Shalby, "Celerity Charter School Founder Who Misspent $3.2 Million Gets 30 Months in Prison," *Los Angeles Times,* May 20, 2019.

151 He did not resign, however, until: Howard Blume and Ben Poston, "How L.A.'s School Board Election Became the Most Expensive in U.S. History," *Los Angeles Times,* May 21, 2017.

152 After he won that grant, he violated: Cassie Walker Burke (with the Better Government Association), "The Rise and Fall of Juan Rangel, the Patrón of Chicago's UNO Charter Schools," *Chicago Magazine,* January 8, 2014.

152 "We concluded that these examples": Office of the Inspector General, "Nationwide Assessment of Charter and Education Management Organizations: Final Audit Report," U.S. Department of Education (September 2016), https://www2.ed.gov/about/offices/list/oig/auditreports/fy2016/a02m0012.pdf.

153 Apparently, stealing money from the state: Megan Guza, "Sentencing Set for Pennsylvania Cyber School Founder Nick Trombetta," "TribLive,"

March 29, 2018, http://triblive.com/local/regional/13477147-74/sentencing-set
-for-pa-cyber-charter-founder; Megan Guza, "Former PA Cyber CEO Nick
Trombetta Gets 20 Months in Prison for Tax Fraud," "TribLive," July 24, 2018,
https://triblive.com/local/regional/13897590-74/former-pa-cyber-ceo-nick
-trombetta-gets-20-months-in-prison-for-tax-fraud.

154 Evidently her age and dementia: Martha Woodall, "Former Charter Parents
Countersue Agora Cyber Founder," *Philadelphia Inquirer,* November 4, 2017.

154 One of every twenty-six high school students: Motoko Rich, "Online School
Enriches Its Affiliated Companies, if Not Its Students," *New York Times,* May 18,
2016.

155 Other states, including Oklahoma: Kristen Taketa, Morgan Cook, and Jaclyn
Cosgrove, "Online Charter Schools in L.A. and San Diego Counties to Close
After Indictments," *Los Angeles Times,* May 28, 2019; Will Huntsberry, "Inside
the Charter School Empire Prosecutors Say Scammed California for $80 Mil-
lion," *Voice of San Diego,* July 12, 2019; Tom Ultican, "Charter Scandal a Product of Shabby Law and Ignored Oversight," www.tultican.com/2019/07/07
/charter-scandal-a-product-of-shabby-law-and-ignored-oversight/.

155 Real estate deals like this: Catherine Candiskey, "Ohio Taxpayers Paid $7.7 Mil-
lion to Renovate Charter-School Building Valued at $2.4 Million," *Columbus
Dispatch,* July 29, 2018.

157 Most charter schools in the state perform: Sunil Jo and Amber Arellano,
"Accountability for All: 2016," Education Trust-Midwest, p. 4, https://3revla28w
gij23c9gkypofod-wpengine.netdna-ssl.com/wp-content/uploads/sites/2/2013/10
/The-Education-Trust-Midwest_Accountability-for-All-2016_February-11-2016
.pdf; Jennifer Dixon, "Michigan Spends $1B on Charter Schools but Fails to
Hold Them Accountable," *Detroit Free Press,* June 22, 2014.

157 By 2018, third graders in Michigan: Lori Higgins, "Michigan Students Slid-
ing Fast Toward the Bottom," *Detroit Free Press,* May 18, 2016; Brian A. Jacob,
"How the U.S. Department of Education Can Foster Education Reform in the
Era of Trump and ESSA," Brookings Institution, February 2, 2017; "2018 State
of Michigan Education Report, Top Ten for Education: Not By Chance," Education Trust-Midwest, 2018; "On National Reading and Math Test, Michigan
Only State Where Students Have Not Improved," Michigan Public Radio, February 21, 2017, http://michiganradio.org/post/national-reading-and-math-test
-michigan-only-state-where-students-have-not-improved.

157 "Charters continue to be sold in Michigan": Mark Binelli, "Michigan Gambled
on Charter Schools. Its Students Lost," *New York Times Magazine,* September 5,
2017.

158 Charters did not cure: Kate Zernike, "A Sea of Charter Schools in Detroit Leaves
Students Adrift," *New York Times,* June 28, 2016; Douglas N. Harris, "Betsy
DeVos and the Wrong Way to Fix Schools," *New York Times,* November 25, 2016.

158 The Civil Rights Project at the University of California: "Choice Without
Equity" (2009), https://www.civilrightsproject.ucla.edu/research/k-12-education/
integration-and-diversity/choice-without-equity-2009-report.

158 Charters are the gateway: Steve Suitts, "Segregationists, Libertarians, and the Modern 'School Choice' Movement," SouthernSpaces.org, June 4, 2019.

159 Independent evaluations of voucher programs: Kevin Carey, "Dismal Voucher Results Surprise Researchers as DeVos Era Begins," *New York Times,* February 23, 2017; Mark Dynarski, "On Negative Effects of Vouchers," Brookings Institution, May 26, 2016. Dynarski summarizes the voucher studies up to 2018: Mark Dynarski and Austin Nichols, "More Findings About School Vouchers and Test Scores, and They Are Still Negative," Brookings Institution, July 13, 2017; Mark Dynarski et al., "Evaluation of the D.C. Opportunity Scholarship Program: Impacts Two Years After Students Applied," Institute of Education Sciences, U.S. Department of Education, 2018, https://www.washingtonpost.com /local/education/study-students-in-only-federally-funded-voucher-program -perform-worse-on-math/2018/05/30/4b6f00c8-6415-11e8-a768-ed043e33f1dc _story.html?utm_term=.fb50d77e00c9.

159 "the students who use vouchers to attend": David Figlio and Krzysztof Karbownik, "Evaluation of Ohio's EdChoice Scholarship Program: Selection, Competition, and Performance Effects," Thomas B. Fordham Institute, 2016, https://edex.s3-us-west-2.amazonaws.com/publication/pdfs/FORDHAM20Ed 20Choice20Evaluation20Report_online20edition.pdf.

160 Vouchers for a tiny number of students: "Indiana Spends $153 Million on School Voucher Program," *U.S. News & World Report,* March 12, 2018; Stephanie Wang, "Indiana Still Has the Nation's Largest Voucher Program. But Growth Is Slowing Down," *Chalkbeat,* March 1, 2018. For a useful summary of current voucher programs as of 2018, see EdChoice, "School Choice in America Dashboard" (2018), www.edchoice.org/school-choice/school-choice-in-america.

161 Some evangelical schools teach: Rebecca Klein, "Voucher Schools Championed by Betsy DeVos Can Teach Whatever They Want. Turns Out They Teach Lies," *Huffington Post,* December 20, 2017, https://www.huffingtonpost.com/entry/school -voucher-evangelical-education-betsy-devos_us_5a021962e4b04e96f0c6093c.

161 Between 2012 and 2016, these schools: Rebecca Klein, "Inside the Voucher Schools That Teach L. Ron Hubbard, but Say They're Not Scientologist," *Huffington Post,* December 20, 2017, https://www.huffingtonpost.com/entry /scientology-schools_us_5a2d8b9ee4b069ec48ae4109.

161 How did the school know that Christ: Rebecca Klein, "These Schools Get Millions of Tax Dollars to Discriminate Against LGBT Students," *Huffington Post,* December 16, 2017, https://www.huffingtonpost.com/entry/discrimination-lgbt -private-religious-schools_us_5a32a45de4b00dbbcb5baobe.

162 The only district that scored: Alan J. Borsuk, "Rising Tide of Concerns Are Greater Than the Debate About One Charter School," *Milwaukee Journal-Sentinel,* January 26, 2018; Alan J. Borsuk, "Milwaukee's Education 'Sector Wars' Move Toward a New Place—Stability," *Milwaukee Journal-Sentinel,* November 10, 2017; The Nation's Report Card, 2017, U.S. Department of Education, 2017, https://www.nationsreportcard.gov/reading_math_2017_highlights/. In eighth

grade reading, two districts scored below Milwaukee: Detroit and Cleveland. In fourth grade reading and fourth and eighth grade mathematics, only Detroit had lower scores than Milwaukee.

10. THE RESISTANCE FIGHTS BACK

165 Over a year, they enhanced: T. C. Weber, "A Conversation with Nashville School Board Member Amy Frogge," "Dad Gone Wild blog," August 19, 2016, https://norinrad10.com/2016/08/19/a-conversation-with-nashville-school-board -member-amy-frogge/.

167 What it truly needed was more funding: Amy Frogge, Testimony to Education Sub-Committee of the Tennessee Legislature, February 13, 2013, https://www .youtube.com/watch?v=7Mjwmo2JTLM.

167 "Last year, I voted against charter schools": Joey Garrison, "Amy Frogge Delivers Strongest Remarks Yet in Charter School Fight," *Tennesseean,* April 24, 2014.

168 "When you're called to service": Weber, "A Conversation with Nashville School Board Member Amy Frogge."

169 What chance did ordinary citizens: "Hijacked by Billionaires: How the Super-Rich Buy Elections to Undermine Public Schools," Network for Public Education, 2018.

171 "The backers of inBloom pitched": Parent Coalition for Student Privacy, "inBloom Background," n.d., https://www.studentprivacymatters.org/back ground-of-inbloom/.

172 "Education technology software for": Natasha Singer, "Deciding Who Sees Student Data," *New York Times,* October 5, 2013; Andrea Gabor, "inBloom, Educational Technology, and the Murdoch-Klein Connection: A Son-of-Frankenstein B-Movie Sequel?," "Andrea Gabor blog," October 8, 2013, https://andreagabor .com/2013/10/08/inbloom-education-technology-and-the-murdoch-klein-con nection-a-son-of-frankenstein-b-movie-sequel/.

173 By April 2014, having lost every state: Benjamin Herrold, "inBloom to Shut Down Amid Growing Data-Privacy Concerns," *Education Week,* April 21, 2014.

174 Leonie Haimson's sharp eye: Leonie Haimson, "Is the Company Due to Receive a $2 Billion Contract from the DOE the Same as Implicated in a Huge Scandal in 2011?," "New York City Public School Parents Blog," February 22, 2015, https://nycpublicschoolparents.blogspot.com/2015/02/was-company-due-to -receive-125-billion.html; Yoav Gonen, "DOE Hiring Tech Firm Linked to Kickback Scheme," *New York Post,* February 24, 2015; Juan Gonzalez, "Department of Education Does an About-Face, Cancels Firm's $637 Million Contract to Provide Computer Services to City Schools," New York *Daily News,* March 19, 2015. Leonie Haimson continues to monitor the Department of Education's spending: "Problems with DOE Contracts Including Lack of Information on Vendors or Those with Problematic Records and Unanswered Questions re E-Rate Consent

Decree and Amplify," "New York City Public School Parents Blog," May 16, 2016, https://nycpublicschoolparents.blogspot.com/2016/05/problems-with-doe-contracts-including.html.

175 The teachers won a pay raise and blocked: "Chicago Teachers Union Karen Lewis: Deal Ending Strike a Victory for Education," Democracy Now!, September 19, 2012, https://www.democracynow.org/2012/9/19/chicago_teachers_union_president_karen_lewis.

176 "When schools closed, it severed": "School Closings in Chicago: Staff and Student Experiences and Academic Outcomes," University of Chicago Consortium on School Research, 2018, p. 4; Kalyn Belsha, "Study: After Mass School Closings, Impacted Students Lagged Academically," *Chicago Reporter,* May 22, 2018.

177 This upheaval and turmoil hurt: Curtis Black, "Chicago School Policy Is a Driver of School Violence, Advocates Say," *Chicago Reporter,* August 16, 2018.

177 She had returned only a week earlier: Megan Crepeau, "Prosecutors Allowed to Use Gang Evidence in Hadiya Pendleton Slaying," *Chicago Tribune,* June 7, 2017.

177 Chicago lost over 200,000: Marwa Eltagouri, "Black Exodus Accelerates in Cook County, Census Shows," *Chicago Tribune,* June 22, 2017.

177 "In Chicago, when we were hit": Norman Stockwell, " 'Education Must Be Available to Every Child': An Interview with Jitu Brown," *The Progressive,* December 1, 2017.

180 Jitu Brown was there to help: Meredith Ogilvie, "Dyett Re-Opens as an Arts-Focused High School," *Hyde Park Herald,* September 6, 2016; Marwa Eltagouri and Juan Perez Jr., "After Hunger Strike, Dyett Reopens as Arts-Focused Neighborhood High School," *Chicago Tribune,* September 6, 2016.

180 The real goal of the closings: Eve L. Ewing, *Ghosts in the Schoolyard: Racism and School Closings on Chicago's South Side* (University of Chicago Press, 2018).

181 At a salary of $280,000: Frederick M. Hess and Max Eden, "The Most Interesting School District in America?: Douglas County's Pursuit of Suburban Reform," American Enterprise Institute, September 2013, pp. 4–5.

182 He returned to D.C.: William J. Bennett, "A Model for the Nation? School Reform in Douglas County, Colorado," https://docplayer.net/16560078-A-model-for-the-nation-school-reform-in-douglas-county-colorado-by-william-j-bennett.html.

183 The Koch brothers' Americans: Colorado Public Radio, "DougCo School Board Election Gets National Attention," 2013, http://www.cpr.org/news/audio/dougco-school-board-election-gets-national-attention.

184 *Education, Inc.* was shown to parent groups: Malone Media Group, *Education, Inc.,* https://edincmovie.com.

185 One of the three judges dissented: Zahira Torres, "Judge: Douglas County School District Violated Fair Campaign Laws," *Denver Post,* December 27, 2013; Jane Reuter, "Judge's Ruling May Impact Allegations," *Highlands Ranch Register,* January 6, 2014; Jane Reuter, "Court Says District Didn't Violate Campaign Law," *Lone Tree Voice,* May 8, 2015.

185 In the highest band: The bands for teacher pay are portrayed in Benjamin DeGrow, "Douglas County: Building a Better Education Model," Independence Institute of Colorado, September 2013, p. 19. https;//i2i.org/douglas -county-building-a-better-education-model/.

185 Many who left the district: Mike DiFerdinando, "Douglas County School District: Why Are Teachers Leaving?," March 30, 2016, http://castlerocknewspress .net/stories/douglas-county-school-district-why-are-teachers-leaving,210598.

186 A parent said, "To say": Stephanie Simon, "Valuing Physics Over P.E., Colorado Schools Test Novel Pay Scale," Reuters, June 10, 2013; Mike DiFerdinando, "Douglas County Schools: The Two Sides of Teacher Pay, Evaluation: District Says Its System Puts Best People in Place, While Some Educators Say It Creates Turmoil," *Colorado Community Media,* June 28, 2016.

187 The victorious challengers were concerned: Todd Engdahl, "DougCo Incumbents Go Down to Defeat," *Chalkbeat,* November 3, 2015.

187 But parents and students knew: Barry J. Koch, "Douglas County School Board Has It Wrong," *Denver Post,* April 25, 2016.

187 When teachers were interviewed: DiFerdinando, "Douglas County School District: Why Are Teachers Leaving?"

188 "The pay-for-performance fad": Ibid.

189 The board president later said: John Aguilar, "Student Claims Intimidation by Douglas County Board Members," *Denver Post,* April 20, 2016; Jenny Brundin, "How a 'Stubborn' Student's Secret Recording Led to Calls for School Board Resignations," Colorado Public Radio, May 11, 2016, http://www.cpr.org/news /story/how-stubborn-students-secret-recording-led-calls-school-board-resig nations.

189 However, she was the Humble board's: Elizabeth Hernandez, "As Superintendent Liz Fagen Departs, Douglas County Parents Celebrate and Texas Parents Petition," *Denver Post,* May 25, 2016; Emily Humble, "In-Depth with the New Humble ISD Superintendent," *KP Times,* September 6, 2016, https://kptimes .com/2192/news/an-interview-with-the-new-superintendent/.

190 Run by former Republican congressman Bob Schaffer: Marianne Goodland, "Douglas County School Board Races Could Be Nation's Most Watched," *Colorado Independent,* August 3, 2017, https://www.coloradoindependent.com /2017/08/03/douglas-county-school-board-race-most-watched/; Leadership Program of the Rockies, https://www.leadershipprogram.org.

190 The victorious candidates said: Monte Whaley, "In Thorny Douglas County School Board Races That Drew National Scrutiny, Anti-Voucher Candidates Prevail," *Denver Post,* November 8, 2017.

190 In January 2018, the Colorado Supreme Court: Erica Meltzer, "The Douglas County Voucher Case is Finally Over," *Chalkbeat,* January 26, 2018.

191 His first order of business was: Monte Whaley, "New Douglas County Schools Superintendent Promises to Ease Tensions, Move Forward," *Denver Post,* August 6, 2018.

191 Public confidence in the public schools: Erica Meltzer, Melanie Asmar, and

Ann Schimke, "Wins, Losses, and Split Decisions: Here's How Colorado School District Tax Measures Fared," *Chalkbeat,* November 7, 2018.

II. THE RESISTANCE GOES NATIONAL

193 The Task Force held hearings: NAACP, Task Force on Quality Education, July 2017, http://www.naacp.org/wp-content/uploads/2017/07/Task_ForceReport _final2.pdf.

193 Presenters in Detroit and New York: Ibid., pp. 5–6.

194 "We have thirteen elementary": Ibid., p. 26.

195 Furthermore, charter schools should be required: Ibid., pp. 28–29.

195 The ACLU warned that these: ACLU Southern California, "Unequal Access: How Some California Charter Schools Illegally Restrict Enrollment," July 31, 2016.

196 "When high-performing charter schools": Melissa Steele, "ACLU: Charter Schools Are Resegregating Delaware Schools," *Cape Gazette,* January 9, 2015; Jessica Bies, "Here Are the 7 Charter Schools at Top and Bottom of Delaware Testing," *Delaware News Journal,* August 3, 2018.

196 " 'School choice' means that families": ACLU of Arizona, press release, "Many Arizona Charter Schools Have Illegal or Discriminatory Enrollment Policies," December 14, 2017, https://www.acluaz.org/en/press-releases/many-arizona -charter-schools-have-unlawful-or-discriminatory-enrollment-policies-aclu; ACLU Arizona, "Schools Choosing Students: How Arizona Charter Schools Engage in Illegal and Exclusionary Student Enrollment Practices and How It Can Be Fixed," December 14, 2017.

197 In Minneapolis, he wrote: John Hechinger, "Segregated Charter Schools Evoke Separate but Equal Era in U.S.," *Bloomberg News,* December 22, 2011.

197 The Civil Rights Project at UCLA: Erika Frankenberg, Genevieve Siegel-Hawley, and Jia Wang, "Choice Without Equity: Charter School Segregation and the Need for Civil Rights Standards," Civil Rights Project at UCLA, January 2010.

197 The school, Hobgood Academy: Jenn Ayscue, Amy Hawn Nelson, Roslyn Arlin Mickelson, Jason Giersch, and Martha Cecilia Bottia, "Charters as a Driver of Resegregation," Civil Rights Project at UCLA, January 30, 2018, https://www .civilrightsproject.ucla.edu/research/k-12-education/integration-and-diversity /charters-as-a-driver-of-resegregation; Valerie Strauss, "A New Story of School Segregation in North Carolina: A Private White-Flight Academy Is Turning Charter," "Answer Sheet," *Washington Post,* March 11, 2019 (the story is based on this post: Justin Parmenter, "Private White Flight Academy Turns Charter, Set to Deprive Some of N.C.'s Neediest Students," "Notes from the Chalkboard," March 7, 2019).

198 The fiscal pressure on public schools: Gordon Lafer, "Breaking Point: The Cost of Charter Schools for Public School Districts," In the Public Interest, 2018, pp. 3–5, 13, 15.

199 In 2016, it won a parent-initiated lawsuit: Education Law Center, "Principles for
      Charter School Reform," https://www.elc-pa.org/wp-content/uploads/2013/12
      /ELC_PrinciplesforCharterSchoolReform_9_20_12.pdf (2012); http://edlaw
      center.org/litigation/in-re-n.j.a.c.-6a8/ (2019); http://edlawcenter.org/news/ar
      chives/secondary-reform/njdoe-implements-consent-order-providing-gradu
      ation-testing-relief.html (2019); "ELC Applauds Ruling Declaring Nevada ESA
      Vouchers Unconstitutional," Education Law Center, September 29, 2016.

199 "This court should not be": In the Supreme Court of Mississippi no. 2018-ca
      -00235-sct *Charles Araujo, Cassandra Overton-Welchlin, Arthur Brown, Evelyn
      Garner Araujo and Lutaya Stewart v. Governor Phil Bryant, JPS, MS Depart-
      ment of Education, Gladys Overton, Andrew Overton, Sr., Ella Mae James, Tiffany
      Minor, the Mississippi Charter Schools Association, Midtown Partners, Inc. and
      Midtown Public Charter School.*

12. DARK MONEY IN MASSACHUSETTS AND CONNECTICUT

202 No on 2 was led by: To see the list of supporters and opponents of Question 2, as
      well as polling results for the measures, see Ballotpedia, "Massachusetts Authori-
      zation of Additional Charter Schools and Charter School Expansion, Question 2
      (2016)," https://ballotpedia.org/Massachusetts_Authorization_of_Additional
      _Charter_Schools_and_Charter_School_Expansion,_Question_2_(2016).

204 Nearly $800,000 came from: Massachusetts Office of Campaign and Political
      Finance, "Financial Reports for Families for Excellent Schools," https://www
      .ocpf.us/Filers/Index; David Sirota, Avi Ascher-Schapiro, and Andrew Perez,
      "Wall Street Firms Make Money from Teachers' Pensions—And Fund Charter
      Schools Fight," *International Business Times,* October 26, 2016; Shira Schoen-
      berg, "Who Is Funding Massachusetts Question 2, on Charter School Expan-
      sion?," November 5, 2016, https://www.masslive.com/politics/index.ssf/2016/11
      /who_is_funding_massachusetts_question_2_charter_schools.html.

204 The largest donations by out-of-state individuals: Massachusetts Office of Cam-
      paign and Political Finance, "Financial Reports for Save Our Public Schools,"
      https://www.ocpf.us/Filers/Index.

204 Within days, the organization: Michael Levenson, "Pro-Charter School Group
      Pays State's Largest Campaign Finance Penalty," *Boston Globe,* September 11,
      2017; Eliza Shapiro and Caitlin Emma, "Charter Champion's Firing Came After
      Sexual Harassment Allegations," *Politico,* February 2, 2018; Kate Taylor, "Charter
      School Group, Known for Battling Mayor, Will Close," *New York Times,* Febru-
      ary 5, 2018.

205 a resolution stating that "Massachusetts Democrats": Citizens for Public Schools,
      "Massachusetts Democratic Committee Votes No on 2!," August 17, 2016, https://
      www.citizensforpublicschools.org/ma-democratic-committee-votes-no-on-2/.

205 "Slice it any way you want": Jonathan Kozol, "Vote 'No' on Charter Schools,"
      Boston Globe, October 27, 2016.

206 "Our charter school assessment": Martin J. Walsh, "Vote 'No' on Question 2," *Boston Globe,* October 18, 2016.

206 In Boston, Worcester: "Massachusetts Question 2—Expand Charter Schools—Results: Rejected," *New York Times,* August 1, 2017.

206 They had already absorbed: Phil Demers, "Massachusetts Charter School 'No' Vote: Fiercest Question 2 Opponents Often from Communities with Existing Charter Schools," November 13, 2016, https://www.masslive.com/news/index .ssf/2016/11/some_of_the_fiercest_question.html.

206 Molly O. McCullough, a member: Scott O'Connell, "Pitch to Voters Rises on Charter Schools," Telegram.com (Worcester, Massachusetts), October 23, 2016.

206 The Yes on 2 cause was damaged: "Charter School Vote May Hurt Ratings, Credit Agency Says," *Boston Globe,* November 2, 2016.

207 She was, as an admirer wrote: Dan Clawson, "The Legacy of Barbara Madeloni," *Jacobin,* June 28, 2018.

208 She told Winerip: Michael Winerip, "Older, Wiser, and Not Giving in to Fear," *New York Times,* October 1, 2012.

208 She told legislators: Clawson, "The Legacy of Barbara Madeloni."

209 Only 27 percent of Democrats: Jeff Plaut, Angela Kuefler, and Robin Graziano, "Question 2: What Happened and What Happens Next?," Global Strategy Group, March 2017, https://www.scribd.com/document/394182449/Walton -Question-2-Full; Matt Barnum, "Internal Memo Offers Candid Postmortem of Charter Fight in Massachusetts," *Chalkbeat,* April 19, 2018; Matt Barnum, "Walton Memo Recommends Charter Advocates Do More to Persuade Democrats and Appease Unions," *Chalkbeat,* April 19, 2018. The latter two articles contain a link to the original memo by Global Strategy Group.

212 He was a donor to campaigns: Maurice Cunningham, "Great Schools or Great Scheme?" "MassPoliticsProfs Blog," WGBH, July 15, 2016, http:// blogs.wgbh.org/masspoliticsprofs/2016/7/15/great-schools-or-great-scheme/. A year later, Cunningham discovered that Seth Klarman was one of the largest holders of the debt of Puerto Rico, owning nearly $1 billion worth, purchased through a shell company to avoid public scrutiny. "Your Dark Money Reader, Special Edition: Seth Klarman," "MassPoliticsProfs Blog," WGBH, October 4, 2017, http://blogs.wgbh.org/masspoliticsprofs/2017/10/4/your-dark -money-reader-special-edition-seth-klarman/.

213 "Tracing this money is no casual task": Maurice Cunningham, "The Hidden Money Behind Great Schools: Strategic Grant Partners," "MassPoliticsProfs Blog," WGBH, August 2, 2016.

213 The groups, he reported, were associated: Maurice Cunningham, "Dark Money in the Great Schools MA TV Ad," "MassPoliticsProfs Blog," WGBH, August 10, 2016, http://blogs.wgbh.org/masspoliticsprofs/2016/8/10/dark-money -great-schools-ma-tv-ad/.

213 "If you're thinking low pay and lousy benefits": Maurice Cunningham, "Democrats Using Republican Money for Education Reform Now to Advance Obama's Legacy on Charter Schools," "MassPoliticsProfs Blog," WGBH, December 14,

2016, http://blogs.wgbh.org/masspoliticsprofs/2016/12/14/democrats-using-re
publican-money-education-reform-now-advance-obamas-legacy-charter
-schools/.

214 Cunningham observed that: Maurice Cunningham, "Dark Money Sharks
Devour Mass. Education Policy," "MassPoliticsProfs Blog," WGBH, April
11, 2017, http://blogs.wgbh.org/masspoliticsprofs/2017/4/11/dark-money-sharks
-devour-mass-education-policy/.

214 None of the funders in Massachusetts: Campaign and Political Finance, Disposi-
tion Agreement, September 8, 2017, http://files.ocpf.us/pdf/actions/fesadafinal
.pdf; Massachusetts Office of Campaign and Political Finance, "Schools Organization & OCPF Resolve Charter School Ballot Question Funding Source Issue,"
September 11, 2017, http://files.ocpf.us/pdf/releases/fesaprfinal.pdf.

215 And it recognized a legitimate rationale: Opinion of the Massachusetts Supreme
Judicial Court, *Jane Doe v. Secretary of Education* (2018), pp. 26, 34, http://
d279m997dpfwgl.cloudfront.net/wp/2018/04/ruling.pdf.

215 It pointed out that the small number: "Who Is Buying Our Education System? Charter School Super PACs in Connecticut," Common Cause, December 19, 2018, http://www.commoncause.org/connecticut/wp-content/uploads
/sites/12/2018/12/Charter-school-PAC-report-121818-final_19012.pdf.

13. THE MIRACLES THAT WEREN'T:
NEW ORLEANS AND FLORIDA

219 Only 26 percent of students: Louisiana Department of Education, LEAP
Scores, Spring 2018, https://www.louisianabelieves.com/docs/default-source
/test-results/spring-2018-leap-2025-state-lea-mastery-subgroup-summary.xlsx
?sfvrsn=5. In 2019, the proportion of students in the state who reached "mastery"
on the state tests increased by one point, but remained stagnant or declined
in New Orleans. Della Hasselle, "A Dip in LEAP: New Orleans Area Schools
See Lower or Stagnant Scores as Tougher Standards Continue," *New Orleans
Times-Picayune*, July 15, 2019. For a full listing of New Orleans charters and
their 2019 academic performance, see New Schools for New Orleans, "LEAP
Scores Stall: As Schools Retain Teachers and New Curriculum Takes Root, the
City Will See Change," 2019. https://www.newschoolsforneworleans.org/leap
-scores-stall-as-schools-retain-teachers-and-new-curriculum-takes-root-the-city
-will-see-change/.

219 Forty percent of the charters: Mercedes Schneider, "State-Run New Orleans
High School ACT Results: Nowhere Near What Is Necessary for Guaranteed,
Four-Year College Admission," *Huffington Post,* August 21, 2017; Mercedes
Schneider, "New Orleans Post-Katrina: Rebirth or After-Birth?," Network for
Public Education, pp. 5–7, https://networkforpubliceducation.org/wp-content
/uploads/2018/07/NOLA-Rebirth.pdf; Stanford Center for Opportunity Policy
in Education, "Educational Inequities in the New Orleans Charter School Sys-

tem," https://edpolicy.stanford.edu/sites/default/files/docsonly/scope-nola-info
graphic.pdf; F. Adamson, C. Cook-Harvey, and L. Darling-Hammond, *Whose Choice? Student Experiences and Outcomes in the New Orleans School Marketplace* (Stanford University, Stanford Center for Opportunity Policy in Education, 2015), pp. 44–45, https://edpolicy.stanford.edu/publications/pubs/1374.

219 Test scores were up: Douglas N. Harris and Matthew F. Larsen, "What Effect Did the New Orleans School Reforms Have on Student Achievement, High School Graduation, and College Outcomes?," Education Research Alliance, Tulane University, July 15, 2018.

219 On the day after the report: News Release, "Tulane University Awarded $10 Million Grant to Launch National School Choice Research Center," Tulane University, July 17, 2018.

219 A New Orleans reporter: Jessica Williams, "Post-Katrina School Reforms in New Orleans Led to Widespread Improvement, Report Says," *The Advocate,* July 16, 2018; Jessica Williams, "A Tiny Hop in LEAP: New Orleans Public School Systems Mostly See Gains on State Test Scores," *The Advocate,* July 10, 2018.

220 That "future review" appeared in 2019: Douglas N. Harris, Lihan Liu, Alica Gerry, and Paula Arca-Trigatti, "How Is New Orleans School Performance Evolving, and Why?" Education Research Alliance, Tulane University, 2019, p. 1.

220 A large share of the new resources: Bruce D. Baker, "What Should We Really Learn from New Orleans After the Storm," Network for Public Education, September 2018, p. 9, https://networkforpubliceducation.org/wp-content/up loads/2018/08/BBaker.NPE_.NOLA_.pdf. See Carol Burris's introduction to Baker's paper, "The Real Story of New Orleans and Its Charter Schools," "Answer Sheet," *Washington Post,* September 4, 2018.

221 Baker wrote that "population change": Baker, "What Should We Really Learn from New Orleans After the Storm," pp. 11–14.

221 "New Orleans was uniquely situated": "What Effect Did the New Orleans School Reforms Have on Student Achievement, High School Graduation, and College Outcomes?: A Q&A with NEPC Fellow Douglas Harris," National Education Policy Center, Newsletter, August 14, 2018, p. 3.

222 "For all its youthful, twenty-first century": Andrea A. Gabor, *After the Education Wars: How Smart Schools Upend the Business of Reform* (New Press, 2018), pp. 196–97.

225 When Corcoran was term-limited: Zac Anderson, "Florida Leads Nation in School Vouchers, and There Are More to Come," *Sarasota Herald-Tribune,* March 31, 2018; Leslie Postal, Beth Kassab, and Annie Martin, "Schools Without Rules: An Orlando Sentinel Investigation," 3 Parts, *Orlando Sentinel,* October 17, 2017.

225 In 2016, twenty-six new: National Alliance for Public Charter Schools, "Estimated Charter Public School Enrollment, 2016–17," p. 4, http://www.public charters.org/sites/default/files/migrated/wp-content/uploads/2017/01 /EER_Report_V5.pdf.

226 In Alachua County, a group: Kathleen McGrory, "Senate Kills Parent Trigger Bill in Dramatic 20–20 Vote," *Miami Herald,* April 30, 2013.

226 Several key legislators had egregious: Florida League of Women Voters, "Statewide Study on School Choice and Consensus Report on charter Schools," April 20, 2014, http://files.ctctcdn.com/9e023c2e001/312a667d-ca9e-4dc6-be723 eb1d9d47c25.pdf; Shirley Arcuri, "Charter Schools Fail to Boost Achievement," *Tampa Bay Times,* April 1, 2014.

227 The report estimated that: Pat Hall and Sue Legg, "The League in Action on For-Profit Charters," October 1, 2016, Florida League of Women Voters.

227–28 Thanks to the legislature's actions: Alan Stonecipher, Brad Ashwell, and Ben Wilcox, "The Hidden Costs of Charter School Choice: Privatizing Public Education in Florida," Integrity Florida, September 2018, pp. 1–6.

14. COMMON CORE AND A GAGGLE OF OTHER FAILED REFORMS

230 Standardization would serve: Lyndsey Layton, "How Bill Gates Pulled Off the Swift Common Core Revolution," *Washington Post,* June 7, 2014; Lyndsey Layton, "Bill Gates Calls on Teachers to Defend Common Core," *Washington Post,* March 14, 2014.

232 Most states were not so scrupulous: Layton, "How Bill Gates Pulled Off the Swift Common Core Revolution"; Jack Hassard, "Why Bill Gates Defends the Common Core," "The Art of Teaching blog," March 15, 2014, http://www.artofteachingscience.org/why-bill-gates-defends-the-common-core/; Peter Elkind, "Business Gets Schooled," *Fortune,* December 23, 2015; "U.S. Education Reform and National Security," Council on Foreign Relations, 2012; Diane Ravitch, "Do Our Public Schools Threaten National Security?," *New York Review of Books,* June 7, 2012; Valerie Strauss, "Former Education Commissioner Blasts Common Core Process—Update," *Washington Post,* February 13, 2013.

234 "In a move likely to cause": Catherine Gewertz, "Cut-Off Scores Set for Common Core Tests," *Education Week,* November 17, 2014.

234 Both testing consortia: Steven Sawchuk, "PARCC Sets the Tougher Bar Among Shared Tests, Study Shows," *Education Week,* May 31, 2018.

234 By 2018, only a small number: Catherine Gewertz, "Which States Are Using PARCC or Smarter Balanced?," *Education Week,* February 15, 2017.

235 He noted that most students: Tom Loveless, "The NAEP Proficiency Myth," Brookings Institution, June 13, 2016.

235 The only beneficiaries were: Five states did not adopt the Common Core standards: Texas, Virginia, Nebraska, Alaska, and Minnesota (which adopted the English standards, but not the math standards).

236 The fourth grade NAEP: Lyndsey Layton, "Common Core Standards Spark War Over Words," *Washington Post,* December 2, 2012; National Assessment

of Educational Progress (2017), https://www.nationsreportcard.gov/reading_2017 /#/nation/scores?grade=4; https://www.nationsreportcard.gov/reading_math_2017 _highlights/.

236 "Do you know the two": David Coleman, "Close Reading of Text: Letter from Birmingham Jail, Letter from Martin Luther King Jr.," New York State Education Department, "EngageNY," 2011, https://vimeo.com/2705 6255; Fred Klonsky, "David Coleman to Our Kids: Nobody Gives a Shit What You Think," "Fred Klonsky's Blog," August 2, 2015 (video included), https://preaprez.wordpress.com/2015/08/02/david-coleman-to-our-kids-no body-gives-a-shit-what-you-think/.

237 The folks at Fordham: Tom Loveless, "Has Common Core Influenced Instruction?" Brookings Institution, November 24, 2015; Jamie Gass, "A Misguided Social Experiment, Common Core Deprives Students of Classic Fiction," Masslive.com, February 28, 2018, https://www.masslive.com/opinion/index .ssf/2018/02/mary_shelley_guest_viewpoint.html; "Dumas' Writings Lost to State Students," *Berkshire Eagle,* July 20, 2018; David Griffith, with Ann M. Duffett, "Reading and Writing Instruction in America's Schools," Thomas B. Fordham Institute, July 2018, pp. 35–37.

239 Johnston, however, refused: Jeremy P. Meyer, "Colorado Teacher Bill Ignites Firestorm of Support, Opposition," *Denver Post,* April 24, 2010; Van Schoales, "Time to Reflect on Colorado's Teacher Evaluation System (SB 191)?," February 13, 2017, http://apluscolorado.org/blog/time-reflect-colorados-teacher-eval uation-system/; Van Schoales, "How We Got Colorado's Teacher-Evaluation Reform Wrong," *Education Week,* April 4, 2017; Nic Garcia, "State Sen. Michael Johnston Reflects on Six Years of Education Reform as Term Ends," *Chalkbeat,* December 12, 2016.

239 However, the teachers lost: Motoko Rich, "Florida Teachers Sue Over Evaluation System," *New York Times,* April 13, 2013; Leslie Postal, "Federal Court Turns Down Teacher Union Appeal in Evaluation Lawsuit," *Orlando Sentinel,* July 7, 2015.

240 Disrupters immediately hailed: Annie Lowrey, "Big Study Links Good Teachers to Lasting Gain," *New York Times,* January 6, 2012; Raj Chetty, John N. Friedman, and Jonah E. Rockoff, "The Long-Term Impacts of Teachers: Teacher Value-Added and Student Outcomes in Adulthood," NBER Working Paper no. 17699, issued December 2011, revised January 2012, published in the *American Economic Review* 104, no. 9 (September 2014): 2593–2632.

241 Adler noted that the Chetty findings: Moshe Adler, "Review of Measuring the Impacts of Teachers," National Education Policy Center, April 2014.

241 This narrative was echoed by: Amanda Ripley, "How to Fix America's Schools," *Time,* December 8, 2008.

242 The case was silly: Haley Sweetland Edwards, "The War on Teacher Tenure," *Newsweek,* October 30, 2014.

242 In a report published in 2016: Leib Sutcher, Linda Darling-Hammond, and Desiree Carver-Thomas, "A Coming Crisis in Teaching? Teacher Supply,

Demand, and Shortages in the U.S.," Learning Policy Institute, September 15, 2016.

243 "negatively affects student achievement": Ibid., p. 41.

243 It warned that teachers: American Statistical Association, "ASA Statement on Using Value-Added Models for Educational Assessment," April 8, 2014, http:// www.amstat.org/asa/files/pdfs/POL-ASAVAM-Statement.pdf.

243 The courts began to step in: Emma Brown, "New Mexico Judge Hits Pause on Controversial Test-Based Teacher Evaluations," *Washington Post,* December 3, 2015; Audrey Amrein-Beardsley, "Breaking News: A Big Victory in Court in Houston," "VAMboozled!," May 5, 2017.

244 The RAND-AIR report concluded: "Improving Teaching Effectiveness: Final Report: The Intensive Partnerships for Effective Teaching Through 2015–2016," RAND Corporation, 2018, https://www.rand.org/content/dam/rand/pubs/re search_reports/RR2200/RR2242/RAND_RR2242.pdf.

245 "Its program alone cost": Carol Burris, "How the Gates Foundation Could Have Saved Itself and Taxpayers More Than Half a Billion Dollars," "Answer Sheet," *Washington Post,* July 17, 2018.

245 "The project failed because evaluating teachers": Burris, "How the Gates Foundation Could Have Saved Itself and Taxpayers More Than Half a Billion Dollars."

246 The parent trigger idea: Gary Cohn, "Public Schools, Private Agendas: Parent Revolution," *Capital & Main,* April 2, 2013.

247 The judge ruled against: Ibid.; Yasha Levine, "Pulling the Trigger," "NSFWcorp," April 16, 2013, https://www.nsfwcorp.com/dispatch/parent-trigger/.

248 By 2018, studies by Vanderbilt researchers: Gary Henry, Ron Zimmer, Adam Cho, and Samantha Viano, "Evaluating the Impact of Tennessee's Achieve-ment School District: 1st Annual Report to the Walton Family Foundation," https://peabody.vanderbilt.edu/research/tnedresearchalliance/HenryZimmer _Walton_Y1.pdf; Gary Henry, Ron Zimmer, Adam Cho, Lam Pham, and Samantha Viano, "Evaluating the Impact of Tennessee's Achievement School District: 2nd Annual Report to the Walton Family Foundation," https://peabody .vanderbilt.edu/research/tnedresearchalliance/HenryZimmer_Walton_Y2.pdf; Lam Pham, Gary T. Henry, Ron Zimmer, and Adam Kho, "School Turnaround After Five Years: An Extended Evaluation of Tennessee's Achievement School District and Local Innovation Zones," Tennessee Education Research Alliance, June 2018; Gary Rubinstein, "After Seven Years, the Failure of Tennessee's ASD Is Finally Made Official," "Gary Rubinstein's Blog," September 23, 2018.

248 As more charter schools opened: Dakarai I. Aarons, "Crisis Financial Man-ager Tries to Fix Detroit Schools' Budget," *Education Week,* July 31, 2009; Curt Guyette, "After Six Years and Four State-Appointed Managers, Detroit Public Schools' Debt Has Grown Even Deeper," *Detroit Metro Times,* February 25, 2015.

248 Covington abandoned Kansas City: Joe Robertson, "What Really Happened When Covington Resigned, Leaving KC School District on the Brink," *Kansas City Star,* March 31, 2016.

249   Michigan State University professor: Jonathan Oosting, "Senate Leader: EAA Set to Be Eliminated," *Detroit News,* February 3, 2016; Sarah Cwiek, "The EAA Is Dead. What Does That Mean for the Bigger Detroit Schools Picture?," Michigan Public Radio, February 8, 2016; April Van Buren, "After Six Years, Education Achievement Authority Leaves Behind Lackluster Legacy," Michigan Public Radio, June 26, 2017; Carolyn Kohls, "The Success of the Education Achievement Authority: How the State Set Itself Up for Failure," Senior Thesis, Eastern Michigan University, December 2, 2016, https://commons.emich.edu/cgi/view content.cgi?referer=https://www.google.com/&httpsredir=1&article=1501&con text=honors.

15. THE TEACHERS REVOLT

251   The states that cut state funding the most: Eric Figueroa, "A Punishing Decade for School Funding," Center on Budget and Policy Priorities, November 29, 2017.

251   The American Federation of Teachers: American Federation of Teachers, "A Decade of Neglect: Public Education Funding in the Aftermath of the Great Recession," 2018.

255   The biggest victory for the teachers: Ryan Quinn and Jake Zuckerman, "WV House Sends Senate New Omnibus Bill Allowing 3 More Charters Every 3 Years," *Charleston Gazette-Mail,* June 19, 2019; Erin Beck, "Charter School Advocates 'Perturbed,'" *The Register-Herald* (West Virginia), August 17, 2019.

255   One of the strike leaders: Eric Blanc, "What the Teachers Won: An Interview with Emily Comer and Jay O'Neal," *Jacobin,* March 6, 2018. Some readings on the West Virginia teachers' strike: Lou Martin, "The Bloody Fight," *Jacobin,* March 27, 2018, on the Battle for Blair Mountain; Michael Mochaidean, "The Other West Virginia Teacher Strike," *Jacobin,* April 9, 2018, on the 1990 teachers' strike; Jane MacAlevey, "The West Virginia Teachers' Strike Shows That Winning Big Requires Creating a Crisis," *The Nation,* March 12, 2018; Benjamin Wallace-Wells, "The New Old Politics of the West Virginia Teachers' Strike," *The New Yorker,* March 2, 2018; Cathy Kunkel, "Anatomy of a Victory," *Jacobin,* March 9, 2018; Campbell Robertson and Jess Bidgood, "'All-In or Nothing': West Virginia's Teacher Strike Was Months in the Making," *New York Times,* March 2, 2018; Steven Greenhouse, "The West Virginia Teacher Strike Was Just the Start," *New York Times,* March 7, 2018.

256   There, the situation for teachers: Center on Budget and Policy Priorities, "State General Funding Per Student Still Far Below 2008 in at Least 12 States," November 2017, https://www.cbpp.org/state-general-funding-per-student-still-far-below -2008-in-at-least-12-states; Rachel M. Cohen, "Teacher Unrest Spreads to Oklahoma, Where Educators Are 'Desperate for a Solution,'" *The Intercept,* March 6, 2018; Sarah Jones, "The Next Big Battle for Worker Rights Is in Oklahoma,"

The New Republic, March 8, 2018; Rivka Galchen, "The Teachers' Strike and the Democratic Revival in Oklahoma," *The New Yorker,* June 4, 2018.

256 Overnight, the group enrolled: Rivka Galchen, "The Teachers' Strike and the Democratic Revival in Oklahoma," *The New Yorker,* June 4, 2018.

257 This was the devil's bargain: Eric Levitz, "Oklahoma Now No. 1 in Earthquakes," *New York,* November 11, 2015; Rivka Galchen, "Weather Underground," *The New Yorker,* April 13, 2015.

257 "The scene had the high spirits": Rivka Galchen, "The Teachers' Strike and the Democratic Revival in Oklahoma," *The New Yorker,* June 4, 2018.

258 In addition, teachers helped to elect: Eric Levitz, "Oklahoma Teachers Just Purged the Statehouse of Their Enemies," *New York,* August 29, 2018; Dana Hertneky, "Record Number of Oklahoma Educators Will Be in Legislature," November 7, 2018, http://www.news9.com/story/39441272/record-number-of -oklahoma-educators-will-be-in-legislature.

258 The legislature found some new funding: Simon Romero, Jack Healy, and Julie Turkewitz, "Teachers in Arizona and Colorado Walk Out Over Education Fund-ing," *New York Times,* April 26, 2018; Rachel M. Cohen, "Colorado Teachers Are Mad as Hell—and Now They're Out on Their First Strike in Decades," *In These Times,* May 11, 2018.

258 Matt Bevin, the Republican governor: John Cheves, "'Frontline' Documen-tary Investigates Kentucky's 'Pension Gamble' and Teacher Protests," *Lexington Herald-Leader,* October 23, 2018; PBS, "The Pension Gamble," https://www.pbs .org/wgbh/frontline/film/the-pension-gamble/; Mandy McLaren, "Teachers Said They Would 'Remember in November.' Did They?," *Louisville Courier-Journal,* November 7, 2018.

259 In Louisville, special education teacher: Matthew Haag, "Kentucky Math Teacher, Riding Wave of Public Anger, Defeats State House Majority Leader," *New York Times,* May 23, 2018; Olivia Krauth, *Insider Louisville,* November 7, 2018, https://insiderlouisville.com/education/three-louisville-teachers-win-state -seats-while-majority-of-kentucky-educators-lose/. A different Kentucky web-site says that eleven of forty-three educators who ran for office were successful: http://www.wdrb.com/story/39439191/after-uproar-few-ky-teachers-win-seats -in-legislature. Every website gives a slightly different count for the number of educators who ran for office and the number who won.

259 Veteran education writer Dale Russakoff: Dale Russakoff, "Arizona Lawmakers Cut Education Budgets. Then Teachers Got Angry," *New York Times Magazine,* September 5, 2018.

260 Teachers were dubious: Michael Leachman, "State Tax Cuts: A Key Factor in AZ, OK Teacher Pay Crises," Center for Budget and Policy Priorities, March 26, 2018.

261 The strike lasted for six days: Simon Romero, Jack Healy, and Julie Turkewitz, "Teachers in Arizona and Colorado Walk Out Over Education Funding," *New York Times,* April 26, 2018.

261 Democrats wanted to raise: Hank Stephenson, "House Republican Leader: Teachers Get Second Jobs to Buy Boats, Enjoy Finer Things in Life," *Arizona Capitol Times,* April 27, 2017.

261 The legislature passed: Howard Fischer, "Lawmakers Waive Teacher Qualifications," *Capitol Media Services,* April 25, 2017.

262 Governor Ducey was funded: Russakoff, "Arizona Lawmakers Cut Education Budgets. Then Teachers Got Angry."

262 A study by *The Arizona Republic:* Rob O'Dell, "Prop 305: Vouchers Still Mostly Go to Students Leaving Wealthier, Higher-Performing Districts," *Arizona Republic,* October 25, 2018.

263 "Sharon Kirsch, a college professor": Laurie Roberts, "How 6 Women Made Save Our Schools Arizona a Political Force," *Arizona Republic,* May 9, 2018.

264 Both the Koch brothers and members: Laurie Roberts, "Voucher Alert: Here Comes the End Run on Arizona Voters," *Arizona Republic,* May 3, 2018; Laurie Roberts, "Citizens to Block Arizona's Universal Voucher Law? Wow!," *Arizona Republic,* August 8, 2017; James Hohmann, "The Daily Post: Koch Network Laying Groundwork to Fundamentally Transform America's Education System," *Washington Post,* January 30, 2018; Russakoff, "Arizona Lawmakers Cut Education Budgets. Then Teachers Got Angry."

264 As journalist Laurie Roberts noted: Roberts, "How 6 Women Made Save Our Schools Arizona a Political Force."

264 They promised that they would: Rob O'Dell and Yvonne Wingett Sanchez, "Undeterred by Crushing Prop 305 Defeat, School Choice Advocates Double Down on Vouchers," *Arizona Republic,* November 8, 2018; Katie Campbell, "Prop 305 Defeat Doesn't End Fight Over Voucher Expansion," *Arizona Republic,* November 9, 2018; Robert Enslow, "If You're a School Choice Advocate, There Is Good and Bad News in Prop 305's Defeat," *Arizona Republic,* November 9, 2018.

265 "Dear Governor Ducey": Arizona RedForEd Facts, Facebook, https://www .facebook.com/AZRedForEdFACTS/photos/a.940617909431997/107977547218 2906/?type=3&theater.

266 The story accompanying the covers: Katie Reilly, "Thirteen Stories of Life on a Teacher's Salary," *Time,* September 13, 2018; Erin Cullum, "Time Magazine's Cover Sheds Light on the Low Wages Many Teachers in America Face," pop sugar.com, September 16, 2018; Madeline Will, "From 'Rotten Apples' to Martyrs: America Has Changed Its Tune on Teachers," *Education Week,* October 3, 2018; Valerie Strauss, "Three TIME Covers Show How American Attitudes About Teachers Have Changed," "Answer Sheet," *Washington Post,* October 3, 2018; Dana Goldstein, "Teacher Walkouts: What to Know and What to Expect," *New York Times,* April 3, 2018; Robert Gebeloff, "The Numbers That Explain Why Teachers Are in Revolt," *New York Times,* June 4, 2018; Holly Yan, "Here's What Teachers Accomplished with Their Protests This Year," CNN.com, May 29, 2018; Susan Page, Merdie Nzanga, and Caroline Simon, "Even When

Teachers Strike, Americans Give Them High Grades, Poll Shows. Unions Fare Worse," *USA Today,* September 12, 2018.

16. GOLIATH STUMBLES

270 Parents want their children: Nick Tabor, "Mark Zuckerberg Is Trying to Transform Education. This Town Fought Back," *New York,* October 11, 2018; Nellie Bowles, "Silicon Valley Came to Kansas Schools. That Started a Rebellion," *New York Times,* April 21, 2019.

271 "I'll go out on a limb": Paymon Rouhanifard, "Like Most Superintendents I Cared a Lot About Test Scores. Too Much, It Turns Out," *Chalkbeat,* November 13, 2018; Matt Barnum, "In a Shift, More Education Reformers Say They're Worried About Schools' Focus on Testing," *Chalkbeat,* November 13, 2018; Robert Pondiscio, "It's Time to End the Testing Culture in America's Schools—and Start Playing the Long Game to Produce Better Life Outcomes for At-Risk Kids," *The 74 Million,* November 20, 2018.

271 That was what John Dewey had in mind: John Dewey, *The School and Society* (University of Chicago, 1907), p. 7.

271 The Disrupters, as we know: Nick Hanauer, "Better Schools Won't Fix America," *The Atlantic,* July 2019.

272 Charter schools have fallen under a cloud: Jennifer Medina and Dana Goldstein, "Success of Los Angeles Teachers Strike Rocks Charter Schools, and a Rich Supporter," *New York Times,* January 28, 2019.

272 The backlash against charter schools: Eliza Shapiro, "With Democratic Wins, Charter Schools Face a Backlash in N.Y. and Other States," *New York Times,* November 9, 2018; Jennifer Medina and Dana Goldstein, "Success of Los Angeles Teachers Strike Rocks Charter Schools, and a Rich Supporter"; Bruce Mohl, "Charters Facing Backlash All Over Country," *Commonwealth,* January 29, 2019; Valerie Strauss, "There's a Backlash Against Charter Schools, What's Happening and Why," "The Answer Sheet," *Washington Post,* February 11, 2019; Andre M. Perry, "Betsy DeVos's Support of Charters Spells Disaster for Their Democrat Backers," Brown Center Chalkboard, Brookings Institution, April 11, 2019; Jack Schneider, "School's Out: Charters Were Supposed to Save American Education. Why Are Americans Turning Against Them?" *Washington Post,* May 30, 2019; Laura Meckler, "Democrats Abandon Charter Schools as 'Reform' Agenda Falls from Favor," *Washington Post,* June 25, 2019.

273 The number of applications: National Alliance of Charter School Authorizers, "Inside Charter School Growth: A Look at Openings, Closings, and Why Authorizers Matter," March 15, 2017, https://www.qualitycharters.org/policy -research/inside-charter-school-growth/openings/.

274 Somewhat gloomily, she concluded: Robin Lake, "Is Charter School Growth Flat-Lining?" *The Lens,* Center for Reinventing Public Education, February 17, 2017.

274 According to the U.S. Department of Education: National Alliance of Char-
ter School Authorizers, "Inside Charter School Growth: A Look at Openings,
Closings, and Why Authorizers Matter"; Lake, "Is Charter School Growth Flat-
Lining?"; National Center for Education Statistics, Fast Facts, "Closed Schools,"
U.S. Department of Education (2018), https://nces.ed.gov/fastfacts/display
.asp?id=619.

274 In Ohio, which had 362 charters: National Alliance of Charter School
Authorizers, "Inside Charter School Growth: A Look at Openings, Closings, and Why Authorizers Matter." The following year (2018), the National
Alliance for Public Charter Schools reported that the largest number of new
charters were opened in California (65), which also had the largest number
of charter closures (46); Florida opened 36 new charters and closed 31 existing charters; Arizona opened 20 new charters and closed 16 charters: "Estimated Public Charter School Enrollment, 2017–2018," March 2018, https://
www.publiccharters.org/sites/default/files/documents/2018-03/FINAL%20Esti
mated%20Public%20Charter%20School%20Enrollment%2C%202017-18.pdf.

275 Consider, after all the billions spent: Illinois Network of Charter Schools,
https://www.incschools.org/get-the-facts/, accessed December 14, 2018.

275 Two thirds of the state's charters: Ohio Department of Education, "Annual
Report on Ohio Community Schools, July 1, 2017–June 30, 2018," pp. 8–9,
17–24, http://education.ohio.gov/getattachment/Topics/Community-Schools
/Annual-Reports-on-Ohio-Community-Schools/2017-2018-Community
-Schools-Annual-Report.pdf.aspx?lang=en-US.

275 In a state that was a national leader: Julie Mack, "Where Michigan Children
Attended School in 2016–17—Public and Private," Mlive.com, September 25,
2017; Citizens Research Council of Michigan, "Charter School Enrollment Pro-
jected to Decline, First Time in 21 Years," January 15, 2018, https://crcmich.org
/charter-school-enrollment-projected-to-decline-first-time-in-21-years/.

276 The year before, nine: Rebecca David and Kevin Hesla, "Estimated Public
Charter School Enrollment, 2017–2018," National Alliance for Public Charter
Schools, March 2018.

276 Several major counties: Travis Pillow, "Florida's Charter School Enrollment
Jumps to Nearly 296,000," *redefinED,* May 16, 2018.

276 About $1 billion: Carol Burris and Jeff Bryant, "Asleep at the Wheel: How the
Federal Charter Schools Program Recklessly Takes Taxpayers and Students for a
Ride," Network for Public Education, 2019.

Index

Page numbers in *italics* refer to illustrations.

Illustration Credits

A NOTE ON THE TYPE

This book was set in Adobe Garamond. Designed for the Adobe Corporation by Robert Slimbach, the fonts are based on types first cut by Claude Garamond (ca. 1480–1561). Garamond was a pupil of Geoffroy Tory and is believed to have followed the Venetian models. He gave to his letters a certain elegance and feeling of movement that won their creator an immediate reputation.

Composed by North Market Street Graphics,
Lancaster, Pennsylvania

Printed and bound by Berryville Graphics,
Berryville, Virginia

Designed by Cassandra J. Pappas